Computers in Teaching Mathematics

PETER KELMAN
ART BARDIGE
JONATHAN CHOATE
GEORGE HANIFY
JOHN RICHARDS
NANCY ROBERTS
MARY KAY TORNROSE
JOSEPH WALTERS

ADDISON-WESLEY
PUBLISHING COMPANY

Reading, Massachusetts
Menlo Park, California
London · Amsterdam
Don Mills, Ontario · Sydney

Intentional Educations, Series Developer
Peter Kelman, Series Editor
Richard Hannus, Cover Designer
David Shopper, Chapter Opening Photographs

Fig. 1.10 reprinted by permission of Art Bardige; Fig. 2.7 reprinted by permission of Engineering Research Lab, University of Illinois; Figs. 3.1–3.4 reprinted by permission of VisiCorp; Figs. 3.5–3.9 © Software Arts, Inc. Reprinted by permission; text material pages 76–84 and Figs. 3.10–3.14 by Tom Snyder, © McGraw-Hill, reprinted by permission; text material pages 96–100 and Figs. 4.1–4.4 reprinted by permission of Spinnaker Software, Cambridge, MA; Fig. 4.28 from Roberts, INTRODUCTION TO COMPUTER SIMULATION, copyright © 1983 Addison-Wesley, Reading, MA. Reprinted with permission; Figs. 6.10, 6.11, 6.21 Copyright 1979, 1981, Apple Computer, Inc., 20525 Mariani, Cupertino, CA 95014. Used by permission of Apple Computer, Inc.; text material pages 230–231 reprinted by permission of the Weston (MA) School System.

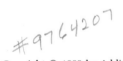

ISBN 0-201-10565-9
ABCDEFGHIJ-AL-89876543

197475

JUL 2 4 1985

Foreword

The computer is a rich and complex tool that is increasingly within the financial means of schools. Like any educational tool, it comes with inherent advantages and disadvantages, is more appropriate for some uses than others, is more suited to some teaching styles than others, and is neither the answer to all our educational ills nor the end of all that is great and good in our educational system. Like any tool, it can be used well or poorly, be overemphasized or ignored, and it depends on the human qualities of the wielder for its effectiveness.

The purpose of the Addison-Wesley Series on *Computers in Education* is to persuade you, as educators, that the future of computers in education is in your hands. Your interest and involvement in educational computer applications will determine whether computers will be the textbook, the TV, or the chalkboard of education for the next generation.

For years, textbooks have dominated school curricula with little input from classroom teachers or local communities. Recently, television has become the most influential and ubiquitous educator in society yet has not been widely or particularly successfully used by teachers in school. On the other hand, for over one hundred years the chalkboard has been the most individualized, interactive, and creatively used technology in schools.

Already, textbook-like computerized curricula are being churned out with little teacher or local community input. Already, computers are available for home use at prices comparable to a good color television set and with programs at the educational level of the soaps. If teachers are to gain control over computers in education and make them be their chalkboards, the time to act is now.

Each book in the *Computers in Education* series is intended to provide teachers, school administrators, and parents with information and ideas that will help them begin to meet the educational challenge computers present. Taken as a whole, the series has been designed to help the reader:

- Appreciate the potential and the limits of computers in education.
- Develop a functional understanding of the computer.
- Overcome apprehension about and fear of the computer.
- Participate in efforts to introduce and integrate computers into a school.
- Use the computer creatively and effectively in teaching and administration.
- Apply a discerning and critical attitude toward the myriad computer-related products offered in increasing volume to the education market.
- Consider seriously the ethical, political, and philosophical ramifications of computer use in education.

Practical Guide to Computers in Education is the basic primer for the series. *Computers in Teaching Mathematics* is one of a number of books in the second tier of the series, each dealing with computer applications in particular educational contexts. Others include *Computers and Reading Instruction, Computers, Education, and Special Needs*, and *School Administrator's Guide to Computers in Education*. Still other titles are planned for this part of the series, including ones on computers and writing, business education, science, social studies, and the elementary school classroom. Each book in this second tier picks up where the *Practical Guide* leaves off. Each is more focused and provides far more practical detail to educators seriously considering computer use in their schools and curricula.

Computers in Teaching Mathematics is an exciting and challenging volume in this series. It recognizes the central role mathematics educators have played in bringing computers into the schools, and it presents a challenge to them to take a leadership role in the next phase of the educational computing revolution. The book is a unique blend of practical suggestions and forward-looking ideas. It provides a wealth of basic information mathematics teachers need in order to integrate computers into their schools and curricula, and it also explores in detail the potential of computers to transform the mathematics curriculum.

As series editor, I am excited to see this book in print. I believe mathematics educators will find it useful and challenging, and I look forward to seeing the next chapter in the educational computing revolution written by those who take up this challenge.

Peter Kelman

Preface

We wrote this book on the premise that mathematics teachers are, and should be, at the forefront of the educational computing revolution. With the exception of two chapters (2 and 8) this book provides mathematics teachers with concrete ideas and suggestions for infusing computers into the mathematics curriculum. Chapter 1, "Transforming the Mathematics Curriculum" establishes the two major foci of the book: transforming process and transforming content. It introduces three themes that permeate the book: problem solving, computer graphics, and programming. Problem solving is the subject of Chapter 3, computer graphics is the focus of Chapter 4, and programming is discussed in Chapter 7.

Computer-based problem solving and computer graphics are presented as aspects of transforming the processes of mathematics. Programming, applied mathematics, and computer science are presented as aspects of transforming the content of the mathematics curriculum.

Each chapter differs in purpose and style, as well as subject. Chapter 2, "Traditional Computer Assisted Instruction," is the only chapter dealing with traditional uses of the computer in mathematics. Through fictional vignettes, it raises issues of educational philosophy and practice with regard to computer use in mathematics education.

Chapter 3, "Problem Solving: Transforming A Process," provides four detailed examples of how commercially available programs can alter traditional problem-solving activities in mathematics classrooms.

Chapter 4, "Using Computer Graphics in Mathematics," is filled with actual activities and exercises that use the graphics computer to teach mathematical concepts. Teachers will find a wealth of ideas with enough detail to implement many of them immediately.

Chapter 5, "Applied Mathematics: Transforming Content," presents two detailed case studies, one a fictional composite, the other true. Both show how the content of the mathematics curriculum could be radically altered by computer use.

Chapter 6, "Computer Science: Mathematics in the Computer," is a mini-course in computer science for teacher and students. Written with humor and in excruciating detail, it takes readers into the heart of the machine, the land of bits and bytes, so that they may understand the mathematics in the computer.

Chapter 7, "Programming and Computer Languages," is a polemic. It urges readers to consider programming not as a language learning activity, but as a construction activity, one in which creativity and problem solving play major roles.

Chapter 8, "The Mathematics Teacher as Computer Sponsor," is a short handbook for mathematics teachers who wish to be, or simply find themselves being, the educational computing leader of their school. It is filled with advice and concrete information to help teachers with that challenging task.

A large resources section assists the readers in that task and with implementing computer activities in their own mathematics courses.

Looking back to when we started work on this book, we find that our ideas on how we should approach the subject of computers in mathematics changed dramatically. We had thought about beginning gently, spending half the book on traditional uses of the computer and traditional mathematics goals and methods. But, as we shared knowledge and experiences with each other, we decided that computers held such great potential for bringing about change in the way we teach and learn mathematics we should dedicate the book to that purpose. So if at times we seem to get carried away, try to understand the excitement of working with so many educators whose experiences with computers are so promising.

As with any book that covers new ground, we were influenced by the work and ideas of many others. We benefitted especially from the suggestions of Bruce Vogeli, Judah Schwartz, Twila Slesnick, and Janet McDonald, but we take full responsibility for the final product and its message. As will be evident when you read the book, we have been particularly inspired by Logo and MicroDYNAMO, programming languages that could stand the mathematics curriculum on its head.

Writing a book with eight authors requires a great deal of logistical support. We could not have completed this book without the herculean efforts of various members of the Intentional Educations staff, most particularly Carol Trowbridge, Carol Nuccio, and Barbara Nielsen. Others at Intentional whose help was important to us include: Jack Reed, Janice Lewbin, Jane Caminos, and Susan Strand.

Finally, the support and patience of our families brought us through when deadlines loomed and meals were missed.

March, 1983

Peter Kelman
Art Bardige
Jonathan Choate
George Hanify
John Richards
Nancy Roberts
Mary Kay Tornrose
Joseph Walters

The Authors

Peter Kelman (Ed.D. Harvard Graduate School of Education) is science coordinator for Intentional Educations, Inc., Watertown, Massachusetts; prior to joining Intentional Educations he was assistant professor of education at Dartmouth College. He frequently lectures and conducts workshops on a variety of topics, and has consulted on or written a number of articles and books, including *Human Sexuality*, *Chemistry for the Modern World*, *Spaceship Earth: Physical Science* and *Dmitri Mendeleyev: Prophet of the Elements*.

Art Bardige (M.A.T. University of Chicago) is president of Learning Ways, Inc., a software development company. He formerly served as Mathematics Curriculum Consultant in the Arlington, Massachusetts public schools, and has taught mathematics and physics in junior and senior high school.

Jonathan Choate (M.A. Bowdoin College) is chairman of the mathematics department at the Groton School, Groton, Massachusetts. He is also the developer of educational software in the area of mathematics; and has worked on other software packages including *Bank Street Writer*.

George Hanify (M.Ed. Antioch College Graduate School of Education) is Senior Consultant, Computer Applications, at Merrimack Education Center, Chelmsford, Massachusetts, and he is an instructor at the Boston College Graduate School of Education. He formerly taught mathematics and computer science in the Billerica, Massachusetts public schools.

John Richards (Ph.D. SUNY Buffalo) is editor and publisher of WINDOW, a disk-based magazine in Watertown, Massachusetts. He formerly served as instructor in the Massachusetts Institute of Technology Division for Study and Research in Education.

Nancy Roberts (Ed.D. Boston University) is associate professor of education at Lesley College Graduate School of Education. She is also associate editor of *Classroom Computer News*, founder and co-chairperson of the Computer Education Resource Coalition and the co-chairperson of the Lesley College Conferences on Computer Use in Precollege Education. She has written numerous articles on computers and education, and is a co-author of *Introduction to Computer Simulation: The System Dynamics Approach*.

Joseph Walters (Ed.D. Harvard University) is a research fellow at Harvard University School of Education. He has taught high school mathematics as well as kindergarten, and most recently served as an instructor at Wheelock College.

Mary Kay Tornrose (M.Ed. Northeastern University) is Coordinator of Mathematics, K–8, for the Newton (Massachusetts) Public Schools, and she has taught mathematics in grades six through twelve.

Contents

27   1948

Transforming the Mathematics Curriculum 1

Mathematics teachers were first to bring computers into the pre-college curriculum. In the early 1960s, a handful of forward-looking mathematics teachers, scattered across the country, arranged for their best students to have access to terminals of large **timesharing** computer systems. The students learned to program, usually in FORTRAN, the first **high-level computer language.** There was little else to do with computers in education at that time.

We've come a long way in the last twenty-five years. As nearly everyone is aware, computers themselves have changed dramatically, declining incredibly in size and cost, and increasing comparably in power and flexibility. As a result, computers have become part of virtually every aspect of our lives, including education in schools and at home.

Once again, mathematics teachers are at the forefront of computer implementation in schools. In fact, they have never ceased to be. Mathematics educators were among the first to use computers as an aid to instruction in the traditional curriculum. They pioneered so-called **computer assisted instruction** (CAI). The first large-scale computerized curriculum projects were in mathematics. The first educational computer games were mathematics games. And now, the entire mathematics curriculum appears to be the first of the traditional school curriculum areas to be undergoing substantial transformation because of computers.

All of this may not seem very surprising, since computers were designed to do mathematics and are fundamentally mathematics machines. Nevertheless, the inventive imagination mathematics educators have brought

1

to educational computing is impressive, and the resulting innovations far from inevitable. Educational computing in mathematics might have remained dominated for some time by CAI and BASIC programming courses, if it hadn't been for the commitment of mathematics educators, in schools and universities, to unlocking the full educational potential of computers.

This is not meant to imply that there is anything wrong with CAI or BASIC programming courses; it is simply that these applications make only limited use of the vast capabilities of today's computers. Nevertheless, until very recently, educational computing consisted exclusively of these two types of application. As with all technological breakthroughs, people first viewed computers in terms of what they were used to. Just as the first automobiles were called horseless carriages and were designed to look and feel like buggies, the first computerized curricula were called drill and practice and tutorials and were designed to look and feel like workbooks and textbooks.

But, a new day is dawning for educational computing; traditional CAI is slowly giving way to a new generation of educational **software** and a new image of how the computer can be used educationally. The new software, dubbed "learningware" by some, do not emulate traditional curricular methods and materials: textbooks, workbooks, chalkboards, filmstrips, overhead projectors. Rather, they exploit the vast memory, logical structures, and impressive graphics capabilities of computers to produce an interactive, flexible, and powerful medium for teaching and learning. The corresponding new image of the computer in education is as a tool for learning, rather than as the latest audiovisual device. And for mathematics education, this new image includes the computer as a tool for *doing* mathematics.

However, in the last thirty years, new technologies and techniques have promised similarly dramatic changes in the way students are taught and learn. Radio, typewriters, film, mimeograph stencils, spirit masters, television, overhead transparencies, film strips, slide-tape presentations, film loops, Polaroid cameras, photocopiers, electronic calculators, thermofax machines, videotape, and others all have raised high hopes for educational improvement. And, all have failed to make much of a difference in children's learning or even in the ways we teach. So, teachers have a right to be skeptical about claims that computers will usher in a new age in education.

Nevertheless, the potential exists for computers to transform how and what is taught and learned in schools, and mathematics educators are the most likely group to play a major role in unlocking that potential for their students and themselves.

TRANSFORMING THE PROCESSES OF MATHEMATICS EDUCATION

The Computer as Problem-Solving Tool

Computers were originally designed to be used to solve scientific and business problems. As a result, they are powerful problem-solving devices with which students can probe problems, store and retrieve data, test out solutions, simulate problem situations, and calculate results. These problem-solving capacities of the computer enable students to work with much more interesting and complicated problems than they were able to before. They can ask "What if?" questions and attack problems in any number of ways. Most important, with computers, students have a new-found freedom to explore, to test strategies, and to play, all of which are at the heart of problem solving.

In the past, the difficulties of teaching problem solving have prompted educators to invent various recipes for it, some resembling old snake oil cures. The "scientific method," the best known of these recipes, has had surprising vitality despite the insistence of creative scientists that it is pure fiction and that, as a method, it hinders the problem solver more than it helps. These recipes each offer the one "true" path to all problem solving. But there is no one way to solve problems; there are many paths, many techniques, and many tools for exploring problems, identifying patterns, and finding solutions. People who learn problem solving well are like actors who play many different roles. They have wide and varied repertoires of tools with which to define and solve problems. The computer culture has appropriated, incorporated, and enhanced many of the most powerful of these tools. These exist primarily in sophisticated forms as business software that can be used by high school students. But, some problem-solving tools are available now which are designed explicitly for educational settings, and more of this type will be coming soon.

Numerical-analysis tools developed for business and scientific applications, such as *VisiCalc* and *TK!Solver*, can be adapted for use by students

	A		C		D		E		F		G		H		I		J		K		L
1																					
2		0		1		2		3		4		5		6		7		8		9		10
3																					
4		1		1		2		3		4		5		6		7		8		9		10
5		2		2		4		6		8		10		12		14		16		18		20
6		3		3		6		9		12		15		18		21		24		27		30
7		4		4		8		12		16		20		24		28		32		36		40
8		5		5		10		15		20		25		30		35		40		45		50
9		6		6		12		18		24		30		36		42		48		54		60
10		7		7		14		21		28		35		42		49		56		63		70
11		8		8		16		24		32		40		48		56		64		72		80
12		9		9		18		27		36		45		54		63		72		81		90
13		10		10		20		30		40		50		60		70		80		90		100
14																					
15																					

Fig. 1.1

in mathematics classes. With them, students can keep track of and separate variables, store and display data, or even generate arithmetic tables, such as the multiplication table in Fig. 1.1. Generating such tables can give students insight into their construction, and may enable them to recognize useful arithmetic patterns. One of the most powerful features of *VisiCalc* is the ease with which students can alter programs so that, for example, a whole number multiplication table can be easily and instantly converted into a decimal multiplication table, as in Fig. 1.2. Numerical analysis programs can also help students solve problems by making it easy for

	A		C		D		E		F		G		H		I		J		K		L
1																					
2|	0		.1		.2		.3		.4		.5		.6		.7		.8		.9		1
3																					
4|	.1		.01		.02		.03		.04		.05		.06		.07		.08		.09		.1
5|	.2		.02		.04		.06		.08		.1		.12		.14		.16		.18		.2
6|	.3		.03		.06		.09		.12		.15		.18		.21		.24		.27		.3
7|	.4		.04		.08		.12		.16		.2		.24		.28		.32		.36		.4
8|	.5		.05		.1		.15		.2		.25		.3		.35		.4		.45		.5
9|	.6		.06		.12		.18		.24		.3		.36		.42		.48		.54		.6
10|	.7		.07		.14		.21		.28		.35		.42		.49		.56		.63		.7
11|	.8		.08		.16		.24		.32		.4		.48		.56		.64		.72		.8
12|	.9		.09		.18		.27		.36		.45		.54		.63		.72		.81		.9
13|	1		.1		.2		.3		.4		.5		.6		.7		.8		.9		1
14																					

Fig. 1.2

them to sort out variables and formulas, keep track of intermediate solutions, and even record their mistakes. Appropriately used, these professional programs can make problem solving more structured and less frustrating for many students.

One of the first problem-solving tools developed explicitly for education, *SemCalc* (Semantic Calculator), is designed to help students use dimensional analysis to solve problems. Described in detail in Chapter 2 of *Practical Guide to Computers in Education*, *SemCalc* keeps track of the dimensions (units) of each number used in the problem and assists the student, through prompting and display, to decide whether the answer has the appropriate units. Problems like "If you keep $500 in a bank at 7.5% interest per year for 5 years, how much interest will you earn?" confuse many junior high mathematics students and teachers alike. With *SemCalc*, students can check their answers to such problems instantly by noting the units in which the program reports them, as in Fig. 1.3. In this

```
          HOW MANY?    WHAT?
  A          500          $
  B          .075        1/yrs
  C           5          yrs
OPERATION:  B × C/A
THE UNITS OF THE ANSWER ARE 1/$
DO YOU WISH TO CARRY OUT THE CALCULATION? (TYPE Y)
OR INDICATE A DIFFERENT OPERATION? (TYPE N)
N
OPERATION: A × B × C
THE UNITS OF THE ANSWER ARE $
DO YOU WISH TO CARRY OUT THE CALCULATION? (TYPE Y)
OR INDICATE A DIFFERENT OPERATION? (TYPE N)
Y
500 $ × .075 1/yrs × 5 yrs = 187.50$
```

Fig. 1.3

Note: In the example above and throughout the book, wherever a program is presented as it would appear on a computer terminal being used, the user's input will appear in bold type, while the computer's output will appear in regular type.

problem, since the student's problem-solving method initially resulted in an answer reported by the program in units of "one over dollars," the student knew the answer and the method for getting it were wrong. On the other hand, when the answer was given in units of "dollars," the student could be fairly sure the answer and the method were correct.

SemCalc performs the arithmetic, so since the student set the problem up correctly, the answer is correct, as well. This suggests a change in role for students doing problem solving. No longer need they be concerned with making trivial arithmetic errors that cause them to "get the problem wrong." Instead, they can focus on figuring out how to solve the problem. Of course, this runs counter to the traditional pattern of providing students with a model solution and then asking them to solve a set of virtually identical problems. Instead of this rote-practice approach to problem solving, *SemCalc* promotes thinking through problems each time they are encountered.

Students can use *SemCalc*, as well as the more complicated *VisiCalc* and *TK!Solver* programs, to check their own work as they wind their way through complex problems. As a result of using such programs, students can approach formula-based problem solving as a structured, planned activity, rather than as a guessing game based on trial and error. Students can take problems one step at a time and see what they have done in each step. Seeing their work neatly displayed in a standard format also can make it easier for students to see their mistakes.

Moreover, the next generation of educational problem-solving tools is just around the corner. With these, students will be able to input problems as English sentences, separate the elements of the sentences, collect those elements, and later join them together as the solution to the problem. The programs will directly assist students to explore problem situations, keep track of what they have learned, and find patterns in what remains to be done. The students will make the decisions and do the thinking; the programs will be the working tools. These programs will be, in essence, powerful but limited computer languages that students would use to program their own problem solving. Using such programs, students will be able to solve surprisingly complex and realistic problems, extrapolate results, and do trial runs on new data. Such power will be in the hands of students sooner than most of us expect.

The use of the computer as a problem-solving tool has the potential to transform how problem solving is taught and learned in mathematics courses. Tool programs such as *VisiCalc, TK!Solver*, and *SemCalc* are already causing some teachers and students to reconsider the meaning of finding solutions, to question the need for a single correct answer to a problem, and to focus instead on problem-solving methods and the notion of finding a range of possible solutions.

This new view is being reflected in educational software development, as well as in classroom practices. Courseware packages such as the *Search Series* promote group cooperation and record keeping as problem-solving activities. Simulation languages, like MicroDYNAMO, permit students to model problem situations and to test their solutions against real-world data. And in classrooms, some mathematics teachers are beginning to alter their lesson objectives, assignments, and grading practices. They are encouraging and rewarding student creativity. They are asking students to try alternative approaches to problems, even when they have arrived at appropriate solutions. They are recognizing that some problems cannot be completed within a class period or even a week. And they are giving students credit more for setting up problems than for getting answers.

These departures from standard practice in mathematics classes are not yet widespread. They may never be. There may be too much inertia in school and classroom traditions to be overcome. But, if ever there was an opportunity to transform classroom problem-solving activities so that they become more like real-world problem solving, the computer appears to be providing it. The onus is on mathematics educators to take up this challenge.

The Graphics Revolution

Prior to the development of video displays, computer terminals could only print output on paper. This led educators to write programs that used the computer more or less like an automated workbook or reading machine. Video computer monitors have changed all that. Now high-resolution color displays enable students to create, see, and manipulate images and to use them to discover patterns, trends, and alternative perspectives.

Students can use the graphics capabilities of computers in a wide variety of ways in mathematics, ranging from traditional graphing activities to informal geometric explorations to sophisticated three-dimensional designing. Teachers can encourage students to put visual images of mathematical phenomena on the computer for study and manipulation. For example, students can graph information and equations to help them visualize these problem elements.

A variety of graphing programs are commercially available, from simple ones that can be used for graphing particular equations to complex and elegant general programs like *VisiPlot*. Most of the best plotting programs are still those developed for business, but there are beginning to be some excellent, sophisticated, general graphing programs specifically designed for education. Mathematics teachers who have not yet seen these graphing programs are in for a pleasant surprise. Finding the best program for current use is less important than getting started and encouraging students to graph problem solutions to see if their answers are reasonable.

Students can also visualize problem elements by using one of the increasing number of two-dimensional drawing programs. For example, students can draw, or even animate on the screen, the common geometry problem which asks students to calculate the angles at which a ladder of a given length leans against a house at various heights. Using more sophisticated three-dimensional drawing programs, now available for even low-cost microcomputers, students can draw three-dimensional figures, manipulate them, and solve problems involving such shapes.

Drawing programs can also be used with elementary school children to help them visualize arithmetic problems. Teachers, or even students, can create shapes, such as circles or squares, which can then be used in traditional exercises like: two circles + four circles makes how many circles? Really imaginative teachers could use drawing programs to create screen-based manipulables like Cuisenaire Rods for students to work with.

In fact, several commercial programs have been developed for children that provide problems to solve using screen-based Cuisenaire Rods and Geo-boards. *Numberforms* even allows the students to create their own "three-dimensional" rods and blocks out of a two-dimensional number line. Such visual representations of numbers not only give students concrete cues for more abstract processes, but also enable them to more easily recognize patterns in numerical relationships, such as fibonacci numbers and perfect squares.

Such supplementary use of the computer's graphics capabilities in the curriculum only scratches the surface of possible applications. Entire units or even courses can be built around the graphics computer. Logo, a high-level computer language, with a powerful graphics component called **turtle graphics,** can be used to teach programming to elementary school children, geometric and algebraic concepts to junior high and high school mathematics students, and vectors to high school or college physics students. With minimal instruction from the teacher, students at all grade levels can adopt Logo as a personal and powerful problem-solving tool with which they can translate abstract and complex problems into accessible, concrete, and simple forms.

The graphics capabilities of computers offer teachers and students a learning tool of nearly infinite flexibility and variety. Even an activity as straightforward as learning graphics programming in BASIC can provide mathematics students with dozens of practical applications of concepts ordinarily covered in high school mathematics courses. Mathematics educators have only just begun to tap the vast educational potential that could emerge from the marriage of computer and video screen.

A New Medium for Teaching and Learning

Harvey Katz stepped into his classroom from the corridor filled with students running to get to their next class before the bell rang. As he closed the door, his eyes took in the scene before him: his entire business math class huddled over the five microcomputers at the back of the room, talking eagerly but quietly to each other. The bell rang.

"Incredible!" Harvey thought. This was the class he had dreaded since the math department chair told him last spring that, due to declining enrollments, one of his advanced algebra II sections would be cancelled and he would have to teach business math. Harvey smiled. He remembered his awful summer. Instead of feeling his usual enthusiasm for planning next year's courses, he had barely been able to open the textbook that was used in the business math course. The thought of it had even put a damper on the enthusiasm he felt for his new computer science course.

And now the business math course was shaping up to be the best, most exciting, most rewarding course he had ever taught. There they were: twenty of the toughest, supposedly dumbest, least-motivated students in the school, racing to get to class early to work on the computers. And they were using *VisiCalc*, not playing PACMAN!

Harvey remembered how it had started. It was the second week of school. The business math course was every bit as bad as he had feared. He was not interested in the material and the students knew it. They were unruly, nearly out of control most of the time. He hadn't felt so bad about his work since his first week of teaching, thirteen years ago.

Then one day, Sallie Young and Debra Phillips, two of the less troublesome members of the class, got to class early and wandered over to the computers at the back of the room where Bill Jones, first-string quarterback and math whiz, was running a program he had written for his advanced algebra II course. When the bell rang and fewer than half the class had as yet straggled in, Sallie and Debra asked if they could continue to watch Bill work. Convinced that they were probably more impressed by Bill's good looks than by his programming skills, Harvey said *no*. Whereupon, various members of the class complained loudly that only the smart kids, preppies, and jocks got to use the expensive equipment in the school, and it wasn't fair that the rich kids got to work with computers in school since their parents could afford to buy them for them. The argument grew louder and more heated, gradually drawing in the stragglers who appeared suddenly, like sharks attracted by blood. Harvey felt himself losing control of the class, of the argument, and of his emotions. Suddenly, he stopped in mid-sentence and thought, "Why not?"

From that point on, events moved quickly. He told the students that the next day they would use the computers, but, to prepare for it, they had to fill out the inventory charts in Chapter Two of their textbooks. The idea of using *VisiCalc* with the class came to him in a flash, and the inventory charts they had skipped over because he had thought them too boring suddenly seemed the perfect topic of study.

Harvey quickly divided the class into five groups of four and assigned each of them a retail store: a drug store, a record shop, an automobile supply store, a pizza shop, and a shoe store. He provided each group with information on five products in their store: the name of the item, the number of each item sold in a week, the wholesale cost of each item, and the selling price of each item. Harvey made the values up as he reeled them off. He instructed each group to draw up a chart like the one in their texts, to write in the values he told them in the appropriate spaces, and then to calculate the two missing quantities for each item: the markup and the total profit for the week. The students groaned at that last instruction; they wanted to use the computers to do the calculations. "Isn't that what they're for?" they demanded. Harvey acknowledged that it was, but that first the computers had to be programmed to carry out particular calculations, and since the idea of using them in the class had just come up, they weren't so programmed. The class accepted his explanation and proceeded to work on the assignment. When the bell rang, the entire class remained in their seats, working furiously to complete the tables. Harvey was stunned.

That night Harvey created a *VisiCalc* template like that in Fig. 1.4 to replicate the table in Chapter Two of the text, but as he was doing so, his pedagogical creativity led him to make modifications that would open up various avenues of inquiry for the students. The template produced a table like that shown in Fig. 1.5.

|A|	B			D		E		F		G		H		I	
1					WHOLE									ITEM
2		ITEM		SALE	%MARKUP	RETAIL	PROFIT	SOLD	PROFIT
3	=====================		===
4	1.					D4*(1+E4)	F4–D4		H4*(F4–D4)
5	2.					D5*(1+E5)	F5–D5		H5*(F5–D5)
6	3.					D6*(1+E6)	F6–D6		H6*(F6–D6)
7	4.					D7*(1+E7)	F7–D7		H7*(F7–D7)
8	5.					D8*(1+E8)	F8–D8		H8*(F8–D8)
9	6.					D9*(1+E9)	F9–D9		H9*(F9–D9)
10	7.					D10*(1+E10)	F10–D10		H10*(F10–D10)
11	8.					D11*(1+E11)	F11–D11		H11*(F11–D11)
12	9.					D12*(1+E12)	F12–D12		H12*(F12–D12)
13	10.					D13*(1+E13)	F13–D13		H13*(F13–D13)
14	=====================		===
15							TOTAL PROFIT: $ SUM(I4:I13)
16				

Fig. 1.4

|A|	B			D		E		F		G		H		I	
1					WHOLE									ITEM
2		ITEM		SALE	%MARKUP	RETAIL	PROFIT	SOLD	PROFIT
3	=====================		===
4	1.					.00	.00		.00
5	2.					.00	.00		.00
6	3.					.00	.00		.00
7	4.					.00	.00		.00
8	5.					.00	.00		.00
9	6.					.00	.00		.00
10	7.					.00	.00		.00
11	8.					.00	.00		.00
12	9.					.00	.00		.00
13	10.					.00	.00		.00
14	=====================		===
15							TOTAL PROFIT: $ .00
16				

Fig. 1.5

Harvey stayed up late that night cranking out additional information for the class to use. He provided each group with data on ten new items for their stores. This time he gave them number sold, wholesale price, and percent markup.

The next day, Harvey passed out the additional data, and before the class could complain about having to do more calculations, he told them they could enter the data directly on the computers. He briefly showed the class how to do this on the *VisiCalc* chart on the computer screen, and turned them loose. Within a minute, one of the students called out, "Hey, the computer filled in the retail price, profit, and item profit columns by itself! How come?" Harvey explained that he had programmed it to do so on the *VisiCalc* template, just as he had said was necessary the day before. Again, the students turned back to the task of entering the values on the screen and *VisiCalc* did the calculations, as shown in Fig. 1.6. While they did so, Harvey wrote on the board:

- Which of these stores would you prefer to own? Why?
- Which items are the most profitable in each store?

|A|	B			D		E		F		G		H		I	
1				WHOLE				#	ITEM
2		ITEM		SALE	%MARKUP	RETAIL	PROFIT	SOLD	PROFIT
3	==============		==
4| 1.RADIAL TIRES		78.00	.35	105.30	27.30	40	1092.00
5	2.CHAMPION SPARK PLUGS		2.15	.55	3.33	1.18	56	66.22
6| 3.GREASY-LUBE OIL		.85	.65	1.40	.55	128	70.72
7| 4.FLARES		.35	.65	.58	.23	30	6.83
8| 5.OIL FILTER		.95	.54	1.46	.51	68	34.88
9| 6.AM-FM/CASSETTE		235.00	.35	317.25	82.25	55	4523.75
10| 7.TOOL KIT		115.40	.45	167.33	51.93	23	1194.39
11| 8.CAR COVER		36.00	.37	49.32	13.32	22	293.04
12	9.RE-LINED BRAKE SHOES		27.80	.65	45.87	18.07	44	795.08
13|10.MUFFLER		85.50	.44	123.12	37.62	17	639.54
14	==============		==
15						TOTAL PROFIT: $	8716.45
16							

Fig. 1.6

As each group finished their data entry, Harvey switched their computer to the printer, which was shared by all five machines, and printed out five copies of their results. By ten minutes before the end of class, all five groups were poring over each other's results, mentally comparing the two profit columns. As the bell rang, groans chorused through the room. Harvey smiled and said, "Tomorrow we'll discuss the questions on the board. Think about them."

"Ringgg." the bell startled Harvey out of his revery. He looked over at the clock. The period was over. He'd spent the whole time remembering how his business math class had started working with computers. He looked at the class. They'd worked entirely on their own for the full class period, oblivious to their daydreaming teacher. Now his problem was to get them to remove their programs from the computers so his next class could work on them. That was a nice sort of problem to have. Harvey smiled again. He'd done a lot of that this year.

Harvey Katz may be an exceptionally creative and flexible mathematics teacher, but what he did in his business mathematics course lies well within the capabilities of most inexpensive computers and within the boundaries of traditional curricular goals. As in Harvey's class, computers can provide an exciting new medium for teaching and learning mathematics, largely because of their flexibility and potentially interactive nature.

Computers are flexible. Most are capable of carrying a veritable tool kit of programs that can transform the computer now into a word processor, now into a sophisticated calculator, now an accounting worksheet, now a set of drafting tools, now a slide projector, now a primitive animation device, and more. Most of these capabilities are generic. They can be applied to any field—engineering, creative writing, economics; to any task—typing a letter, estimating costs, projecting election results; to any situation—home, school, business, government; and to any student—gifted and talented, unmotivated, handicapped.

Computers can be used interactively. Students can test out their own solutions and hypotheses on the computer, receiving immediate and appropriate feedback. They can explore microworlds to discover mathematical patterns, system dynamics, logical relationships, or natural laws. They can program computers to solve problems or perform tedious tasks, such as calculations, or difficult ones, such as drawing diagrams. They can use computers to query data bases, store and retrieve information, manipulate and analyze data, and display results in myriad forms.

Or, they can do none of this. Mathematics teachers can disregard the interactive capabilities of computers. They can use them to provide students with drill and practice of basic mathematics skills or with tutorials that lead students through a series of brief questions and answers to arrive at some statement of a mathematical concept. They can use computers as electronic page turners and grade books, as "high tech" demonstration screens or arcade-like behavior modification devices. It is up to mathematics teachers to decide how they will use computers. Interaction is only potential in computers; if it is to become actual in classrooms, teachers must release it.

TRANSFORMING THE CONTENT OF THE MATHEMATICS CURRICULUM

The 1980s promise to be a watershed for the K–12 mathematics curriculum. Pressures from society and from within the mathematics community, coupled with the revolutionary potential of the computer, are already changing how some mathematics teachers are teaching some topics in the curriculum. And this may be only the beginning of far more pervasive changes. All indications are that such a transformation is underway.

Public figures from government, industry, and academia have, for the past few years, been calling attention to the need for many more high technology workers, from engineers and inventors to technicians and computer programmers. At times, these public pronouncements have reached a fever pitch, akin to the scare that followed the Soviet Union's launch of Sputnik and precipitated herculean crash programs to upgrade science and mathematics education in the 1960s. Indeed, members of the science, mathematics, and education communities appear to be hoping for and encouraging a similar reaction to the technology gap of the 1980s. This time the scare is less military than economic, less symbolic than real. Politicians like former California Governor Jerry Brown and the so-called "Atari Democrats" in Congress are claiming that many of our economic woes are a result of our failure to replace traditional industrial activities with high technology, to replace steel and automobiles with semiconductors and computers. They warn that unless the United States takes quick and drastic action to develop and adequately capitalize new high technology industries, we will experience a serious technology gap in which other industrial countries such as Japan and Germany will dominate the world economy. In the pessimistic version of this scenario, the economy of the United States is reduced to a shambles with chronic high unemployment and a state of almost perpetual recession.

While such dire warnings are undoubtedly dramatized for political purposes, the pressures to close the technology gap are real, as are the concommitant needs of people for skills and knowledge befitting citizens of the 1980s. Unfortunately, the majority of the K–12 curriculum in all subjects reflects values and needs more appropriate to the 1950s, or even the 1940s. This is especially true in science and mathematics where many of the innovations of the ill-fated "new science and math" curricula of the 1960s have been abandoned or so diluted as to be unrecognizable and largely ineffective.

Equally unfortunate is the shortage of qualified science and mathematics teachers to prepare people for life and work in a high technology society. The conventional wisdom regarding this shortage is that industry is so desperate for people with science and mathematics training that they are luring them away from teaching with high salaries and excellent benefits. This line of thinking leads inevitably to proposals for financial incentives for science and mathematics teachers and crash programs to train them.

While neither of these approaches to the problem is particularly objectionable, they suffer some drawbacks and more importantly, they do not address the more significant problem: the outmoded content of today's science and mathematics curricula. No increase in numbers of science and mathematics teachers, particularly if many of them are overnight converts from the "breadlines" of English teachers, can produce technologically literate high school graduates if the curriculum doesn't reflect this as a goal. Yet, technological literacy is not currently a central feature of the K–12 curriculum, either in words or deeds.

Indeed, many would argue that there is no room in the K–12 curriculum for yet another set of goals and objectives. It is hard enough to attain basic literacy objectives in reading, writing, and arithmetic without worrying about high technology objectives in data base utilization, word processing, and computer programming. Others counter that the so-called basics have changed; that computer-accessed data bases and interactive video are permanently altering what it means to read; that with word processors, educators may at last really be able to teach people to write; and that electronic calculators and computers make basic arithmetic skills unnecessary. According to such educational futurists, basic skills are indeed important, but they must be the skills students will need for life and work in the 1980s and beyond, not those of a pre-technological era.

While it is uncertain that such a view of basic skills and needed educational objectives will prevail, it is clear that computers stand ready to be the vehicle for implementing such a vision in all areas of the curriculum. In the mathematics curriculum alone, computers offer opportunities to learn new content, in different sequences, and with a higher degree of sophistication at every age level. They provide mathematics educators with an unprecedented opportunity to reconsider why they teach what they teach and whether they should be teaching other skills and ideas altogether.

Computers do not merely change the size or the quantity of the numbers that can be handled by students in mathematics classes. (If such magnified numbers were ever interesting, the pocket calculator now provides an easy means of handling them.) Computers can take us far beyond the realm of magnified numbers to problems with new dimensions of richness and reality, problems in which mathematics intersects with other disciplines, and problems that involve the theory of mathematics. Further, computers suggest the need for entirely new topics and even new courses in the mathematics curriculum.

Realistic Mathematics Problems

A typical seventh-grade mathematics textbook problem asks students to find the time it would take a car traveling at 40 miles per hour to go from New York to Boston, a distance of 212 miles. Such a problem is then usually followed by another that asks the same question for other cities and then another and another, always asking the same basic question. Because of limited space available on problem-solving pages and because of a textbook's inability to check answers, textbook authors must rely on such repetition, and cannot build either realism or complexity into their problems. (When was the last time someone drove a car at 40 mph from New York to Boston?)

But, using a computer, it would not be difficult for a teacher with some programming experience to create a program that generates a variety of more realistic and complex problems. Such a program might begin with the same sort of question, but would include a map of a region familiar to the student, state the problem in terms of that region, and display a car traveling along the roads on the map so that students could get a visual sense of the problem. A clock on the screen and the moving car could then simulate the situation, providing students with a visual means to check their solution. The computer wouldn't need to tell them if their solution were right or wrong. They would be able to see it on the screen.

This idea could form the basis of a more elaborate commercial program that might add a "window" to provide the student with a scratchpad for doing calculations on the screen, as well. (See Fig. 1.7.)

Such a program might also have provisions to branch to a tutorial or to ask the same question for two different towns, if the student got the answer wrong, and to pose the same problem but for different routes between the same cities if the student got the problem right. The program could also add each successfully calculated route to the map as a mark

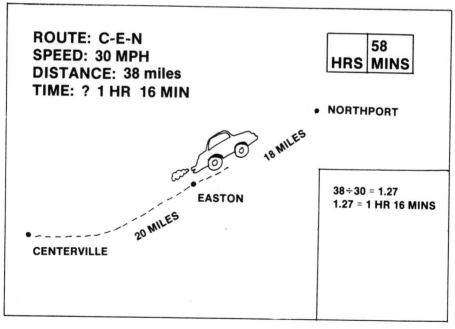

Fig. 1.7

of the student's progress and keep a record of distances, times, and speed limits correctly calculated for each route in a table. For some routes the computer could change the speed limit; for others it could add obstacles and towns, which slow a car up. Students would thus be solving similar but increasingly sophisticated problems, while at the same time building up a realistic road map and a table of useful information. (See Fig. 1.8.)

Becoming even more sophisticated, such a program could ask students to become travel agents, plotting a family's vacation, stopping points, the fastest possible route, and gas savings. This is the sort of problem involved in planning school bus routes, mail delivery routes, or a traveling salesperson's route. To solve such problems, students would have access to similar maps and tables of information as in earlier problems but for a new region. The program could also provide a simple authoring language that would allow students to transform all the roads into straight lines and all the stops into points. This would move students to a new level of abstraction in understanding and visualizing a problem.

Such a powerful and flexible program would give teachers the ability to create different problems for different students and to save a student's

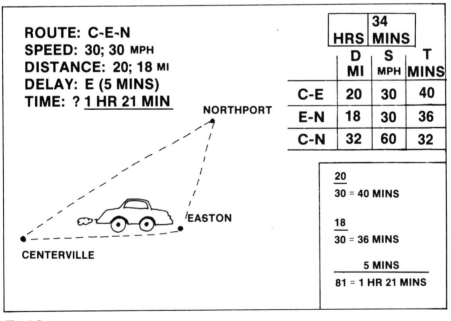

Fig. 1.8

work for later use. Although this program does not exist, it easily could—the product of a talented teacher-programmer or a forward-looking curriculum developer and publisher. But educators need to let publishers know that this is the direction mathematics curriculum materials should be taking.

Real World Mathematics Problems

In the vignette about Harvey Katz, his students forced him to recognize a painful truth about his use of computers with students, a truth that unfortunately applies in many schools: computer use is provided primarily to the college-bound, usually wealthier segments of the school population. Harvey's snobbery about business mathematics is typical. Yet, experience in using computers is clearly appropriate for students who will be going straight to work after high school. Many of them will work directly with computers in the office, on the assembly line, or in stores. If one of the missions of American public education is to prepare young people for the world of work, then today's public schools must provide a reasonable degree of computer education to all of their students.

This admonition is particularly directed toward mathematics educators who, in their curriculum projects, have tended to focus their attention on college-bound students and on their understanding of the underlying structures of mathematics. While it is certainly worthwhile for some students to learn and appreciate the more abstract aspects of mathematics, the vast majority of students will have little use for such knowledge after graduation. In contrast, all students will need to use mathematics in a variety of settings, many of them involving computers as well. Yet, aside from business mathematics texts, mathematics materials rarely provide applications or examples from life.

Because computers are real-world tools and do not belong to any one field or academic discipline, they are an ideal medium through which students may learn to use mathematics skills they will encounter in their lives. For example, the classic business mathematics unit on income taxes can be transformed from a mechanical task into a creative activity that may raise issues and questions about tax laws and tax fraud, both matters of relevance to most citizens.

There are already business computer programs that fill out the 1040 form, and hardcopy versions of the forms themselves are free, in quantity, at IRS offices, banks, and post offices, so that students can work with pencil and paper, as well as with the computer. Students could be given various parameters for income tax problems by using a computer's random number generator. These parameters would include income, number of family members, expenses, business losses, stock market gains, and so forth. The students would then use the computer to fill out their tax forms and find out what their income tax would be. The teacher could pursue many creative variations of this problem; for example, tell students to find ways for someone with a large income to pay little or no taxes, or ask students to determine the difference between the taxes paid by a married couple with two incomes filling out a joint return and those paid by two single persons with the same combined income. This relatively traditional business mathematics topic could then be extended beyond what is ordinarily treated in high school courses to problems dealing with the stock market, the start-up of new companies, business accounting, or car sales. Software publishers have been coming out with new and improved simulations much like the classic *Lemonade*, which do just this.

But why stop there? The same kind of simulations that business schools have used for years in their courses can be adapted for use by high school students using microcomputers. In one such simulation, *Fast Freight*, a small group of students run their own trucking company. They start with a small bank loan with which they try to build a successful business. They compete with other students, running similar companies, much as actual trucking companies would compete in the real world. In order to be successful, the students must learn a great deal about the trucking industry, business practices, and financial management. They must take actions based on mathematical information and calculations, such as deciding whether to buy or lease their trucks, figuring how much to bid on a job, or borrowing additional money to take advantage of a promising opportunity. All of these are realistic activities similar to those most adults are faced with sometime in their lives.

Presumably, the great concern for basic mathematics competency for high school graduation is a function of the need for citizens to successfully manage such mathematically based actions. Yet, so much mathematics instruction ignores the practical context in which the skills to be mastered will be practiced. Computer simulations like *Fast Freight* provide effective and motivating means of learning practical mathematics for a wide range of students.

But real world problem solving need not be limited to simulations. Students can use problem-solving tools like *VisiCalc* and *TK!Solver* for real-world problem solving for their family, their school, their organizations, and themselves in such diverse areas as: energy conservation, budget management, investment strategies, purchasing, strategic decision making, efficiency studies, and many others.

One of the important reasons for learning mathematics is to be able to use it in the real world. Computers make it much easier for students to do so now, while they are being taught the mathematics, and thus make it more likely that they will actually learn the needed skills and use them later.

Interdisciplinary Problems

But how will there be room in the curriculum to include these additional problems and approaches to problems? As it is, there are ever more increasing demands on schools to provide coverage of new subjects: drug education, driver education, health education, environmental studies, women's studies, various ethnic studies, and so on. This is coupled with competing and often opposing pressures to spend more time on the basics and less on such "frills" as lab sciences, social studies, art, and music.

Now, computers can provide at least one approach to settling some of these competing demands through meaningful interdisciplinary problem solving. Not that computers are required for interdisciplinary activities, but they certainly make such problem solving more interesting, more realistic, and more useful to students.

Moreover, much interdisciplinary problem solving is difficult to implement with traditional curriculum materials because the problems are often complex; useful data bases are generally too large to incorporate into textbooks; and books are a static medium. Computers can be very effective in helping to overcome these barriers to solving problems derived from other disciplines.

The sciences are the most fertile source of problems for treatment in mathematics courses. For example, among the laws of physics is the relationship between the speed of a wave, its frequency, and its wavelength: the speed (v) equal the frequency (f) times the wavelength (l), $v = f \times l$. Using this law involves simple multiplication or division, just like the multiplication and division problems students do in routine problem sets. A program for junior high students using this equation could begin by graphically showing the definitions of speed, wavelength, and frequency. Two or more waves might be displayed simultaneously, with a chart indicating v, f, and l. Students could change one variable, while holding a second constant, and watch the change in the third, as in Fig. 1.9.

Students might then be asked to solve multiplication and division problems involving one of the variables as an unknown. The students could use the computer as a scratchpad and the program could be written to check their answers when they finish filling out a table such as the one to the right of each wave on the screen in Fig. 1.9. This table could

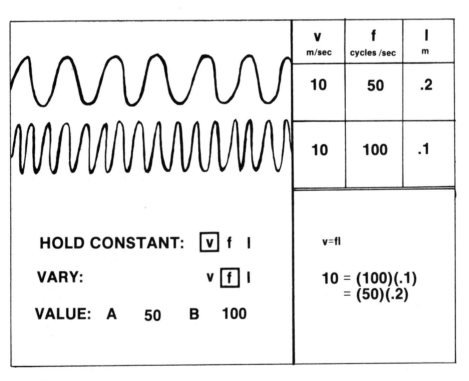

Fig. 1.9

then be used as the basis for relevant interdisciplinary problem solving. For example, some students could study sound waves, solving problems connected with the design of musical instruments; others could study ocean waves, determining where to place a wave barrier to prevent beach erosion; others could apply this approach to radio waves, calculating the size of an antenna to get a stronger signal from their favorite radio stations. A more elaborate program could provide on demand special tutorial instruction about the content for each area of study. Although such a program would focus on using mathematics skills for problem solving, students would necessarily learn some physics, which they might then wish to continue exploring.

One of the great attractions of the computer as an educational tool is the relative ease with which most students can learn to write simple programs. Interdisciplinary problems provide an ideal opportunity for students to develop their own computer learning materials through programming. For example, junior high students now spend significant amounts of their time doing countless sets of problems involving fractions, ratios, and proportions. The manipulation of these three mathematical concepts happens to be required to use the basic principles of Mendelian genetics. It is a relatively simple matter for students to calculate the proportion of white and black mice that will be born to a given set of parent mice. However, the simplicity of the basic principles of Mendelian genetics quickly disappear in their application to real situations after just a few generations. Using computers, with their visual display capabilities and memory, teachers can guide junior high students to solve such problems through programming. Even a computer without color graphics could be programmed by students and teachers with little programming experience to show sex-linked inheritance. Each line of the screen could represent one generation, with a white or black box representing one mouse. A whole series of problems involving fractions, ratios, and proportions could be formulated and answered, beginning with the calculation of the fractions of white and black mice in each generation.

Chemical composition problems provide another science topic simple enough for students to program, yet ideal for teaching, in this case, the rudiments of chemistry and fractions. For example, one law of chemical composition states that chemical substances combine in simple and constant ratios by weight. Students easily could create a program to determine the weight of one substance needed to combine with a given weight of another substance, if their combining ratio is known. Similar programs could be created by students for the other laws of chemical composition, providing them with useful programming activities, practice manipulating ratios, and a means of solving the sort of problems that ordinarily bedevil students and plague science teachers.

Although science is the most obvious discipline with which to combine mathematics, the social sciences, and even the arts provide exciting possibilities for interdisciplinary computer applications involving mathematics as well. Two commercially developed programs, *Songwriter* and *Pattern-maker*, use mathematics in an intuitive way with music and art. Designed to teach music and mathematics simultaneously, *Songwriter* displays music like a player piano and lets the user invent or change the music in significant ways (see Fig. 1.10). In the program, the student sets the length of a note either by using the number keys alone or in combination with an operation key (addition, subtraction, multiplication, or division). The student changes

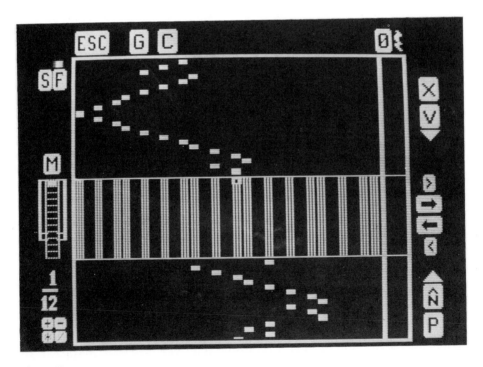

Fig. 1.10

the length of a measure in the same way. Musical notes are fractions; thus, while students learn music with *Songwriter* they also learn fractions. Not only do they see how mathematical operations with fractions are performed, they see them in a graphic and dramatic way.

With *Patternmaker,* students design and explore tesselation (tiling) patterns and symmetry. Students can view these patterns artistically and mathematically. The program enables students to take patterns of boxes and perform on them any of the symmetry operations: translation, rotation, or reflection. These operations are carried out on the screen graphically where students can observe the resulting changes in patterns. They can specify a series of operations that combine artistic design with some fundamental algebra. In this way, students can use *Patternmaker* to solve design problems mathematically, or mathematical problems graphically.

These few examples have but scratched the surface of the possibilities for cross-fertilization of mathematics and other disciplines through computer-based learning activities. Computers offer curriculum developers, teachers, and students opportunities to use real data, to display it graphically, and to test out results of calculations in dramatic and realistic ways. Many interdisciplinary problems can be easily programmed by teachers or students. Others may be approached via problem-solving programs like *TK!Solver,* and still others may be built into commercially developed courseware such as simulations.

Real Mathematics Problems

Traditional mathematics instruction rarely provides opportunities for students to make their own discoveries. Most mathematics curricula are taught axiomatically. The text and teacher present the concepts and problems and develop the methods of solution, usually providing models of solved problems. The students are expected to follow the logic of the theorem or derivation and to solve problem sets given them by imitating the models also provided. Only rarely are elements of discovery incorporated into mathematics materials, and even then such inclusion is often contrived.

With computers, students are much more able to make genuine discoveries and to seek the solution of problems that they themselves identify. Even very young children can pose problems for their own explorations. For example, many students are fascinated by numerical patterns such as fibonacci numbers. Computers make it "child's play" to search out patterns among the prime numbers or the perfect squares or the multiples of 9 or the factors of consecutive numbers.

Even a novice programmer can develop a simple program that searches prime numbers for relationships. The first element of the program would extract prime numbers from the natural numbers using the Sieve of Eratosthenes, in which each whole number is tested to see whether it is divisible by the whole numbers before it.

In the next step of the program, the prime numbers could be grouped by 100s, those from 1 to 100, 101 to 200, and so forth, and the primes in each group counted. These results could then be displayed on a graph to see whether they show any patterns or tendency. This is precisely the method used by mathematicians through the centuries in searching for elusive relationships among primes. But with computers, even elementary school children stand a better chance of finding a relationship than the best mathematicians of earlier days. Students can generate an almost infinite number of primes, group them in as many different ways as they can think of, perform any mathematical operation on them or on the intervals between them, display them in a wide variety of ways graphically, and all of this effortlessly and errorlessly. What power to be in the hands of students! With computers, the once mysterious realm of number theory can become a reasonable subject for exploration throughout the K–12 curriculum.

Similarly, sophisticated graphics packages make it possible for students to explore geometric patterns and relationships instead of waiting for these to be presented to them as a series of theorems whose significance is usually unclear. Whether students "discover" relationships that are already known or really make new discoveries is irrelevant. The importance of such explorations is the genuine sense of discovery students get when they pose their own problems, devise their own methods of solution, and recognize some pattern or relationship that they never noticed before. This can help students to see mathematics as a living, changing discipline of which they can be a part.

Computer Science

For some time now, at the university level, mathematics departments either have offered a computer science major or have split into two departments: mathematics and computer science. The trickle-down effect is beginning to be felt in secondary schools, reinforced by the interests of students who have home computers and parents who want their children to be prepared for a computerized world. High school mathematics departments are slowly responding to these pressures, primarily by integrating the computer into existing courses. However, mathematics departments will soon need to offer entire courses in computer science. Some computer enthusiasts are even suggesting computer science departments at the high school level.

Courses in computer science would include far more than programming, just as programming should be part of many courses besides computer science. Much of what is loosely classified as "computer literacy" would be included as objectives in most computer science courses: consideration of social, economic, political, and ethical issues related to computing; an awareness of important historical developments in computer technology; the ability to use computers for a range of purposes, including programming; understanding how computers work, from the level of electronic switches to high-level programming languages.

Of course, the treatment of topics will vary in sophistication depending on the age, experience, abilities, and goals of the students, but every student in school today needs a modicum of exposure and skill in these areas. The world in which they are living and will be working is dominated by computers and is certain to be more so. They will need computer know-how simply to exercise their basic rights and responsibilities as citizens: voting intelligently, obeying and being protected by laws, working, being informed and informing others, engaging in financial transactions, participating in military activities, and so on. Every aspect of our society and culture will be affected by computers. Today's students need to know and understand as much as they can about this major influence in their lives, and mathematics teachers will be expected to take a leading role in the creation of lessons, units, and courses that address this need.

Programming

Programming can be viewed as a vocational skill, and for some students it will be a valuable preparation for work. Programming may also be viewed as an important element of computer literacy. Like reading and writing, most people in our society will do some programming in their lives, even if it is only programming a microwave oven, a programmable hand calculator, a telephone, or a television. However, programming can also be regarded as a fundamental mathematical activity.

Programming is problem solving and problem solving is at the heart of mathematics. Seen in this way, learning to program involves far more than learning the rudiments of some computer language and using it to perform trivial tasks, such as generating the squares of the integers from one to one hundred, printing "HI" on the computer, or drawing Snoopy on a screen with character graphics. Programming also involves more than mastering a computer language such as BASIC or Logo and applying it to more complex traditional programming tasks.

Programming is a creative activity, involving the exploration of a range and variety of mathematical problems. To engage in such activity, students need not master any one computer language. They need to understand the underlying structure of all programming, so they can learn to use new programming tools as they need them. Such an understanding of programming enables students to make creative and effective use of tools, ranging from word processors to numerical analysis programs like *VisiCalc*, from graphics packages and drawing programs to full-fledged programming languages like BASIC and Logo.

Viewed in this way, teaching programming is teaching problem solving. To write programs, students must explore the problem situation, define the problem, and work on various solutions until they have the simplest one. Almost any problem can be programmed a myriad of ways. Each way permits the programmer more or less flexibility, and is susceptible to more or fewer problems and bugs. As in all problem solving, the simplest solution to a programming problem often comes from exploring and working with a number of alternatives. Some of these are complicated and some are simple and elegant. The joy of programming as a problem-solving activity is that when students have solved the problem, they know it. The program runs.

BASIC is easy to manipulate and thus an easy language with which to try out problem solutions. Logo is an easy language with which to construct mathematical ideas. Pascal can be used to help students understand complex problems. And students can achieve major insights into how the computer works by doing some assembly language programming. All programming languages are fundamental means of expressing problems.

With this view of programming as a free-wheeling, exploratory, imaginative, problem-solving activity, teachers can urge students to write simple programs of their own design and to arrive at their own solutions to programming problems. Students can come to understand that there is no one right way, no recipe for programming or problem solving; there are only programming tools and procedures that make problem solving easier, faster, and more elegant.

A New View of Mathematics Content

Timothy Sterling is the Mathematics Department Chairman at The Palfrey School, an exclusive New England prep school. He is a computer enthusiast and an accomplished programmer in BASIC, Pascal, FORTRAN, Logo, LISP, Forth, and C. Programming for Tim is almost as natural as speaking. He dreams about computer applications in mathematics, doodles programs at faculty meetings, and inserts programming into his mathematics courses on every possible occasion.

Tim's algebra II course is a case in point. He begins the year assuming no programming knowledge on the part of his students. In truth, most students who know they'll be in his course try to pick up a little BASIC prior to the course. Early and often, Tim sends his students to the computer to use BASIC programs he has written to illustrate or explore some topic in the course.

One of the first programs he gives them asks the students to input values for *A, B, C,* and *D* on a cartesian plane, as in Fig. 1.11. The

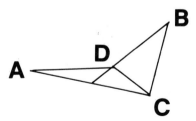

Fig. 1.11

program plots the image created by the points and then plots an image under the transformation $T(x,y) = (-3x + 8y, 8x - 2y)$, as in Fig. 1.12.

Tim gives this program to the students so they can use it to understand the phenomenon under study, linear transformations. It also starts the students thinking about programming as a skill and an art. Tim encourages the students to look at the program (Fig. 1.13) by typing the LIST command.

At this point, Tim gives the students no formal instruction in BASIC; that comes later. Even so, they begin to pick up some of the rudiments of BASIC in much the same way that a foreigner picks up bits of a new language by hearing it spoken and by reading public signs and newspaper headlines.

Another of the simple programs Tim gives his students at an early stage evaluates a polynomial and searches for solutions to a variety of polynomial equations. Again, Tim encourages the students to look at the simple program that provides this.

About two months into the course, Tim gives the students a quick one-week introduction to BASIC programming in which he uses, as examples, a few of the numerous programs that students have seen. Having seen the examples before helps the students to pick up BASIC programming very quickly, and, more importantly, it helps them to recognize the connection between programming and the mathematics concepts themselves. In fact, Tim selects his mathematics topics for their programmability. His curriculum does not follow the traditional sequence of topics.

When the class gets to the study of vectors, Tim teaches them Logo, which the students catch onto instantly. After fifteen minutes, Tim's

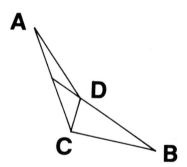

Fig. 1.12

```
10   REM ...THIS IS LINEAR TRANSFO
     RMATION DEMONSTRATION PROGRA
     M
15   DIM P(7,2): DIM NP(7,2): DIM
     C(2,2)
17   READ N
20   FOR I = 1 TO N: FOR J = 1 TO
     2: READ P(I,J): NEXT J: NEXT
     I
25   HGR : HCOLOR= 3
30   REM ...THIS READS IN TRANSFOR
     MATION
40   INPUT "A ";C(1,1): INPUT "B "
     ;C(1,2): INPUT "C ";C(2,1): INPUT
     "D ";C(2,2)
60   GOSUB 500
70   PRINT "A DIFFERENT TRANSFORMA
     TION (Y/N)?": GET A$: PRINT

80   PRINT "A CLEAR SCREEN (Y/N)?"
     : GET B$: PRINT
90   IF B$ = "Y" THEN  HGR : HCOLOR=
     3
100  IF A$ = "Y" THEN 40
105  DATA   7,0,0, 10,0, 3,2, 0,7
     ,              0,0, 3,2, 5,0

110  END
500  REM ...THIS PLOTS TRANSFORMA
     TION
510  FOR I = 1 TO N: FOR J = 1 TO
     2:NP(I,J) = C(J,1) * P(I,1) +
     C(J,2) * P(I,2): NEXT J: NEXT
     I
520  FOR I = 1 TO N - 1: HPLOT 14
     0 + NP(I,1),80 - NP(I,2) TO
     140 + NP(I + 1,1),80 - NP(I +
     1,2): NEXT I
530  RETURN
```

Fig. 1.13

Fig. 1.14

students are writing vector programs in Logo and gaining a deep, experiential understanding of vector properties.

Later in the course, Tim gives the students a variety of polygon problems in Logo, some of which would be very difficult without a computer. For example, he asks the students to use Logo to draw a regular heptagon and all of its diagonals, as in Fig. 1.14. Problems such as this require the students to apply trigonometric concepts they learned earlier in the course.

To Timothy Sterling, programming is fundamental to all mathematical study. Different languages are appropriate for different purposes. For rapid calculations and point-to-point drawings, he uses BASIC. For vector drawings, he uses Logo. His students spend almost no time studying computer languages as languages. Rather, he introduces the languages as they are needed to clarify mathematics content.

In today's educational world, Timothy Sterling might be considered an unusual mathematics teacher. His command of a half dozen programming languages and his ability to infuse appropriate programs of his own creation into his curriculum almost effortlessly are not skills many mathematics teachers have. However, the educational world of the future will have many Timothy Sterlings, teachers capable of recasting traditional mathematics topics in terms of computer programming. Over time, such teachers may shape a totally new mathematics curriculum, as different from today's "new math" as those reforms were from the traditional mathematics curricula of the first half of this century. This newest mathematics curriculum would almost certainly be heavily influenced by computers and computer languages. It would move away from abstract axiomatic approaches toward real-world problem-solving applications. It would be oriented more toward graphic representations than toward symbolic ones. Topics formerly avoided because they required tedious calculations would emerge in the curriculum, as would approaches to topics such as motion, which involve transformations and changes with time.

One of the most interesting and provocative side effects that has already emerged from using computers with elementary school children is the challenge this use poses to traditional concepts of cognitive development. Child-appropriate programming languages like Logo, powerful simulation languages like MicroDYNAMO, the various graphics capabilities of computers, and their capacity to handle very large and complicated calculations quickly, all provide children with tools and the means to think and learn differently from the way children learned even five years ago. This makes possible, and perhaps necessary, a radical alteration in the way mathematics topics have been sequenced in the curriculum.

Topics can now be taught much more often on a need-to-know basis, rather than according to some logical hierarchy or cognitive developmental framework. Computers can make accessible, even to young children, concepts from integration, differential geometry, topology, and number theory. Mathematics teachers may have to shift their expectations about what children of a certain age can and cannot learn. They may also have to change their modes of communication and methods of instruction to better fit the new learning styles of children reared on television, computers, and video games.

A Future Scene

Anne had been fascinated by the weather for years. During summer evenings in Washington State, she loved to watch the clouds that appeared over Mt. Ranier, as moist air was forced over the summit where, as it cooled, it sank, then warmed up and formed a cloud which finally disappeared into the sky. Her family called this the Mt. Ranier Cloud Show.

Anne, now in the sixth grade, had just gotten home from school. She had thought of Mt. Ranier today in geography class because they had been discussing weather. Her teacher had stated at some point during the class that a good rule of thumb to remember was "go north, go cold; go south, go warm." Anne had just finished reading about Napoleon's disasterous invasion of Russia, when most of his troops froze to death. She realized that Napoleon had gone east and had gotten very cold indeed. Her teacher's rule of thumb bothered Anne, and she wanted to find out more about how temperatures are distributed globally.

Anne turned on her family's computer terminal and selected the LIBRARY option. A prompt appeared on her screen, telling her that she had successfully hooked into the National Data Bank and asking for her account number. She responded, and a menu with many options appeared on the screen. She selected CATALOG and then WORLD TEMPERATURES. After a pause, the screen filled up with possible sources. She selected the DATA option and requested a list of average temperatures for all the major cities of the world. A message appeared on the screen telling her to turn on her printer, and shortly she had a complete list of all the major cities, arranged alphabetically, with their average temperatures.

She was puzzled by the list because the temperatures were all about the same. Ann thought about this for a moment and realized that she had requested the wrong data. She had just finished some work in her math group at school on statistics in which the teacher had explained averages. She now realized that the statistic she wanted was the average coldest temperature per year for each city, or the "average extreme cold." The data she had did not give her this.

She sat and thought for a couple of moments and was startled when her older brother David came into the room and asked her what she was up to. She told him, and explained the problem she was having. David told her about a special map he had seen at his school, called the Dymaxion Air Ocean Map, designed by Buckminster Fuller. He said it was a weird shape, but it contained a great deal of information, like temperatures.

Anne asked for another CATALOG, and this time requested information about the Dymaxion Air Ocean Map. In a couple of seconds she had a list of sources in front of her. Unfortunately, most of them sounded pretty technical so she asked to see a copy of the map.

David was right; it was weirdly shaped and certainly didn't look like any map she had ever seen before. Anne typed in a command that caused a colored copy of the map to appear on her printer, but she couldn't make much sense of what the colors represented. When the computer displayed the explanation of the colors on the screen, Anne knew she had found what she was looking for. The map was color-coded to show the average extreme low temperature for each place on the globe. The map showed clearly that, in many cases, the temperature gets colder as you go east, not as you go north. As one moved from Paris to Moscow, the colors became progressively bluer. Anne thought for a moment about what would have happened if Napoleon had used this map.

The more she looked at the map, the more fascinated she became. All the land masses seemed to be the proper size, with Greenland appearing as the relatively small island that it is. Also, there were no longer three oceans but only one. Anne noticed also that the shortest distance from Chicago to Europe and points East was over the pole.

As Anne sat staring at the screen, David took the color printout of the map and cut it out. He then folded it and joined the edges, making a solid object, called an icosahedron. David held it up for Anne and said, "I've got the whole world in my hands." Anne laughed, appreciative of the joke.

The map continued to amaze Anne, and she wanted to learn more about it.

"David, how does it work? Why doesn't it distort the shapes of the continents like other maps do?"

David had just finished a unit on transformations in his math course, so he had a partial answer to her question.

"I know why other maps are distorted; it has to do with the method of projection that is used."

"What do you mean by projection?" Anne asked.

David sat down at the terminal and requested information on Mercator projections. He asked for a demo and then said to Anne, "Watch. This will show you how one type of projection works."

A white sphere appeared on the screen. Below it appeared a question

DO YOU WANT LINES OF LATITUDE (LA) AND/OR LONGITUDE (LO)?
LA and LO

The computer drew the great circles on the sphere as requested by David. It then asked a second question.

DO YOU WANT POLITICAL BOUNDARIES DRAWN ON THE LAND MASSES?
Yes

Again the computer responded to the request, filling in the territorial lines of the countries of the world.

The sphere now rotated slowly around the poles and stopped after one revolution. Beneath the sphere appeared a brief description of the

Mercator projection process, which then began to happen on the screen. The sphere was enclosed in a translucent cylinder that was tangent to the sphere at the equator. A ray originating at the center of the globe appeared with its end on the equator. The tip of the ray traced out the equator and then moved on to trace out all the other lines of latitude and longitude on the cylinder. Points on the sphere were being transformed to points on the cylinder.

As this was happening, Anne could see why Mercator maps were so distorted: lines of latitude are equally spaced on the sphere, but their projections on the cylinder become further and further apart as they get closer to the poles.

The computer now traced each country onto the cylinder and colored it appropriately. It did not include anything above 70 degrees North or below 70 degrees South, because there would be too much distortion.

Once the tracing process had finished, a cut appeared on the cylinder and the cylinder slowly unfolded into a rectangle. There it was: a Mercator map of the world. Anne asked for a copy and now had two maps in front of her, the dymaxion map and the Mercator map.

It was getting late, so Anne and David signed off from the Data Bank. As she left the room, she made a mental note to ask her teacher about icosahedrons, because she wanted to know how Buckminster Fuller had made the Dymaxion map.

Although the preceding vignette is fictional, all the technology referred to in it now exists. Large data bases are getting easier and easier to access. Solid modeling systems are being perfected. Multicolored printers capable of printing the maps Anne used are now available. Of course, all of these are relatively expensive at the present time, but in the near future these features and more are likely to be available to schools and to many homes, at relatively low costs.

Developments such as these promise to bring about dramatic changes in how mathematics and other subjects are learned and taught. One major change, evident in this vignette, is that more and more learning is likely to take place at home, at least for families with the means to buy the latest in computer technology. The impact of such a shift, on schools and on society, is difficult to predict at this time. Will schools become less important as more learning takes place at home? Or will they take on even more critical roles as equalizers by providing computer access to lower socioeconomic groups who may not be able to afford elaborate home computer systems? Will teachers become mere computer technicians, or will they need to be even more creative, developing curricula capable of exploiting computer capabilities? Will students develop more creative learning styles as in the exploration carried out by Anne in this vignette? Or will parents view computers as a way of providing their children with a competitive edge over their classmates, and so insist that they be used to reinforce skills and knowledge learned in school?

Largely because of computers and related technologies, we stand at a crossroads in our educational system. The potential is there for computers to bring on the next Guttenberg Revolution in society and in education. Computers can open up vast new areas of knowledge and understanding to all the citizens of the world. But the potential is also there for computers to spur on an Orwellian nightmare in which they help "Big Brother" and the "thought police" to limit our knowledge and understanding, and so our control over our own lives. Which road we take is in our hands, as citizens and educators of a free society.

Traditional Computer **2** *Assisted Instruction*

While the future of educational computing holds exciting possibilities, many current uses of computers in mathematics classes are also impressive. Some of these applications are breaking new ground in the mathematics curriculum. Others are simply computerized versions of traditional mathematics content and methods. Both challenge mathematics teachers and offer them the chance to improve the quality of mathematics education.

Traditional computer assisted instruction originated in the early 1960s on large **mainframe** computers at universities, but it has been evolving and improving along with the evolution of computers themselves. Today's CAI programs, most of which are available on popular microcomputers, are more pedagogically and technologically sophisticated than their mainframe forebears. Still, they employ traditional teaching methods in pursuit of traditional educational goals.

DEMONSTRATION PROGRAMS

Interactive Demonstration

As the students arrived, they took their usual seats chattering curiously about the three TV sets in the front of the room. Mr. Mendoza began the class with a short review of their work on factoring whole numbers. He explained that the TV sets before them were connected to a computer that contained a program to help them find common factors, and in fact the greatest common factor, of any two numbers, even very large ones. He divided the class into three groups, each positioned in front of a monitor, and asked for two numbers to start.

"1287," someone called out; "2745," offered another. Mr. Mendoza sat down at the computer keyboard and hit the Return key. The program responded with an introductory statement on each of the three monitor screens:

> I AM A FACTORING MACHINE.
> I WILL FACTOR ANY TWO NUMBERS.
> WHAT IS THE FIRST NUMBER? (ENTER WITH RETURN).
> **1287**
> WHAT IS THE SECOND NUMBER?
> **2754**

"No!" called the class, followed by some confusion. "The second number was supposed to be 2745," pointed out one student. For a moment Mr. Mendoza couldn't remember how to interrupt the program to correct the error. Then he pressed the Escape key and the program returned to the original prompting statement. He typed in "1287" and "2745" correctly this time.

The computer responded to these inputs as follows:

> 1287 = 3 × 3 × 11 × 13
> 2745 = 3 × 3 × 5 × 61
> WHAT ARE THE COMMON FACTORS?

"Can anyone see a common factor? Yes, John?"
"How about 3?"
Mr. Mendoza typed "3", and hit Return. The computer responded by printing a "3" in a small box at the top right of the screen and then:

> 1287 = 3 × 3 × 11 × 13
> 2745 = 3 × 3 × 5 × 61
> ARE THERE OTHER COMMON FACTORS?

"What do you think? Do we have them all?" Mr. Mendoza asked the class.

A chorus of voices responded, "Another 3 should go inside the box."

Mr. Mendoza smiled, and finished by typing, YES and then "3".

The computer responded, by printing a second "3" in the small box and then:

$$1287 = 3 \times 3 \times 11 \times 13 = 9 \times 11 \times 13$$
$$2745 = 3 \times 3 \times 5 \times 61 = 9 \times 5 \times 61$$
9 IS THE GCF OF 1287 AND 2745.

"That's how the program works. Let's try it again with some really hard numbers."

With this simple demonstration program, the computer played the combined role of a dustless chalkboard and a convenient hand-held calculator: it displayed numerical data and performed routine calculations. Freed from the distractions of calculations and recording, the teacher could then respond to questions and observe the reactions of the class.

The computer has several attributes that make it a worthy assistant in demonstrations: it is neat, organized, and very fast. In the example, this speed, together with the ability to enter numbers of one's choosing, created an interactive demonstration. It would not have been feasible to calculate the factors of large numbers in class, and calculating them ahead of time would have defeated the purpose of the demonstration, which was to induce the insight that, by factoring any two numbers regardless of their size, one can find their greatest common factor. In this demonstration, the class drew conclusions from experimentation, not from illustrations of previously calculated examples.

The dramatic quality that most enhances classroom demonstrations is the computer's graphics and animation capabilities. Pictures in textbooks are static. Illustrations on the chalkboard or overhead projector often require artistic talent and/or hours of preparation. In contrast, the computer can create colorful, clear, and precise displays quickly and easily. Numbers take on a new meaning and reveal new relationships when they become visual. Interactive computer demonstrations in which shapes are changed or rearranged, or variables are controlled and the resulting images compared, make hidden mathematics visible with the touch of a key.

Function plotting programs illustrate these features of graphics in demonstrations. Instead of laboriously plotting a particular function on the chalkboard, the teacher can use the computer. The teacher enters the function and sets the scale for the x and y axes and the program plots

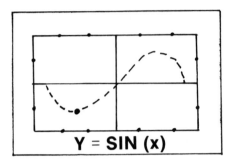

Fig. 2.1

the function. Then the axes can be changed, the function can be altered, or a second function can be added to the display. For example, the teacher can dynamically illustrate the effect of changing numerical coefficients of functions because the computer speeds up the process of plotting them (Figs. 2.1 and 2.2). Then more direct comparisons may be made by graphing both functions on the same axes (Fig. 2.3).

Other characteristics make the computer particularly appropriate for mathematics demonstrations as well. For example, demonstrations that depend upon frequent random inputs become dynamic when the random numbers are generated by computer, while they would remain abstract concepts if described verbally. In science demonstrations, the computer can collect data from sensors measuring quantities such as heat, light, and pressure via its game-paddle ports or other interfacing devices. The computer may also act as a timing device during such demonstrations. Other programs can organize the data collected and display them graphically.

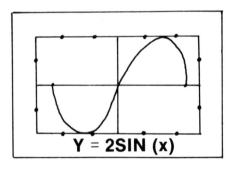

Fig. 2.2

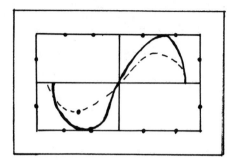

Fig. 2.3

Using the computer for demonstrations also has disadvantages. The setup of the computer and multiple display screens for large group demonstrations can be inconvenient, and hardware can fail at inopportune times. Some demonstrations may fail when unexpected responses bring out bugs in the program. Other programs simply do not demonstrate adequately. In this sense, the computer demonstration is not unlike the science experiment or presentations in other media. This only underscores the need for preview, planning, and preparation.

Powerful demonstration programs require elaborate and time-consuming programming. Thus, programs in a commercially acceptable form, including debugged software and adequate documentation, can be relatively expensive to purchase. However, some simple programs, such as Mr. Mendoza's "Factoring into Primes" program, could be written by a teacher or student who has some knowledge of BASIC. Teacher-developed special purpose programs need not necessarily have every bug removed, since such programs might run with certain restrictions and still be adequate. In some schools, student programmers choose interesting demonstration ideas as programming assignments. Once tested, and found relatively free of bugs, these programs have been used for class demonstrations, and as part of a student-prepared software library.

The decision to use the computer for demonstration also involves answering some more fundamental questions about all applications of computers in schools. One must always ask these two questions: "Is this activity worth using the computer for?" and "Is this activity taking advantage of the special capabilities of the computer?" Demonstration programs that are not interactive, but run by themselves, requiring no response from the user, merely convert the computer into an expensive "page flipper." Such programs fail to take advantage of the computer's other unique capabilities and demonstrate primarily that for such applications the old technologies, the overhead or movie projector, the chalkboard, and the textbook, can accomplish the same objectives as the computer, and in most cases, more efficiently.

Nevertheless, when used appropriately, the computer can expand greatly the realm of demonstrations. For example, demonstration programs become even more exciting when they are taken over by students. Often, students are quite insistent that they run the program themselves; at that point the teacher must decide whether to turn over control of the computer to them. Students can easily run many of these programs with little additional explanation; the programs then become significant learning devices, often in unexpected ways.

DRILL AND PRACTICE
AND TUTORIAL PROGRAMS

In the early 60s, under the guidance and endorsement of behavioral psychologists, the idea of a personal teaching machine emerged and became the embodiment of one view of the future in education. These "machines" were originally simply drill and practice or tutorial programs, in a book or in a cardboard box with a window, that guided students through the lessons. With the advent of computers, large systems of so-called computer assisted instruction, were implemented in elaborate detail. Systems like PLATO, developed at the University of Illinois, TICCIT, developed at the University of Texas and Brigham Young University, and Patrick Suppes' Computer Curriculum at Stanford University, offered an extensive library of programs stored in large mainframe computers. Later, some of these became commercially available as integrated hardware and software systems from companies like Computer Curriculum Corporation and Control Data Corporation, and were implemented widely throughout the country.

In typical drill and practice programs, students are presented with problem sets, reflecting a sequence of skills and requisite subskills to be practiced. In its most sophisticated forms, drill and practice programs contain elaborate branching routines, based on the individual child's responses, which present the appropriate problems.

In contrast, tutorials usually attempt to teach new information and new conceptual understandings. A typical tutorial lesson starts by presenting information and follows with a series of questions that guide the student to an understanding of the information and ideas presented. When students successfully answer questions, more information is presented; when students are unsuccessful in responding to questions, either a hint or repetition of previously stated details is given, followed by more questions. Resemblance to the classic Socratic dialogue is not coincidental, but is a result of carefully thought-out pedagogical structure incorporated into the lessons.

Tutorial programs are usually more sophisticated than drill and practice programs. Although tutorials are certainly not one-to-one human dialogues, most have built in responses to sets of anticipated correct and incorrect student answers. To narrow the range of these answers, many tutorials employ a multiple choice format in their questions.

Some programs combine drill and practice and tutorial with a management system. As the student progresses through the skill sequences, the computer monitors and maintains records that can be transformed into detailed reports for the teacher. This record keeping capability is often called **computer managed instruction** (CMI).

The early development of drill and practice and tutorial programs for mainframes has provided a legacy of abundant, debugged software that is currently being converted to run on less expensive microcomputers. Combined with a profusion of drill and practice software newly developed for microcomputers, teachers and administrators now have a wide choice of comprehensive programs focused on mathematics skill and concept development.

Three essential assumptions are at the heart of all drill and practice and tutorial programs: first, that basic skills are learned like physical skills through repeated practice; second, that more complex ideas and skills can be learned by being broken down for the student into appropriate sequences of sub-ideas and subskills; and third, that students will replicate behaviors that are reinforced with a pleasant experience. According to this learning theory, students learn by repeating problems that are grouped in a developmental sequence, when their correct responses are reinforced.

One Student's Reaction to CAI

Every day at 10:30 I go to another room for help with math. Usually I go to the resource room, which I hate, but on Thursdays, like today, I go to the computer lab, which is OK, but not great.

When I get to the computer lab, the first thing that happens is that the aide, Miss Connor, gives me a program disk which I put into the computer. The computer asks for my name, and I type in "Carole" with an "e" because that's how I spell my name. At first I had to type it in wrong or the computer made me do it over again. That was fixed.

Then it asks, "Do you want to do some problems?" which is really a joke—I mean what am I supposed to say, "No"? Well, anyway, today I typed in "Yes" and it started giving me fractions problems, you know, the hard ones where the bottom numbers are different and you have to add? But yesterday I got some help from the teacher so today I knew how to do them and got most of them right.

The way you can tell that you got them right is that a funny little man dances around in the corner when the answer is right. I don't know why, I guess it thinks that kids would like that stuff. Actually I would like it better if it just said, "Right."

Well, after I did a bunch of those fractions, it asked if I wanted to do some more and I typed "Yes", because, see, the period wasn't over yet. Then it started giving me a different kind of fraction—the ones where there is a big number beside the fraction when you add? I thought I remembered how to do those from last year, but I guess not. I got them all wrong. I wanted Miss Connor to help, but she was busy doing something else with another kid . . . and the computer wouldn't let me stop or skip problems. If you don't answer, it marks the problem wrong anyway, and if you don't know how to do it, and just guess, then it marks that wrong too.

So, anyway, I got them all wrong, and the computer said something sarcastic to me, like, "I guess you need review, Carole." I mean, that isn't fair, is it? I knew I needed help, but the dumb computer just kept giving me problems and marking them wrong! And then it got sarcastic too, just like Nancy Murphy, boy do I hate her!

Well, when the period was finally over, I gave my disk to Miss Connor and she made it print out a grade sheet for me. Sometimes I ask for a second copy and take it home to show my mom, but today I think I just forgot it. I don't know what the grade sheet says. I guess the teacher knows because sometimes she looks at it when she helps me with problems the next day.

Even at its best, drill and practice does not pretend to teach; it provides well-organized, self-correcting drill on skills the student has been taught already. In this vignette, the student worked with a computer managed program, in which the teacher pre-selected the problems sets. When the student had demonstrated a particular response level for the given skill, the program moved on to the next lesson. But in the next lesson, the student became frustrated because the problems were inappropriate, and there was no provision for skipping over them. The teacher might have avoided this frustration for the student by making better use of the program's management system or by selecting the software more carefully.

In general, critics of drill and practice maintain that it is monotonous and boring; yet, for many students drill may become much more tolerable when lessons provide self-paced problems, and when creative graphics, animation, and sound are effectively employed for motivation. Carried to an extreme, however, the same techniques may become distracting to the student, or actually reinforce incorrect responses to problems.

Similarly, tutorials are often criticized for being limited, not only by the imagination of the designers, but also by the computer technology itself. Although historically large tutorial systems, such as the PLATO system, have been used in college-level courses or as training systems in business and the military, the mass storage restrictions of low-cost microcomputer systems have limited the scope of tutorial programs for use in elementary and secondary schools. However, some of the less storage-intensive PLATO programs have been adapted for use on microcomputers and some more innovative tutorial programs have been developed for smaller systems as well, including those by Alfred Bork at the Educational Technology Center of the University of California at Irvine. Moreover, hardware developments are beginning to make much larger amounts of mass storage available at relatively low prices, so that even sophisticated tutorials will soon be available on smaller, less expensive computers.

Bork's research in the development of instructional dialogues indicates that there are specific design features that appropriately enhance computer-generated tutorials. These include sophisticated branching; innovative screen design that employs timed display of text, graphics, and animation; and the ability of the computer to recognize and respond to answers in short phrases and sentences. Bork's programs also store unexpected student responses so that he and his colleagues may determine whether or not these answers indicate a deficiency in the program.

Proponents of drill and practice and tutorials cite the opportunities for success these programs provide. The computer gives immediate and personal feedback to student answers while being patient and flexible. It is always available and quick to respond.

Drill and practice programs in mathematics are most often designed to exercise arithmetic computations, but there are other areas that exploit this technique as well. For instance, there are factoring programs that exercise skills in solving equations, and a *Base Ten Blocks* program that gives elementary school children practice with problems of place value. This is done imaginatively by displaying numbers as either individual blocks, rows of ten blocks, plates of one hundred blocks, or cubes of one thousand blocks. The child answers drill questions referring to graphic displays of the cubes.

With minimal tutorial programs of quality available in mathematics, some teachers are attempting to create their own simple tutorials by using special authoring systems. PILOT, an authoring language available on most popular computers, offers teachers one means of developing uncomplicated tutorials without requiring any programming expertise. Other available **courseware** authoring systems provide graphics, sound, and even video tape/disk interfacing capabilities. However, teachers who want to develop tutorials should recognize from the start that it takes many hours to create a few minutes of an effective tutorial lesson. Teachers who are tempted to commit a large amount of their time and effort to designing and using computerized tutorials might ask themselves if their time wouldn't be better spent in human dialogue with their students.

The most serious criticism leveled at drill and practice and tutorial programs is that they cannot instruct as effectively as a human teacher. However, it is not at all clear that this is the case. Some research indicates that significant gains have been realized, above those achieved using traditional techniques, when students in basic skills improvement courses have had regular and frequent sessions with drill and practice programs. In such studies, a minimum of ten minutes of drill was usually prescribed for each day, five days a week. The long-term results of such studies have yet to be determined.

While there is no consensus on the advantages and disadvantages of drill and practice and tutorial programs, it is clear that computers are still a limited resource in many schools, and there are other purposes for which they may be used. Should basic skills improvement through drill and practice and tutorial programs take priority over more innovative uses of this limited resource?

SIMULATION

Like tutorials and drill and practice, simulation, as an instructional application of the computer, began on mainframes in the 1960s. The Huntington Project produced numerous science and social studies simulations for use in the classroom. The *Search Series* and *Three Mile Island* are examples of more recently developed classroom simulations. However, the full impact of simulation in education, particularly in the mathematics classroom, is yet to be realized.

A simulation is a representation of a real-world situation in which a specified number of factors can change; as they do, they produce other changes throughout the simulated world. Since many relationships are complicated and their outcomes often unpredictable, the simulation program produces a problem-solving situation in which decisions are made in light of past experiences and projected into the future. One critical consideration for teachers is the number of variables that have been included in a simulation, since most simulation programs are limited in scope and complexity. The simulation described here, *Lemonade*, is a simple illustration that shows how teachers may adapt existing programs for use as mathematics activities.

The object in *Lemonade* is to make profit. At the beginning of the day, each player decides how many glasses of lemonade to make and how much to sell them for. Each student can also decide to make advertising signs, which add to expenses, but which presumably increase net sales. The weather report informs students of another factor that might effect the demand for lemonade that day.

After all production decisions have been entered, the computer presents the daily "Financial Report" for each player, which lists the glasses made and sold, the price per glass, and the net profit. It computes the total cash on hand for each player. When it has finished displaying all the Financial Reports, the computer begins the next simulated day.

Developing Business Strategies

Four children in Ms. Dodson's seventh grade class had chosen to play *Lemonade* for their activity project. They formed two teams, Bill and George against Kerry and Tracy, and played the game during the regular activity period. After the students had played the game several times, Ms. Dodson introduced a worksheet activity to organize their information in order to make better decisions.

The class had been working on graphing during the past several weeks so the worksheets Ms. Dodson gave the children helped them organize their data by graphing the results of their lemonade sales efforts. For the first worksheet, Ms. Dodson suggested that advertising be controlled; that is, each team should keep constant the number of signs they made each day. The worksheet results from one of the teams is shown in Fig. 2.4.

The next day, Ms. Dodson gave the *Lemonade* teams a second worksheet that included profit as an outcome variable. Again she suggested that advertising be kept the same each day. The graph the girls drew on the second worksheet did not form a straight line and it took several attempts by them to graph it correctly. After studying their results, the girls decided that the top of the curve indicated the best price because that was the point at which the profit was the greatest. Fig. 2.5 shows the graph they drew, and the table on which it was based.

The girls were careful in drawing this graph to use the same number of signs each time. The boys on the other hand had tired of keeping their advertising strategy the same, so on the second day they changed it. Consequently, their graph did not form a recognizable curve. The girls decided from their graph that the price of 10 cents per glass produced the most profit, and using this information, they won the game.

Even a simple simulation like *Lemonade* produces a complex set of data. The worksheets provided by the teacher were important in helping the children organize these data and draw conclusions from them. For example, with all factors acting at once, weather, advertising, price, cost, and so on, the profit at the end of the day is unpredictable. Using the worksheets, the students could simplify the situation in two ways: first,

Worksheet # 1

Weather	Signs	Cost	Glasses Made	Glasses Sold
S	O	8¢	50	34
S	O	10	50	30
S	O	9	50	32
S	O	13	50	17
S	O	11	50	24
S	O	16	50	11
S	O	12	50	20
S	O	6	50	42
S	O	18	50	9
HH	O	13¢	50	35

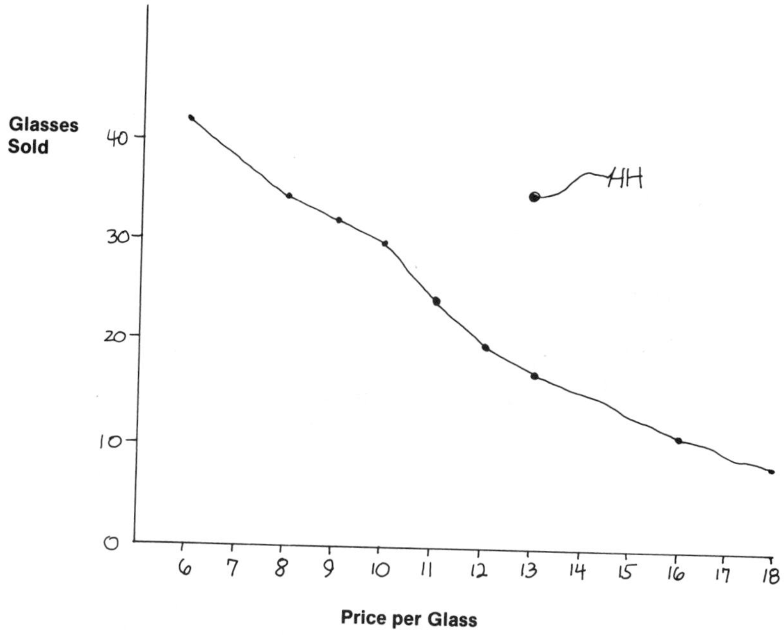

Fig. 2.4

they held constant the variable of advertising; and second, they organized the data obtained from the remaining variables in the form of graphs. As a result, the relationship between price, number of glasses sold, and profit became quite evident.

The concept of isolating variables and the recognition that effects are confounded as long as variables are allowed to change, but become

Worksheet # 2

Weather	Signs	Price	Glasses Made	Glasses Sold	Profit
S	4	8	70	64	1.92
S	4	9	70	60	2.00
S	4	10	70	55	2.10
S	4	11	70	46	1.66
S	4	12	70	38	1.16
S	4	13	70	33	89
S	4	7	70	70	1.50
HD	4	10	70	70	3.60

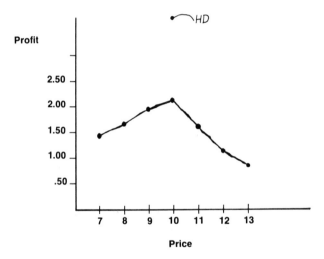

Fig. 2.5

straightforward when variables are controlled, are appropriate for this age group. Ultimately, it is quite important in the logic of scientific reasoning and in everyday problem solving. Some children even arrive at this isolation strategy on their own, but most require some assistance from a teacher.

Simulations like *Lemonade* provide a personally meaningful setting for solving mathematical problems. Students become engaged in problem solving, and the mathematics becomes a means to an end.

One teacher used *Lemonade* with his tenth-grade business mathematics students. He had one microcomputer in the front of the room running the simulation with several lemonade stands operating at once; meanwhile, teams of students analyzed the results of sales and advertising with *VisiCalc* on other microcomputers around the room, and used the results of these analyses to make investment strategies. They also used *VisiPlot* to produce graphic representations of the price/sales relationships.

The *Lemonade* simulation could be made more complicated and, perhaps, more realistic by altering the **source code** of the program. This might make an interesting programming problem for more advanced students. Nonetheless, simulations like *Lemonade* have an intrinsic limitation: they set up a world that is governed by far more limited rules than the real world, and yet students are given little information about the source of, or reason for, these rules. Thus, through interaction with artificial worlds, students learn something about hypothetical thinking, but they do not develop any sense of what is required to construct a simulation in the first place.

There is a specialized programming language called DYNAMO, which does allow the user to construct a simulation of the real world. Given a particular problem, students can decide how the different elements in that problem will interact, and then construct a mathematical model of those interactions. The students then can write up this model in the DYNAMO language, and run it on the computer. The results of the interactions are printed out in graphic form and can be compared with real-life outcomes. This provides students with an entirely different type of simulation, one in which they must learn to cope with the modeling difficulties. Two extensive examples of how this language has been used in mathematics classrooms appear in Chapter 3 and Chapter 5.

There is a profound difference between the canned simulations, like *Lemonade*, and the open-ended simulations possible through languages like DYNAMO. *Lemonade* provides a closed environment where effects are constrained and easily understood. On the other hand, the DYNAMO language provides an opportunity for simulating complex, real-world problems, and consequently is far more difficult to work with and to understand. Teachers considering the use of simulations must judge the advantages and disadvantages of the two approaches for their particular classes.

EDUCATIONAL GAMES

If you have recently walked past an arcade featuring video games, you undoubtedly witnessed the incredible wave of interest in them. The old and familiar pinball machines have been replaced by alien games named

Missile Command, Asteroids, and PACMAN. If you looked closely, you noticed that the crowd playing these games was composed not just of youngsters, but adults, business executives on lunch hour, or just passers-by, lured in by the noise of explosions, laser rays, and missile launches.

No matter what your feelings may be about arcades, you should recognize computer games as potential learning situations for the players. Immediately after the start of play, they must begin to think in terms of survival, what techniques help them to stay alive, to score well, to win a free game. The game presents a finite manageable fantasy world in which players have control, where there is a clear goal, and where, in spite of a rapidly changing environment, players have the possibility of success within the reach of each finger. Computer games represent an important segment of the educational computing market, particularly in mathematics.

New Games and New Players

Max Crosby stopped for a moment in the computer lab where three students huddled over a microcomputer. Max knew immediately from the computer sounds that they were playing an arcade game.

"Hey Mr. Crosby," called one of the on-lookers before Max could duck out again. "Look at this. Mr. Allen put the Green Slime game on its fastest speed, and Butch is almost at the fifth level!"

Butch was staring intently at the screen, firing his laser gun into the Green Slime which threatened the village. He could only shoot at those portions of the slime that displayed the answer to the subtraction problems in a box on the laser gun. The problems changed frequently, as the Slime advanced. The game ended suddenly when Butch missed a problem and allowed the Slime to creep past his defenses and destroy the town. He sat back as the screen displayed his unprecedented score.

"Want to try, Mr. Crosby?" Butch asked with a cocky grin.

"No thanks. I wouldn't stand a chance." As he left, Max tried to think of another time he had seen Butch as intent on solving mathematics problems, or as successful.

Educational games like the Green Slime game, really named *Minus Mission* of the *Arcademics Series,* are drill and practice activities in an arcade format. They are fast-paced tests of cognitive and motor skills. The teacher can adjust the speed so the game can be used by students of varying abilities. The computer provides feedback to "answers" immediately through vivid graphics and sound. The goals are clear: rapid, accurate responses are rewarded, and slower and incorrect ones are penalized. The games challenge students to improve their mastery of basic skills by increasing the difficulty of the problems, as the students' proficiency increases.

Dr. Thomas Malone has identified three characteristics of computer games which, according to his research, make them "intrinsically motivating": challenge, fantasy, and curiosity. He suggests that educators seek ways of incorporating these characteristics in the educational computer games they develop. Challenge and fantasy are clearly involved in *Minus Mission*.

Although such arcade-like games may be intrinsically motivating, they are not intrinsically mathematical. The skills or knowledge exercised could as easily be spelling words or social studies facts as arithmetic problems. However, there are also computer games in which mathematics is inherent in their structure and/or content. There are, for example, a whole group of mathematics computer games based on mathematical puzzles or board games. In one of these, *Diffy*, the student places four numbers at the corners of a square. The student subtracts each adjacent pair (always smaller from larger number) and then places the resulting whole numbers in the corners of a new square. The student repeats the activity until the subtractions result in four zeroes as answers. The object of the game is to choose initial numbers which permit the most squares, or "Diffs," to be completed.

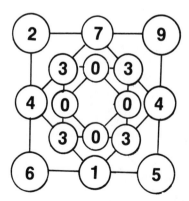

Fig. 2.6

A New Look for Traditional Games

The situation could best be described as Diffy Fever. For about two weeks, the entire fifth grade did nothing but eat, sleep, and talk *Diffy*. PACMAN had all but been forgotten.

Diffy Fever started when Sean discovered a set of four numbers that allowed the game to continue for seven diffs. The computer replaced the old record holder with Sean's name and after each game it stated,

SEAN—RECORD 7 DIFFS.

The contest was on!

Sean's classmates worked hard to find a set of starting numbers that would break the record. They were also anxious to keep the record in their room. When Mr. Johnson's class got their chance to use the computer (the computer was wheeled back and forth between rooms every few days), they too were impressed with the new record, and quickly set to work to break the mark of 7 Diffs.

Meanwhile Sean's class began a systematic search for 8 Diff numbers. Since they did not have access to the computer for several days, they used worksheets with the square patterns drawn on them. The worksheets were often faster because the graphics slowed down the computer version of the game. The worksheets also enabled the students to keep records of past games to analyze. They found, for example, that very large numbers were not always better at prolonging a game than small numbers.

On Wednesday, Sean came to school with a 9 Diff game that he had worked on at home. However, careful examination by a classmate exposed a subtraction error midway through the game. The students saw that the worksheet approach had its drawbacks too, since the computer would not have allowed an incorrect answer to a subtraction problem. By the next week, just as quickly as it had started, Differ Fever died out. *Diffy* was still played regularly by smaller groups, and variations on it with other arithmetic operations were enjoyed by some students, but for most, it had become just another game. . . . The great Diffy Craze was over.

Given that computer games like *Diffy* are roughly the same as their non-computer versions, the educational advantages are about the same. The *Diffy* game exercises subtraction skills in a self-paced and self-initiated way; students rather than the teacher choose the problems. *Diffy* provides opportunities for students to go beyond drill and practice of arithmetic skills; they can develop insights into number theory and problem solving.

The specific advantage of computerizing the game is that the computer rejects arithmetic errors immediately, but does not mark them wrong. The computer also keeps records from one game to the next and displays high scores and the name of the current record holder. The principal disadvantage of the computer version is that only individuals or a small group can play the game, while in the traditional worksheet mode an entire class may play simultaneously, providing a personalized class drill session.

Unlike arcade games, mathematics puzzle games such as *Diffy* may be both intrinsically motivational and intrinsically mathematical, but they may still not be the best use of a computer. There is a third class of games that combines motivation and mathematics with powerful and unique uses of the computer. One example of such a game is *Buggy*. Students select a whole number arithmetic operation, such as vertical addition of multi-digit numbers, for which the computer displays several problems along with answers to those problems. These answers are special, in that the computer calculated them through some systematic misuse of the addition algorithm. That is, there is a bug in the method the computer uses to solve the problems. By analyzing the problems and the answers the computer has generated, the players make inferences about what the bug is. The players then test those inferences by giving the computer several additional problems to solve using the same algorithm. Once players feel the bug can be precisely defined, they ask for a test problem. The computer responds with a problem, the players predict the answer, and the computer determines if that answer is appropriate, given the bug. If it is not, the computer gives additional bugged problems and answers. If the players' prediction is correct, the computer gives a description of the bug in words which the players can compare to their own understanding of it.

Buggy exercises important kinds of thinking: induction and hypotheses testing. Students work backwards from an answer to determine the procedure that produced that answer. In traditional mathematics classes, students generally have little difficulty stating algorithms for producing an answer, but the process of working backwards from an incorrect answer, to produce a hypothetical misuse of the algorithm, is far more complicated, and rarely attempted outside of this game. *Buggy* uses the computer to create a learning situation that would be difficult to create without a computer:

an intrinsically mathematical microworld which challenges cognitive and creative skills.

A number of similar games have been developed in recent years, including the well-known *Darts* and *Green Globs* games. Originally designed for the PLATO system and now available for microcomputers, *Green Globs* combines fantasy, challenge, and curiosity in an intrinsically mathematical activity. Students are challenged to destroy thirteen green globs displayed on a coordinate grid. Students write equations to create graphs that pass through the globs, thereby obliterating them. Points are scored for hitting the most globs with the smallest number of equations.

The computer stores the ten highest scores for the game in a "hall of fame" along with the series of equations that the record holders wrote to achieve the scores. Curious challengers may recall and display the records of the record setting games to develop or improve their own winning strategies.

Instructional games have been and will continue to be a popular approach to involve students actively in the learning process. The computer

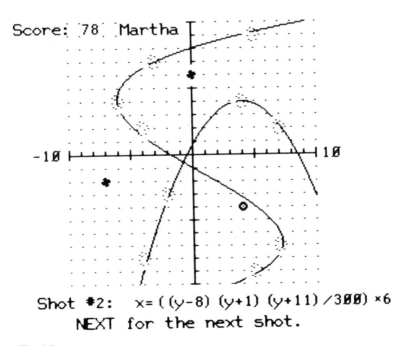

Score: 78 Martha

−1Ø   1Ø

Shot #2:   x= ((y−8) (y+1) (y+11) /3ØØ) ×6
NEXT for the next shot.

Fig. 2.7

offers new dimensions to designers who share this perspective. There is no consensus on the best way to construct the games or on what elements produce desirable effects when incorporated into instructional computer games. Further research is needed to answer the myriad questions that educators must ask, and as this research is carried out, new questions will undoubtedly arise.

PROGRAMMING

As we close this chapter on the traditional uses of the computer in mathematics instruction, we again examine an activity that originated as a part of the mathematics curriculum over twenty years ago: programming. This activity originally was limited to the high school level because the computer that supported it was generally located in large high school complexes so it could be used for centralized administrative purposes. Student programmers were given computer time between scheduling, report cards, and business functions. Today the availability of low-cost microcomputers at all levels of a school district makes it possible for a wider cross-section of the school population to have access to computers for programming.

Traditionally, programming has been taught like a foreign language. Students learn the commands and syntax of a language much as they learn vocabulary and grammar, and then practice, using simple structured exercises. Well-known activities include filling the display screen with the student's name by using PRINT and GOTO statements in a two line program.

```
10 PRINT "HI, MARY"
20 GOTO 10
```

The same program is then usually changed by inserting a comma or semicolon to produce interesting displays that illustrate the effect of punctuation in a PRINT command.

Curious number patterns also provide limitless but repetitive exercises for beginning programmers. Students write programs to generate consecutive integers, lists of multiples, tables of perfect squares, or series of fibonacci numbers to develop programming techniques involving IF statements and conditional branching or FOR-NEXT loops. A simple three-line program can make the computer count by odd numbers from 1 to 99.

```
10 FOR N = 1 TO 99 STEP 2
20 PRINT N
30 NEXT N
```

Teachers frequently choose these types of problems because they offer three advantages: 1) most students, even students in elementary grades, can succeed in writing the programs, 2) teachers can occupy a class for virtually any amount of time with variations on the same problems, and 3) students are usually impressed by the computer's speed in producing large amounts of printed results, especially from short, simple programs. Although many traditional programming texts offer a multitude of such problems, many students and teachers eventually find this approach to the teaching of programming monotonous because it requires mainly low-level cognitive skills in a context that is minimally relevant to most students. More recently, teachers who have recognized the need to provide a more meaningful context for teaching programming skills have viewed programming as a problem-solving activity.

Programming as Problem Solving

During Ecology Week the students in Boris Hamilton's fifth-grade class collected litter from school playgrounds and accumulated over 3000 aluminum beverage cans. To call attention to their efforts, the students decided to build a pyramid-shaped tower with the cans in the community center lobby. To do this, they needed to find the dimensions of the largest triangular pyramid that could be constructed with 3000 cans.

Boris suggested to the class that they write a computer program to solve this problem. The students were very excited by this idea, but were unsure of how to start. Boris proposed that they begin by drawing a rough sketch of the pyramid. Various students began to do so at once. Before long, one of the students called out, "If you add together the cans in each level, you'll get the number of cans in the pyramid."

At the same point, three boys began to build a small can pyramid with five cans on a side of the base. Other students clustered around and a discussion ensued about the relationship of the number of cans on a side to the number in the entire level.

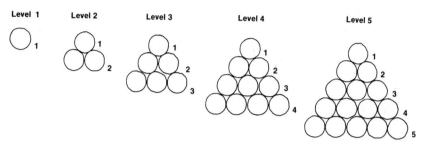

Fig. 2.8

They saw easily that the number of cans on each level is equal to the sum of the cans in each row, but they needed some help from Boris to recognize that this was also equal to the sum of the first n consecutive integers, where n is the number of cans on the side of the triangle. Again with some assistance from Boris, the class wrote the following program to compute the number of cans in a given level.

```
10 INPUT LEVEL
20 FOR CANS = 1 TO LEVEL
30 LET SUM = SUM + CANS
40 NEXT CANS
50 PRINT "CANS IN LEVEL"; LEVEL;" IS "; SUM
```

It was at this point that one of the students exclaimed, "Hey, you have to count cans from the top to figure out how many levels you'll get from the cans." Before long the students developed the appropriate modification of the program so the computer could total the sums of the cans in an n-level pyramid. They did this by changing lines 10 and 50, and inserting lines 15 and 45.

```
10 INPUT HEIGHT
15 FOR LEVEL = 1 TO HEIGHT
20 FOR CANS = 1 TO LEVEL
30 LET SUM = SUM + CANS
40 NEXT CANS
45 NEXT LEVEL
50 PRINT "CANS IN "; HEIGHT; " LEVEL PYRAMID IS "; SUM
```

Some of the students in the class decided to use the program to check their guesses as to the dimensions of a 3000-can pyramid. They ran the program a number of times, using trial and error to find the largest number of levels that would require fewer than 3000 cans.

```
]RUN
?50
CANS IN 50 LEVEL PYRAMID IS 22100

]RUN
?25
CANS IN 25 LEVEL PYRAMID IS 2925

]RUN
?30
CANS IN 30 LEVEL PYRAMID IS 4960

]RUN
?27
CANS IN 27 LEVEL PYRAMID IS 3654

]RUN
?26
CANS IN 26 LEVEL PYRAMID IS 3276
```

Other students in the class wanted to modify the program still further to obtain a more direct solution. They made a few more changes so the program would compute the number of levels and the exact number of cans needed.

In this example, the programming insight had to wait for the mathematical insight. First, the students observed a pattern in the arrangement of the triangular levels which allowed them to write a program to calculate the number of cans in each level, using an algorithm that could be expressed as the sum of consecutive integers. Then they recognized that the calculation of the size of the bottom of the pyramid presupposed the solution of the problem. This led them to writing the program in BASIC such that the process of finding the answer began at the top of the pyramid, not at the bottom as they would actually construct it. It is probably because the intuitive solution doesn't work that this problem has a certain appeal. In exercises such as this one, programming and problem solving are combined in a meaningful new way to find solutions.

CONCLUSION

Despite the evident imagination of Boris Hamilton and the other teachers whose use of CAI has been described in the vignettes, neither their educational goals nor their pedagogical methods deviate from tradition. This is not criticism, but simply a statement of the framework within which CAI should be considered. When and where traditional goals of mathematics education are prominent, traditional methods appropriate, and computer resources abundant, CAI may promote learning and enhance teaching. In those circumstances teachers must carefully assess the software under consideration. Chapter 5 of the *Practical Guide to Computers in Education* provides guidelines for courseware evaluation, and the Resources section of this book describes software that we consider exemplary.

The concerns about all CAI emerge when one of these three circumstances is not in effect. Most CAI is not helpful in pursuing nontraditional educational goals like creative problem solving. Nor is most of it appropriate when student autonomy or initiative is a goal. Of greatest concern is the issue we have raised several times: given limited computer resources, is this the best, most appropriate way to use computers in schools?

Problem Solving: 3
Transforming a Process

No aspect of mathematics or science education has received more attention or more concern than problem solving. And in no area of the curriculum has progress been less. Teaching problem solving has been one of the great dilemmas for educators, most of whom regard it as the most significant preparation for the real world because it teaches students to think. However, the instructional reality is very different. Teachers force students to do masses of repetitive story problems that have no reality to them, in the frail hope that the activity alone will somehow grant them the ability to solve new problems. Curriculum writers invent hints, rules, and charts for systematizing a process that is not really well understood by the students. Teachers press students to take problem solving seriously despite the obvious tedium and mindless repetition of the problem sets assigned. By and large, students who can already solve problems solve them, and those who cannot are as confused as ever. To make matters worse, educators do not even know if the ways they teach problem solving actually make better mathematicians, scientists, businesspersons, teachers, citizens, or even better problem solvers.

As the computer becomes a valuable tool for all of education, perhaps it will be most valuable in the learning of problem solving. Its own problem-solving capacity should at least amplify each student's problem-solving abilities. But the computer is likely to have an even more profound effect than this; it may radically alter what it means for students to solve problems. Freed from the drudgery of long and complex calculations, students will be able to explore problems, not simply obtain answers. In fact, such exploration will often reveal a range of solutions rather than a single answer. Further, with computers, teachers may create complex problem-solving environments in which students act more like real-world problem solvers: cooperating as members of a group and gathering and analyzing information. Finally, students can use computers the way real-world problem solvers do, as a tool for modeling problem situations. In these ways, computers may transform the very nature of problem solving in the mathematics classroom.

SOLVING PROBLEMS, NOT FINDING ANSWERS

VisiCalc

Numerical-analysis software, such as *VisiCalc*, permit teachers and students to explore problems while employing traditional mathematical skills and concepts. A junior high school teacher might present the following problem to a class.

PROBLEM

A motorcycle "daredevil" is designing a stunt in which she must drive a motorcycle up a ramp, and jump over 8 automobiles, landing safely on the other side. The problem is that she has never done this stunt before. She doesn't know how fast to go or how steep to make the jump ramp. To complicate matters further, if she clears 8 cars successfully (189 feet), she will be asked to jump a second time, over 10 cars (235 feet). She knows from previous experience that the motorcycle can be driven off an incline up to 55 degrees at speeds no greater than 75 miles per hour. However, she wishes to do the jump with maximum safety, which means at as little incline as possible, as slowly as possible.

What is the best take-off speed and ramp angle to ensure a safe jump?

VisiCalc is an electronic spreadsheet, a huge matrix, 260 rows by 75 columns. The computer display screen is like a window through which the user can view any part of the sheet. A cursor, controlled by arrow keys, indicates the user's position in the matrix. Each slot on the matrix, identified by a row and column name, can contain a label, a value, or a formula. A label is a word or words such as "income" or "miles per hour" which can head a row or column to make the information in the spreadsheet more easily interpreted. A value is a numerical value such as "13" or "19876." A formula is an expression containing numbers, variables, and arithmetic or trigonometric functions such as (A1 + A2 + A3)/3 or cos(C8). Such formulas do not actually appear on the spreadsheet. They are simply relationships that define the value of a location in terms of other values in the matrix. Variables are actually the names of locations in the spreadsheet that *VisiCalc* automatically computes and lists whenever the numerical value in the position is provided.

To use *VisiCalc* to solve a problem with a junior high school class, the teacher would most likely set up the spreadsheet for the problem ahead of time for the students. Then, when the students use *VisiCalc*, they would load the problem from a problem disk and find a spreadsheet as in Fig. 3.1.

The ramp angle on this sheet is set at 45 degrees. A range of possible speeds is listed in the speed column. The values for the formula computing the distance of the jump (in feet) given a certain speed (in miles per hour) are computed and appear under the distance column. It should be obvious immediately that the speed values are too slow because the corresponding distances are too short. So the students might begin by changing these to "55, 60, 65, 70, and 75". For a ramp angle of 45 degrees, the spreadsheet immediately changes to look like Fig. 3.2.

The table shows distances calculated for the new speeds entered. The students, noticing that these distances are all longer than they need to be might decide to reduce the ramp angle to a safer incline. Entering a new angle of 30 degrees would yield results shown on the spreadsheet in Fig. 3.3.

Now the distances span the target distance of 189 feet, so the students can reduce speed until they find the lowest speed at this angle at which the jump is possible. It appears, from examining the spreadsheet, that 55 miles per hour is not fast enough but 60 miles per hour is too fast, so the students could change the speeds, and get the results shown in Fig. 3.4, which indicate that 57 miles per hour with a ramp angle of 30 degrees would work. However, the students should recognize that this solution is not unique. They could find a new solution with a steeper angle and a

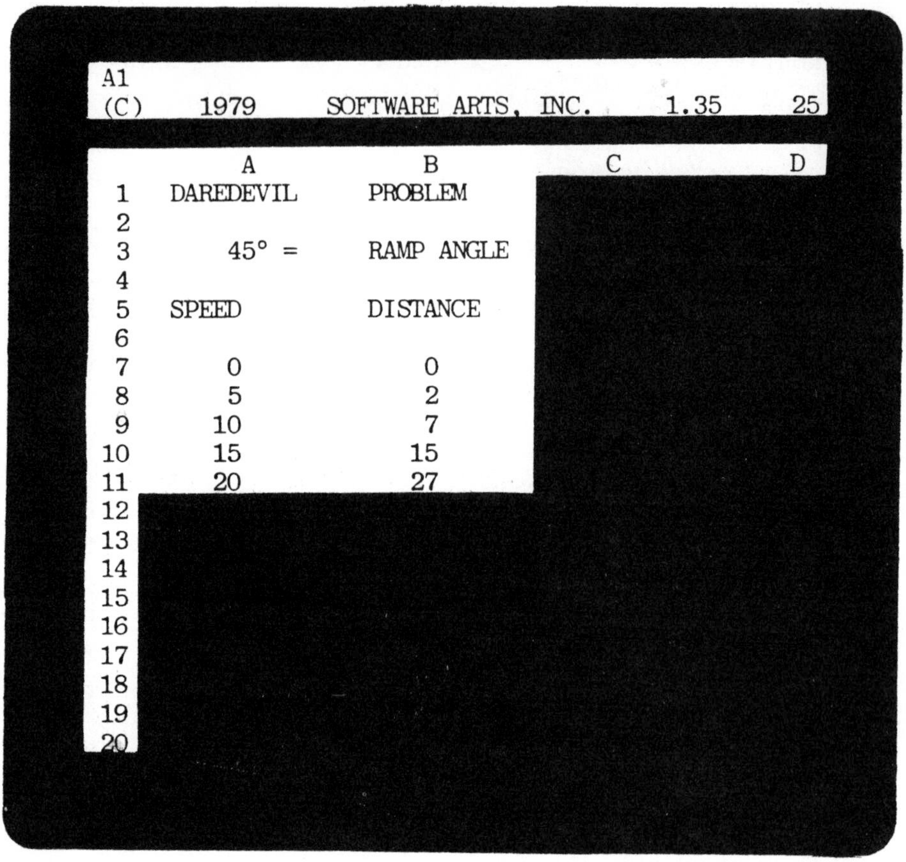

```
A1
(C)    1979      SOFTWARE ARTS, INC.      1.35      25

            A              B              C              D
  1   DAREDEVIL      PROBLEM
  2
  3     45° =        RAMP  ANGLE
  4
  5   SPEED          DISTANCE
  6
  7     0              0
  8     5              2
  9    10              7
 10    15             15
 11    20             27
 12
 13
 14
 15
 16
 17
 18
 19
 20
```

Fig. 3.1

lower speed or with a less steep angle and a higher speed. This is a most important mathematical insight for students to have, and it provides them with an appropriate perspective on real-world problem solving where there are seldom single answers to problems.

The use of *VisiCalc* for problem solving in mathematics classes raises another educational issue. *VisiCalc* operates like a "black box"—the students arrive at answers without even seeing the formulas that provide those answers. In the traditional sense of the word, the students are not solving the problem; *VisiCalc* is. However, in a far more profound sense, the students are acting as problem solvers and are learning mathematics. By using the computer in this way, students can make several dozen complex

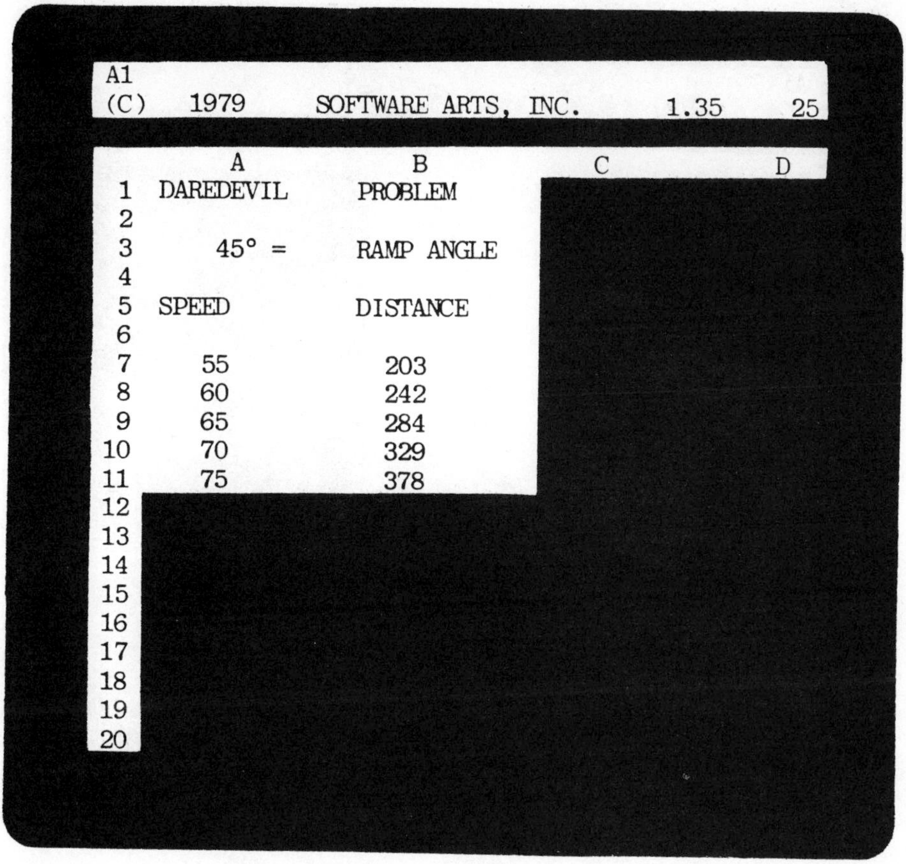

```
A1
(C)   1979      SOFTWARE ARTS, INC.      1.35      25
```

	A	B	C	D
1	DAREDEVIL	PROBLEM		
2				
3	45° =	RAMP ANGLE		
4				
5	SPEED	DISTANCE		
6				
7	55	203		
8	60	242		
9	65	284		
10	70	329		
11	75	378		
12				
13				
14				
15				
16				
17				
18				
19				
20				

Fig. 3.2

calculations quickly and accurately. Freed from the tedium and guaranteed of the accuracy of the computations, students can explore the various problem parameters, and in so doing discover patterns that may lead them to understand fundamental concepts of mathematics.

Consider the Daredevil problem as a way of coming to understand the concept of functions. The problem involves two variables: the speed of the motorcycle and the angle of the ramp. As each set of numbers is entered, the spreadsheet values change in paired fashion. There is no need for students to commit to memory some abstract definition of a function. Instead, they can internalize an operational definition they observe happening on the spreadsheet, such as "A procedure that changes output in some

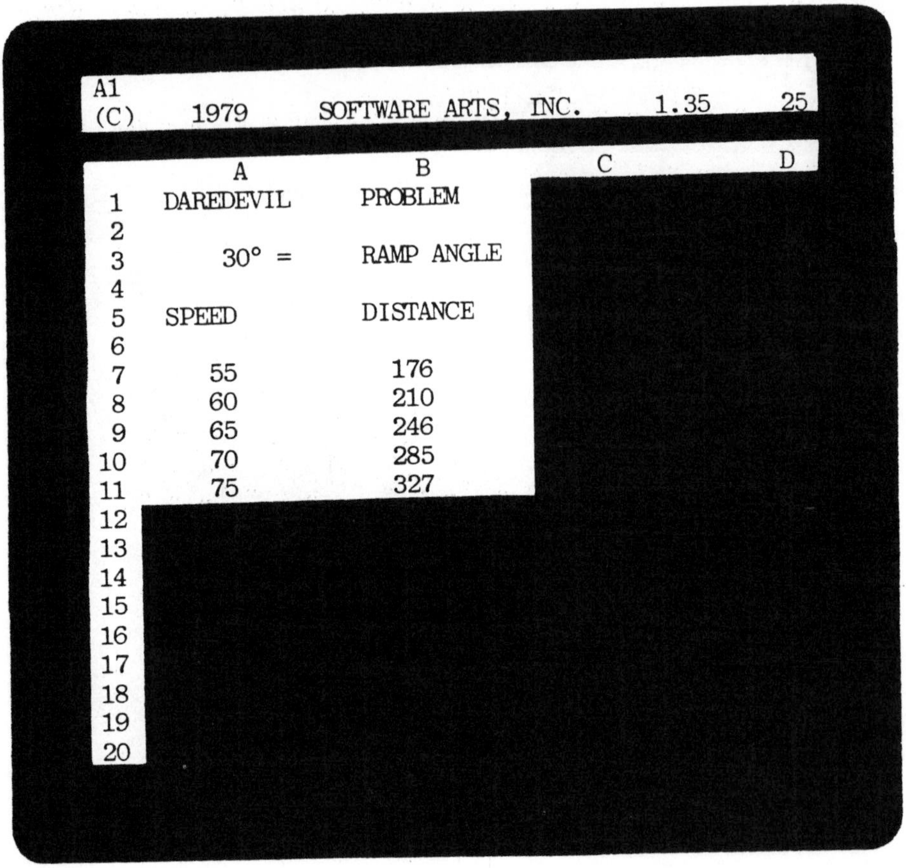

```
A1
(C)     1979        SOFTWARE ARTS, INC.        1.35        25

            A                 B              C           D
  1     DAREDEVIL        PROBLEM
  2
  3        30° =         RAMP ANGLE
  4
  5     SPEED           DISTANCE
  6
  7        55              176
  8        60              210
  9        65              246
 10        70              285
 11        75              327
 12
 13
 14
 15
 16
 17
 18
 19
 20
```

Fig. 3.3

direct and definable way as input varies." The spreadsheet format for this problem is helpful because it emphasizes the function relationship between variables and deemphasizes the process of calculating the values.

It is quite easy for teachers to design problem-solving activities with *VisiCalc*. Unlike a similar problem-solving project done with a BASIC program, neither the teacher nor the students need to have any programming experience.

VisiCalc is a versatile tool. Teachers can introduce students to *VisiCalc* as a way of exploring traditional topics such as functions, equations, and general problem solving. Then, as students become proficient with it, they can enter their own formulas, or alter those provided by the teacher.

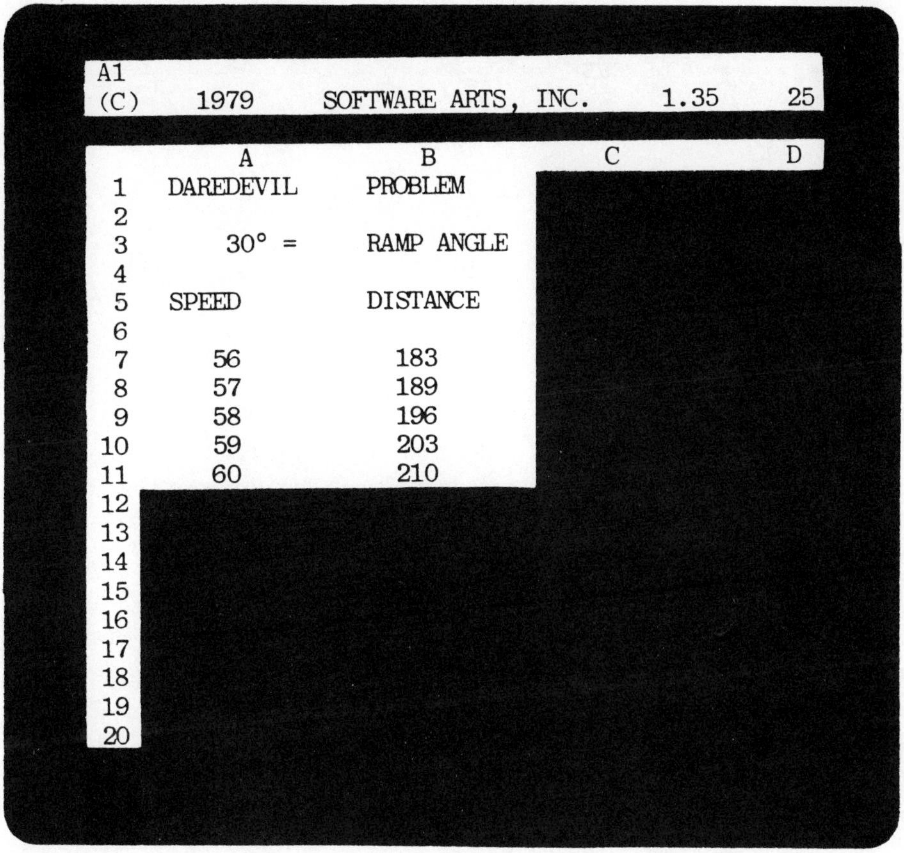

```
A1
(C)    1979      SOFTWARE ARTS, INC.      1.35      25
```

	A	B	C	D
1	DAREDEVIL	PROBLEM		
2				
3	30° =	RAMP ANGLE		
4				
5	SPEED	DISTANCE		
6				
7	56	183		
8	57	189		
9	58	196		
10	59	203		
11	60	210		
12				
13				
14				
15				
16				
17				
18				
19				
20				

Fig. 3.4

Eventually, students can even design their own spreadsheets for solving problems.

TK!Solver

More complex problems may be solved with other appropriate problem-solving software, such as *TK!Solver*, an automatic problem solver. Students using *TK!Solver* begin by listing the different elements of the problem on different screens or sheets. One is for equations or rules, one for variables, one for dimensional relationship units, and a number of others are for specialized applications. Once these sheets have been filled out, students can ask the program to solve problems for any variable. The program

(1r) Rule: **y=vy*t–16*t^2**

```
============RULE  SHEET===============================192/!
S Rule
- ----
* y=vy*t–16*t^2
* x=vx*t
* vy=v*cos (angle)
* vx=v*sin (angle)
* vy–16*t_end=0
* x_end=vx*t_end
```

Fig. 3.5

sorts through the equations provided by the student to determine which are appropriate and in what order they must be used to provide the variable value needed to solve the next equation. The program also converts the dimensions of a variable to correspond to those of other variables in the problem. For the Daredevil problem, the rules sheet might look like Fig. 3.5.

As the student types in these equations on the rule sheet, the variables in each equation are simultaneously displayed in a list on the variables sheet, as shown in Fig. 3.6. The student then defines the variables by typing in comments and identifies the unit of measure for each variable by typing in the unit abbreviation on the variable sheet. Where conversions between units are needed, the student defines the relationships between the units on a similar unit sheet.

```
*
(1 i) Input:  30
```

```
==================== VARIABLE  SHEET ====================192/!
St Input      Name    Output   Unit      Comment
-- -----      ----    ------   ----      -------
              angle
L             v
              t
              vx
              vy
              x
              y
L             t_end
L             x_end
```

Fig. 3.6

```
*
(1i) Input: 30
```

```
==================== VARIABLE  SHEET  ==================192/!
St  Input        Name      Output       Unit      Comment
--  -----        ----      ------       ----      -------
    30           angle                  deg       angle of ramp
L   10           v                      mi/h      vel. leaving ramp
                 t                      s         time
                 vx        37.5         mi/h      x velocity
                 vy        64.951905    mi/h      y initial velocity
                 x                      ft        horizontal distance
                 y                      ft        height
L                t_end     .79385662    ft        final time
L                x_end     5.8216152    ft        final x position
```

Fig. 3.7

Now the problem is ready to be solved. The student enters values for the independent variables and types "!". The program carries out the calculations and outputs values for the dependent variables. Outputs may be obtained for a single condition such as a ramp angle of 30 degrees and a speed of 10 miles per hour, as in Fig. 3.7. Alternatively, the student can obtain outputs for a range of conditions such as speeds of 50 to 75 miles per hour at intervals of 2.5 miles per hour, as shown in the table and plots in Figs. 3.8 and 3.9.

The Daredevil problem is complicated by the number of different equations involved and by the variety of units used in measuring the parameters. Because problems like these are inherently complex, textbooks

v	x_end	t_end
50	145.540380	3.96928310
52.5	160.458269	4.16774726
55	176.103860	4.36621141
57.5	192.477153	4.56467557
60	209.578148	4.76313972
62.5	227.406844	4.96160388
65	245.963243	5.16006803
67.5	265.247343	5.35853219
70	285.259146	5.55699634
72.5	305.998650	5.75546050
75	327.465856	5.95392465

Fig. 3.8

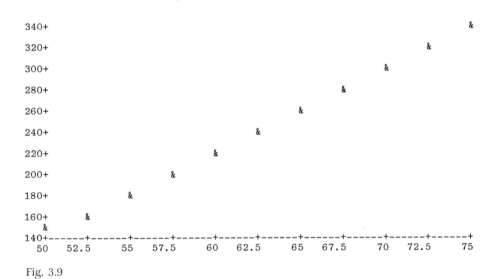

Fig. 3.9

and teachers generally simplify the parameters, point out to the students those equations which should be used, and often add a few hints. All of this makes problems less realistic, less interesting, and more ritualistic.

With *TK!Solver*, students can solve such problems in all their reality and complexity. However, the students' roles in problem solving are now changed substantially. As in the *VisiCalc* example, they are no longer solving problems in the traditional sense of the word. *TK!Solver* does that. Instead, they can engage in problem solving in much the same way engineers and scientists do in the real world. No longer do students have to wade through lists of possible equations to find the right one. No longer need they get bogged down in countless computations that often produce trivial arithmetic mistakes, and no longer need they worry about making sure they have kept all of their units consistent. Now they can think about the problem and begin to explore it creatively.

As with *VisiCalc*, students can explore the problem from a variety of perspectives, instead of focusing on finding a single correct answer. *TK!Solver* is an even more powerful tool than *VisiCalc*; it permits students to backsolve problems. For example, to find the ramp speed required for the jump, students simply type in a selected ramp angle and distance to be jumped, and *TK!Solver* calculates the required speed exactly. *TK!Solver* is a very general program that can be used with problems entered into it by the teacher or by students or with problems contained in commercially developed templates. One template that is now available includes all the basic equations and dimensional relationships necessary for solving problems in kinematics and dynamics.

When students use problem solving software such as *VisiCalc* and *TK!Solver*, teachers will not look so much at their end results, but rather at the methods and directions they have chosen. Correcting problems that require students to create charts is more like correcting written themes than like correcting mathematics problem sets. Students, as well as teachers, may find it hard at first not to get the single right answer many of them have been used to. However, eventually they will discover, probably to their relief, that solutions to many problems are not purely objective but often involve subjective and even aesthetic judgments. Such discoveries may do much to demystify problem solving for students and transform it into an activity in which a wider range of students may actively participate and be successful.

PROBLEM SOLVING ENVIRONMENTS

With computers, educators can create problem-solving environments that promote behaviors important to real-life problem solving, and yet are rarely seen in the classroom: group cooperation and extensive and careful record-keeping. Tom Snyder's *Search Series* is an outstanding example of commercially available software designed with such activities in mind. The programs create an environment that is part simulation, part adventure game, and part arcade-like game, all constructed to involve students in problem solving that demands excellent data organization and a high degree of group interaction. The programs require students to read directions, keep a notebook, do calculations, and plan and interact with members of a group. All of these are important skills that are rarely taught in schools.

One particular program, *Geography Search*, provides an opportunity for mathematical skills to serve as important tools in a geography and social studies context. In this program, a simulation is embedded in an environment taken from history; yet to make decisions and solve problems, the students must apply their practical knowledge of everyday factors, such as the apparent motion of the sun, as well as their mathematical skills.

In *Geography Search*, groups of students, organized into crews of ships, are challenged to find the Lost City of Gold in an uncharted New World. They are to bring back gold which they will sell for profit, but in doing so they must avoid the hazards of starvation and piracy along the way. Central to the simulation is the organization of students as the crew of each ship, with important tasks divided among them: keeping a record of the provisions aboard ship, sounding the depth of the water, finding the position of the ship in terms of latitude and longitude, and recording wind direction.

Problem Solving in Groups

To begin the simulation, the teacher divides the class into crews and briefs them on the different duties of the various crew members and the significance of each task to the overall success of the journey. A student workbook, which accompanies the program, also describes these tasks as well as other useful information on weather, winds, the compass, and sailing techniques.

This division of labor is essential to the group approach to problem solving in this situation. Each group member's responsibility is to observe and record a specific set of information, which must be recorded either in a chart or on a map. In some cases, the recording process also requires a translation of units or scale. Only after all the individual tasks are completed can all information on the chart or map be usefully interpreted. The group approach implies that individuals alone are unable to solve the problem. Each crew member obtains and manipulates only part of the relevant information. Some crew members make arithmetic calculations, while others draw maps; individuals no longer need to have all the skills required for solving the problem.

Students are often unprepared for the full significance of the division of labor. "This is a crummy program," or "It doesn't work," are often the frustrated responses from children when vital information disappears from the computer screen before they have had a chance to record it. But usually after several turns at the computer, the students develop the necessary strategy of dividing up among themselves the recordings to be made during the deliberately brief time the information is on the screen.

The ships begin their journey by sailing west from the home port of Vesuvia. Information from a previous voyage indicates that a prevailing westerly wind can be found to the south which provides an advantage to a south-westerly heading. The first task is to set the course of the ship. This is accomplished through a series of steps involving most of the crew. First, one crew member must determine the wind direction while another crew member studies the screen display of possible sailing directions, presented in the form of a 360 degree compass, as shown in Fig. 3.10. For example, a wind direction of 45 degrees means that the wind is blowing from the northeast.

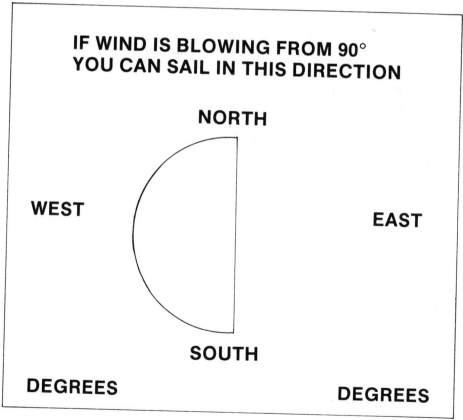

Fig. 3.10

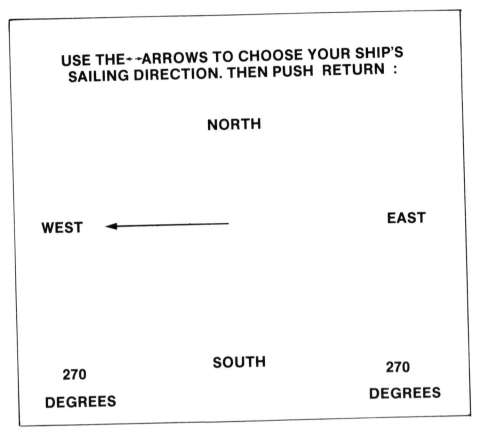

Fig. 3.11

The captain should know from class discussion that a course within 90 degrees of the heading of the wind results in little progress, if any. The captain and crew may try to determine visually what the best course is, or they may calculate the direction mathematically by adding or subtracting 90 degrees from the determined wind heading. Once that is done, the captain indicates the chosen course by using the arrow keys on the computer keyboard to set the compass pointer. The computer then displays the heading in degrees, as in Fig. 3.11.

If the heading for the ship is into the wind (i.e., within 90 degrees of the wind heading), either through oversight or intention, the computer chides the decision with the statement,

THAT HEADING IS ALMOST DIRECTLY INTO THE WIND.
BETTER KEEP MORE CAREFUL RECORDS OF WIND DIRECTION.

The crew must also decide how long to sail at the heading they have chosen: 1/4, 1/2, or 1 sailing day.

At the end of the sailing day, the crew obtains a report of the day's travel in the form of a display with many parts, as in Fig. 3.12. This display provides all the information the crew needs to make their next decision, yet it remains on the screen for only fifteen seconds. Thus it is essential that each crew member be ready to record the information for which he or she is responsible: weather, temperature, wind direction,

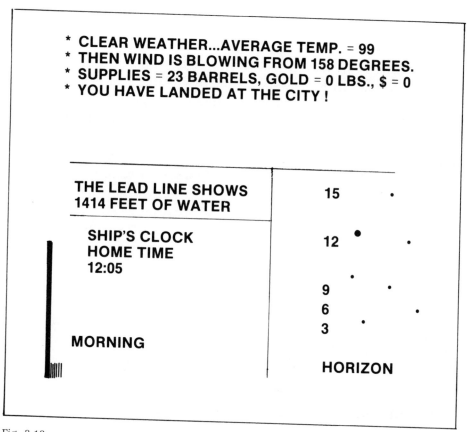

Fig. 3.12

supplies, gold, water depth, home time at noon ship's time, and position of the North Star.

Longitude is calculated by recording home time, as shown on the ship's clock when the sun is directly overhead. An animated shadow grows shorter as noon approaches. When the sun's shadow reaches its minimum length, one member of the crew must glance at the ship's clock on the computer screen to determine the home time at that instant. The crew member must then convert this reading, for example 1:06, into minutes past noon, in this case 66 minutes, to provide the longitude. It is crucial that at least one crew member be ready to make this reading because the animation of the shadow occurs only once during a day's display and failure to observe it results in a loss of information essential for plotting the location of the ship.

Latitude is calculated by determining the position of the North Star above the horizon. The computer displays a portion of the sky as if seen through a window, with a scale at the right of the screen to simulate sighting the stars with a sextant. Again, it is crucial that this sighting be made and recorded before the display disappears for the "day." After the daily report disappears, the computer provides any visual sightings of other ships made on that day; these appear on a compass grid from which the crew can determine an approximate relative position and distance.

While crossing the ocean, the crew's basic decisions involve setting the direction and length of time of the course. After reaching land, the crew must continue to set a course, now relative to the land, as they search for the City of Gold. They may also choose to land to gather provisions, or when they find the City, to gather amounts of gold.

The approach to problem solving designed into *Geography Search* contrasts sharply with traditional approaches to problem solving, in which all students are given all necessary information and expected to solve all the problems. The group approach is more like solving problems in the real world, where most problems are far too complex to be solved by one person alone, and the skills of each group member are highly relevant.

Organizing and Interpreting Information

Geography Search not only demands that students work well as a group, it also requires each individual in the group to organize and interpret collected information. For example, to insure survival, the crew must have adequate supplies of food and water. The rate of consumption of these supplies can be determined only if the provision report is carefully maintained on a day-to-day basis. Using the captain's log form, provided in the student Search Book, as shown in Fig. 3.13, is one way to keep such records.

The crew can then calculate the average rate of consumption by observing the pattern of provisions remaining at the end of each of several days. They can estimate the amount of supplies needed for the return trip by combining this information with the estimated time to cross the ocean. Without careful recordkeeping, the lives of the crew and the success of the trip could be endangered.

Wind direction on different days, when organized properly, can provide similarly important information to the crew. By comparing wind directions and speeds in southern locations with winds in northern locations, the crew may determine that the prevailing winds are found to the south, and so set a southerly course that will shorten sailing time. Temperature and weather conditions can provide a further basis for inferences.

Students can also record important information about the journey on a map. When land is found they can use the recordings of the ship's position as it sails around the New World, together with sighting information

Captain's Log

Day #	The wind is blowing from...	Wind speed	Latitude (north or south)	Longitude minutes east or west	Depth of water	Food Provisions	Temperature
1	130 °	8 mph	8 °	12:22 1324 feet		23 barrels	82 °F
2	281 °	30 mph	8 °	12.27 min 1174 ft		20 bbl	75 °F
3	67 °	29 mph	3 °	12:31 min 1412 ft		18 bbl	79 °F
4	91 °	9 mph	0 °	102 min 1465 ft		16 bbl	90 °F
	°		°				

Fig. 3.13

about the land formations, to construct their own map of the New World, as seen in Fig. 3.14.

A map is a coordinate system whose construction and use require students to understand graphing, unit conversion, and estimation. The longitude of the ship is obtained directly from the ship's clock and shadow display, but this information first must be converted into appropriate units, and then plotted on the map. Plotting requires estimation skill since, in most cases, the recorded longitude will fall between the grid lines of the map. Conversely, latitude, once read, can be plotted exactly, since latitude lines are marked in the same units in which they are recorded, but reading the latitude from the simulated sextant requires estimation.

A map is a valuable cognitive link between the concrete world and the abstract mathematical concept of coordinate systems. In *Geography Search*, the positions of the ship represent concrete distances traveled, yet these distances are recorded in terms of the more abstract concepts of latitude and longitude. For example, as the ship sails west, the quantity longitude gets larger. Since students have a strong intuitive sense of the direction of sail, the activity of charting their course on a coordinate map provides a concrete learning experience which may later be translated into plotting points on a more abstract cartesian coordinate system.

The collection, organization, and analysis of information in this program can also stimulate student discussion of related mathematical concepts. For example, the observation of the length of the shadow at noon may lead to a discussion of telling time by shadows, and thus to an investigation of indirect measurement and proportion. Setting the course of the ship, based upon wind direction, can lead to deeper insights into angular measurement and angle relationships.

Geography Search is a computer-based instructional environment in which students can learn problem-solving skills and strategies that are often overlooked in the contemporary mathematics curriculum. To succeed in this environment, students must carry out problem-solving activities as a group of cooperating team members. The problem is too large and complex for solution by an individual. Consequently, subproblems solved by individuals must be assembled to yield group solutions to larger problems. Further, solutions in this environment require students to record and analyze large quantities of information. This, too, motivates them to break

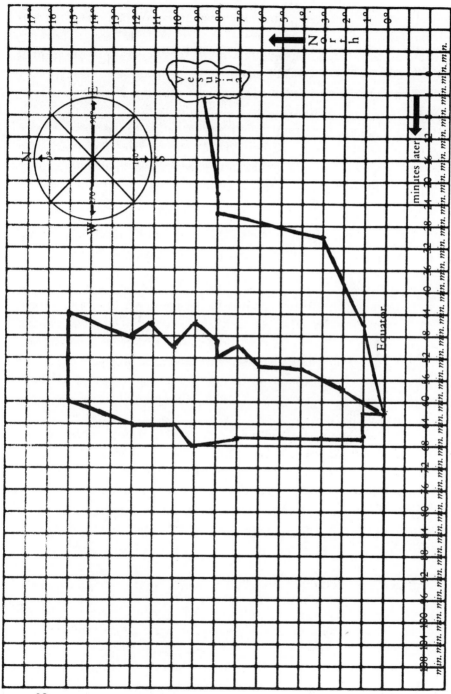

Fig. 3.14

the problem down into subproblems, in which the solutions provide them with patterns and helpful inferences.

One of the outstanding features of the *Search Series* is the design, which creates an elaborate learning environment using only one computer in the classroom. The program manages the activities of many teams of students, providing them with necessary information, doing rapid calculations for them, recording their progress, and storing their current situation to be continued another day. Programs like this promise to transform what it means for students to solve problems in mathematics classes.

MODELING SOLUTIONS TO PROBLEMS

Over the past twenty years, scientists and decision makers in government and industry have increasingly turned to the computer as a tool and to system dynamics as a method for understanding problems and solving them. Now, using microcomputers and MicroDYNAMO, a micro version of DYNAMO—a programming language designed for computer modeling—high school students can engage in very similar problem-solving activities. System dynamics and computer modeling differ significantly from traditional approaches to mathematical problem solving. In the first place, the solutions arrived at, like most real-world solutions, are approximate; they reflect the complexity of real systems, rather than the artificial simplicity of most textbook problems. But more importantly, this approach requires students to formulate hypothetical models that they may test against reality. No such creativity or reality-testing is involved in traditional problem solving. System dynamics and computer modeling clearly offer an opportunity to transform the meaning of mathematics classroom problem solving.

The Coffee Cup Problem

How long will it take a cup of coffee to cool? Specifically, how long will it take the coffee to cool from 190 degrees to 104 degrees if it sits undisturbed in a room at 70 degrees?

Using common sense, we would expect the rate of cooling to change with the temperature of the cup, and indeed Newton's Law of Cooling states that the rate of cooling at a given moment is directly proportional to the difference in the temperature of the room and the temperature of the cup at that moment.

Newton's law:

$$\text{Rate} = K(\text{temp cup} - \text{room temp})$$

We can find an approximation of the constant K in this formula experimentally by measuring the temperature at two times, subtracting these, and then dividing that quantity by the difference between the cooling cup temperature and room temperature. Let's assume for the cup in question that $K = .09/\text{seconds}$. The relationship between the temperature of the cup and the cooling rate can be expressed as:

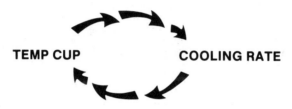

TEMP CUP   **COOLING RATE**

Fig. 3.15

The cooling rate depends on the temperature of the cup, as we have seen. However, the temperature of the cup also depends on the cooling rate—after all, the cooling rate causes the change in that temperature. Thus, the cooling rate can only be calculated if we know the temperature at two different moments, while the temperature at any moment can only be calculated if we assume the cooling rate to be zero. Most mathematics teachers would recognize this situation as one in which we could use integral calculus to find the length of time needed for the cup to cool, given Newton's formula and a coefficient of cooling, $K = .09$.

However, this problem can also be solved by students who have had no calculus whatsoever. They can use a method that solves the initial cooling rate equation by **iteration.** While this approach never produces an exact answer, it does produce approximations that can be made entirely satisfactory by shortening the length of the iterated interval.

For example, if the iteration length is set at an arbitrarily small interval, say .1 minute, then an approximate cooling rate for the short interval can be calculated at 190 degrees; the degrees of cooling resulting from this cooling rate approximation would then be subtracted from 190, and a new cooling rate calculated for the next .1 minute interval. This procedure would be repeated until the endpoint of 104 degrees is reached; the sum of .1 minute intervals required to reach this point would be the (approximate) answer to the problem of how long it would take the coffee cup to cool to 104 degrees. A more precise answer could be calculated in a similar fashion by using intervals of .01 minute each.

Such a procedure is only practical when using a computer. The teacher or students could write a BASIC program like that following to perform the calculations and print out a table of results.

```
10 REM ... COFFEE COOLING SIMULATION USING NEWTON'S LAW OF COOLING
30 TE = 190
50 K = .09:DT = .1
60 PRINT "TIME","TEMP","CHANGE"
70 FOR T = 1 TO 200
80 TC = K * (70 - TE)
100 TE = TE + TC * DT
110 IF INT (T / 5) 〈 〉 T / 5 THEN 130
120 PRINT T / 10, INT (100 * TE) / 100, INT (100 * TC) / 100
130 NEXT T
```

A second programming method for solving this problem iteratively would use the MicroDYNAMO language, as follows:

```
* COFFEE COOLING EXAMPLE
L TEMP.K = TEMP.J + (DT)(CHANG.JK)
R CHANG.KL = (.09)(70 - TEMP.K)
N TEMP = 190
SPEC DT = .1/LENGTH = 20/PLTPER = 1/PRTPER = 1
PLOT TEMP = T/CHANG = C
OPT PR
```

In this MicroDYNAMO program, there are three types of equations: level, rate, and initializing. The level equation (L) in this example computes the temperature of the cup (TEMP.K), which equals the old temperature

(TEMP.J) plus the change in temperature during the interval (DT)(CHANG.JK). The Rate equation (R) computes the cooling rate (CHANG.KL) from Newton's formula, using the approximated temperature at time K (TEMP.K). The Initializing equation (N) sets the starting temperature at 190 degrees. The SPEC line sets the iterations at .1 minute for 20 minutes and the PLOT command sets the labels and variables which will appear in the graph.

Using this MicroDYNAMO program, the students would predict that the cup takes a little over 13 minutes to cool, as shown in Fig. 3.16. The students can now check their dynamic model against reality. Suppose they let a real coffee cup cool, and they measure the temperature at four different points. These temperatures can then be plotted against the time

```
TEMP=T,CHANG=C

        0.00        50.00       100.00      150.00      200.00
      -20.000      -15.000      -10.000     -5.000       0.000
 0.0000 ----------------------C------------------------T--
        •            •            C            •        T        •
        •            •          . C            •      T          •
        •            •            •   C        •    T            •
        •            •            •     C        ,T              •
        •            •            •      C  T.                   •
        •            •            •        CT  •                 •
        •            •            •       T C  •                 •
        •            •            •      T    C.                 •
        •            •            •    T      ,C                 •
10.000 ---------------------------------T---------C----------
        •            •            • T            • C            •
        •            •            • T            • C            •
        •            •            • T            •   C          •
        •            •            ,T             •     C        •
        •            •            T              •     C        •
        •            •            T              •       C      •
        •            •          T.               •       C      •
        •            •        T •                •         C    •
        •            •        T •                •         C    •
20.000 ------------------------T-------------------------C----
```

Fig. 3.16

of the measurement. If the points do not fall on the graph, then it would appear that cooling does not conform to the model of cooling postulated. But since the students are reasonably certain about Newton's law, as well as the accuracy of their measurements, they would immediately suspect the validity of the estimated value for the coefficient of cooling ($K = .09$). They might guess that because of the material in the cup or its surface area, or perhaps because of uncontrolled drafts, the cup in the experimental situation does not have a coefficient of .09. The students may now modify the computer model by changing the .09 to another number and observing the changes in the plotted output. They could continue to make such changes until they find a value for K that brings the model into congruence with the points determined experimentally.

The students can also test the model beyond the range of prediction by heating the cup to 200 degrees and predicting the length of time it takes to cool to 100 degrees. And they can test the meaning of the coefficient of cooling by varying the amount of liquid or the type of cup. In fact, there are numerous experiments the students could do with this model, many of which provide them with possibilities for original problem solving and exploration.

The Flu Epidemic

The use of system dynamics and computer modeling not only creates opportunities for students to do original problem solving, but it also enables them to explore real-world problems and even to propose real-world solutions. Consider the problem of constructing a model that simulates the spread of the flu in a specific population. This problem has actually been explored in just this way at Groton School in a course in applied mathematics (see Chapter 5).

The first relationship the students must analyze is between the size of the susceptible population and the rate at which they become infected with the flu. There is no precise law governing the rate of infection, as there was for the rate of cooling, but students might intuitively conclude that the more susceptible people there are to be exposed, the higher would be the infection rate; and at the same time, the infection rate by definition should decrease the number of susceptible people—once they get sick, they are no longer susceptible. This can be expressed in a diagram like that in Fig. 3.17.

INFECTION RATE   SUSCEPTIBLE

Fig. 3.17

The infection rate also changes the size of the sick population: as the infection rate goes up, the size of the sick population goes up. But, as there are more sick people around (and they are not quarantined) they make others sick, so the infection rate goes up as well. The model can now be diagrammed as in Fig. 3.18.

SICK   INFECTION RATE   SUSCEPTIBLE

Fig. 3.18

But the sick condition is not permanent: the people with the flu stay sick for roughly eight days, after which time they recover and become immune to further infection for at least one year. The more sick people, the higher the recovery rate (the number of people recovering each day), and as the recovery rate increases, the number of sick people obviously goes down. The full model is shown in Fig. 3.19.

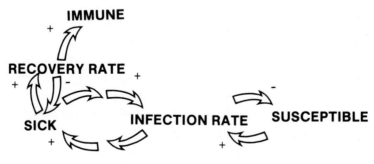

IMMUNE

RECOVERY RATE

SICK   INFECTION RATE   SUSCEPTIBLE

Fig. 3.19

Actually, this particular model of the problem is a simplified version of a more complicated model of a flu epidemic, in which the loss of immunity is taken into account. However, the present version is complex enough to illustrate the issues involved in model building.

The next step in the problem is for students to construct a mathematical model of the relationship designated by the arrows in the diagram. Using MicroDYNAMO notation, the students would write the following equations:

SUSC.K = SUSC.J − (DT)(INFECTR.JK)

SICK.K = SICK.J + (DT)(INFECTR.JK − RECOVR.JK)

RECOVR.JK = (SICK.K)/8

IMMUN.K = IMMUN.J + (DT)(RECOVR.JK)

The new susceptible population (SUSC.K) is the old susceptible population (SUSC.J) minus the number of people who become infected during the interval (DT)(INFECTR.JK). The new sick population (SICK.K) is the old sick population (SICK.J) plus the number who become infected during the interval minus the people who recover during the interval (DT)(INFECTR.JK − RECOVR.JK). The rate of recovery (RECOVR.JK) is simply the number who are sick divided by the average length of the illness, eight days in our example. The new immune population (IMMUN.K) is the old immune population (IMMUN.J) plus the number who recover during the interval (DT)(RECOVR.JK).

However, it is not immediately evident what should be the value for the infection rate (INFECTR.JK) and there is no theoretical model for constructing it. To find this value, the students must resort to an empirical approach. Since the infection rate depends on both the number of sick people and the number of susceptible people (see Fig. 3.18 again), the students could postulate a number of different formulas involving these two factors to obtain values for the infection rate, which could be confirmed empirically. For example, they could try the sum of the two populations, or the products, or more complex relations involving weighted sums or products. Each hypothesized relationship could be entered into the mathematical model, which would generate a graph against which the data from a real flu epidemic could be compared.

Suppose the students knew specifically that at their school, with a total population of 1000 people, an epidemic appeared on the eleventh day after the first reported case. They could then try each hypothesized mathematical relationship for INFECTR.JK until they found one yielding a graph showing an epidemic peaking on the eleventh day. In this case, the following relationship produces that result:

INFECTR.JK = (SUSC.K)(SICK.K)/1000

The initializing equations set the values SUSC.J = 100 and SICK.J = 1 and the MicroDYNAMO program gives the results shown in Fig. 3.20.

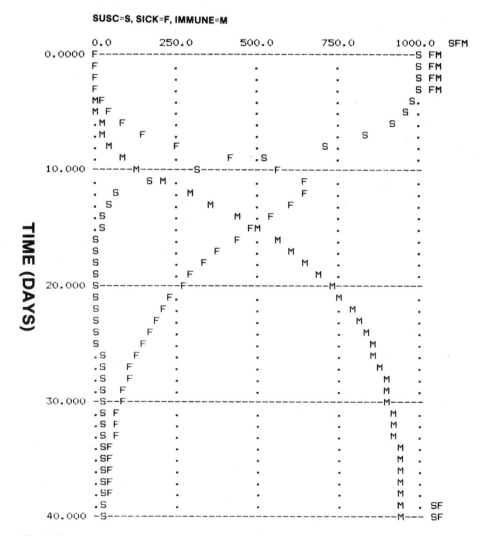

Fig. 3.20

The plot indicates an epidemic resembling the known epidemic emerging around the eleventh day, so the model with its hypothesized formula for infection rate fits the empirical data.

Two important issues remain. First, the students must verify the model with a second population. Since the selection of the formula for INFECTR.JK was determined by its fit to the data for their school, the students cannot verify its correctness on the same set of data. Students could also test other possible variables that might change the model. For example, does the initial number of susceptible people make a difference? In the model, as stated above, it does not. Students can model different situations by starting with a different initial population, observing the outcome, and using that as a prediction to be tested against real populations.

The second issue concerns other possible inferences from and interventions in the model. For instance, suppose that half of the sick population was effectively quarantined and could not spread the illness; would this alter the epidemic significantly? This intervention can be tested by changing the infected rate appropriately:

INFECTR.JK = (1/2)(SICK.K)(SUSC.K)/1000

Other situations could also be tested. What would happen, for instance, if the immune population became susceptible again within a short period of time? This would produce a more complex model in which the SUSC.K formula must include the addition of the people who have lost their immunity. We know that people do not lose their immunity in a short period of time, so in this case the model is not attempting to replicate the real world. Instead it provides, through the simulation of an impossible event, some important information about how disease and immunity are related.

Systems models, such as those for the cooling coffee cup and the flu epidemic, are attempts to represent complex situations. They are not exact and they are often incomplete. In both examples, the model must be tested against independently collected data. The purpose of involving students in such modeling exercises is to give them opportunities to test hypotheses, to reveal assumptions, and to explore alternative interventions. It allows them to investigate the nature of the interactions between factors in systems.

The nature of what we consider to be a solution is quite different here from traditional mathematics problems, like solving simple equations or answering "story problems." In system dynamics, the solution is often the process of exploration and hypothesis generation. It forces students to consider what effects different parts of the problem have on each other, and it allows them to consider those problems in which it makes no sense to talk about static, fixed points. In some cases, the solution that students ultimately derive from attempts at modeling might even imply that the mathematical formula is relatively unimportant.

CONCLUSION

By using computers, teachers and students can engage in an entirely new kind of problem solving, one in which the process, not the product, is paramount. By using numerical-analysis programs like *VisiCalc* and *TK!Solver*, students and teachers will come to recognize that there are always many "right" answers for a given problem. Some of these are better than others, but discovering the unique right answer is not a necessary part of problem solving.

Computers can also provide students and teachers with elaborate problem-solving environments, as in *Geography Search*, where group co-operation and careful record-keeping became crucial problem-solving skills, just as they are in the real world.

With computers, students at pre-college levels can now engage in sophisticated problem solving of complex systems using systems modeling and MicroDYNAMO. Creating computer models has at least two important outcomes. First, it requires a sophisticated analysis of the situation in which different factors affect each other. Second, model designing allows students to explore the results of possible interventions in the model.

Problem solving is an activity; yet, too often we overlook the activity and focus on the outcome, the "right answer." In using the computer for problem solving, the "right answer" becomes much less important than the process of exploring the context of solutions. This is not to say that students need not understand how formulas work or what multiplication means. But it suggests that with the computer doing the calculations, the students' attention can move from the mechanics of problem solving to the important concepts that lie behind those mechanics.

Using Computer Graphics in Mathematics

4

Just as the graphics capabilities of computers propelled them into the living rooms and arcades of America, so are these largely responsible for the increasing presence of computers in mathematics classrooms. And like the profound influence of video games on popular culture, computer graphics may have a profound influence on how mathematics is understood by the next generation of students. Mathematics education has for some time been dominated by "number," while "figure" has played a secondary role. Visualizing geometric and trigonometric relationships is difficult for many students and has been an obstacle in teaching these subjects. Now the graphics computer promises to change all that. As a result, visual topics and methods of analysis may soon emerge from the shadows of algebra and numerical analysis.

For this to happen, mathematics teachers, as well as their students, need experience with computer graphics activities. This chapter is filled with practical suggestions and exercises for using computer graphics in the mathematics curriculum.

TURTLE GRAPHICS

Logo, a new computer language developed by Seymour Papert and others at MIT, has taken the educational world by storm primarily because of its graphics commands, called turtle graphics, which make it easy for students to program the computer to draw complex designs. In the process of writing programs to draw objects on the screen, students can learn a great deal of mathematics in a way impossible before computer graphics became available on most microcomputers. The turtle graphics commands used in Logo to perform graphics tasks are now also available in many other programs and languages.

Turtle graphics allow the user to move a cursor, often called the turtle, around on the screen. Most turtle graphics packages contain commands that will do, at a minimum, the following: move the turtle forward and backward, turn the turtle left and right, allow the turtle to trace its path as it moves, and allow the turtle to move without tracing its path. More extensive packages contain additional commands that will place the turtle at a specified point on the screen, output the current screen coordinates of the turtle, and head the turtle toward a specified point on the screen.

A Turtle Graphics Program: *Delta Drawing*

Delta Drawing is one of several graphics programs that have been inspired by the turtle graphics capability of Logo. *Delta Drawing* was designed to enable very young children to draw pictures on a screen by creating simple programs that they can easily store and recall. It features two outstanding design elements: simplicity of syntax and a direct relationship of graphics to text. Even intricate drawings are achieved by entering a sequence of commands, each of which is but a single keystroke. *Delta Drawing* requires little instruction for students (or teachers) to master, and at the same time its product, programs for drawing pictures or making geometric shapes, can become quite complex.

A small triangular figure, Delta, is manipulated by a set of commands, its movement across the screen leaving traces in the form of straight lines. The drawing commands are Draw (D), Move (M), turn Left (L), turn Right (R), and Fill (F). Typing the D key for instance draws a straight line of about 1 centimeter (on a 9-inch monitor, that is! See Fig. 4.1).

The Move command (M) moves Delta exactly the same distance but without leaving a trace. The Right and Left commands turn Delta 30 degrees in the respective direction; and the Fill (F) command causes the program to fill with color or white (on a black-and-white monitor) the closed figure currently surrounding Delta.

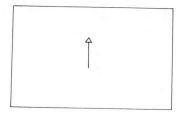

Fig. 4.1

Each command is executed immediately upon pressing the key, causing Delta to disappear. When the execution is finished, Delta reappears at the new position or pointing in a new direction, and gives a chirp sound, indicating that it is ready for the next command. At the same time the command is being executed, a record of that command is stored in the text buffer so that the series of commands, from the first to the last, are stored as a program in text form. A program is closed and given a name by typing a number key. For instance, typing "1" closes the first program which is now named "1" and immediately opens the second program. Nine programs may be created and stored. Each program stored becomes an additional command in Delta's repertoire: Delta will execute the series of commands stored as program 1 when the 1 key is typed. The 1 command or program can then be made part of any other program.

Actually, this is all much easier to do than to describe. Let's look at an example. To draw a 1-unit square, the student types "D RRR D RRR D RRR D".

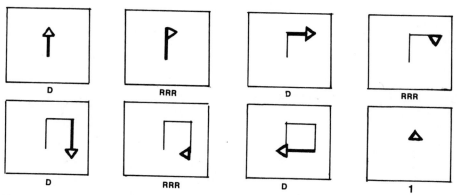

Fig. 4.2

D draws a line 1 unit long and then RRR turns Delta 90 degrees and so on. At the end of this series of commands, by typing "1", the student can store the entire sequence as program 1. Defining and storing the program clears the screen and returns Delta to the starting position. The student can then draw a series of squares by typing "1 1 1 1", as in Fig. 4.3.

The student can edit a drawing, erasing a particular line or an entire sequence of lines and turns with the E command, which simply deletes the previous command and its effect from the screen. For instance, typing "E" after a right or left turn deletes that turn and returns Delta to its previous heading. The student can erase an entire drawing from the screen

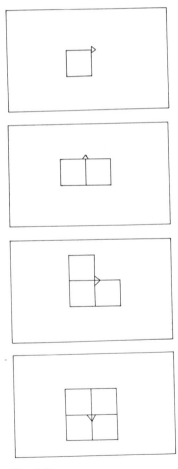

Fig. 4.3

by typing Control/E and an entire drawing session by typing Control/Z. Requiring the use of the Control key with these erase commands prevents students from inadvertently erasing large program elements.

There is also a text capability that accompanies the graphics. For example, the text for drawing the square in the previous example is stored in the text buffer as:

1⟨..1D..3R..1D..3R..1D..3R..1D.....⟩1

When a command or series of commands is erased, the text is also changed. Since text and graphics are updated simultaneously, the student can go back and forth between them at any time during the drawing session by typing "T" for text or "G" for graphics. This one-to-one correspondence between the graphics display and the text representation of the commands which produce the display is a powerful device for helping children (and adults) understand that a program is a series of commands that accomplish a task. There are several other useful features of *Delta Drawing*, including: "bounce mode" which causes Delta to bounce off the boundary of the screen when given a command which exceeds the space available; the "wrap command" which causes Delta to wrap-around the screen; and typing "A" followed by the number of a defined program, which executes the program with automatic repetition until interrupted by typing the Escape key. For example, A 1 would make the same drawing made by 1 1 1 1, but would continue to retrace the same figure until the Escape key was typed. In addition, for the adventurous student, typing "?D" or "?R" causes a random number of executions of that command; using "A" and "?" together in the same program can produce some fascinating results, such as random walks or unusual maze-like patterns (see Fig. 4.4).

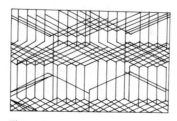

Fig. 4.4

Students may tell *Delta Drawing* to print out or save on disk programs they have written; both the print (P) and save (S) commands print and save the text program, as well as the drawing.

Exercise #1: Introducing Delta Drawing.   Following a brief introduction to the *Delta Drawing* commands, a teacher might suggest that the students experiment with the commands by drawing some figures and then print the figures.

After exploring the nature of drawing with the program, as well as some of the different shapes that can be generated, students might study printouts of their figures and text while discussing what is meant by a closed figure, a convex or concave figure, or a regular polygon, and so on. By using the program as a tool, students can explore the procedural definitions of these terms, in contrast to the traditional definitions which often seem meaningless to them. As a further activity, students might draw some regular polygons; they could experiment to see how many different regular polygons can be constructed with *Delta Drawing*. This could result in the following sort of exploration: DD R DD R DD R DD R....

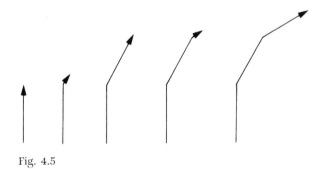

Fig. 4.5

If continued, this will produce a twelve-sided regular polygon (a dodecagon), perhaps a surprising result, since the procedure is simple and yet the resulting figure complex (see Fig. 4.6).

A natural next step might be: DD RR DD RR DD RR.... as in Fig. 4.7.

This will eventually produce a six-sided polygon, a hexagon (see Fig. 4.8). At this point the student might notice that the first figure had twelve sides and the second figure only six. The first was produced with turns of R and the second with turns of RR.

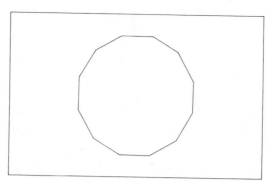

Fig. 4.6

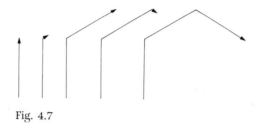

Fig. 4.7

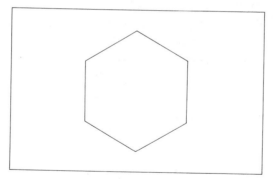

Fig. 4.8

From this it might be reasonable for students to conclude that a triangle would be produced with: DD RRR DD RRR DD RRR.... It isn't; instead this program produces a square as shown in Fig. 4.9. With further experimentation, students would discover that a triangle requires a turn of RRRR.

Fig. 4.9

In these exercises, students could use the text mode as well as graphics to study the relationship between the number of Rs in the angles in each figure and the number of sides produced. These are relatively simple exercises, which introduce students to the drawing features of the program, as well as to some mathematical concepts related to polygons. The program allows students to experiment with shapes directly, by drawing the polygons neatly and quickly, rather than getting bogged down with the requirements of drawing them with straight edge, protractors, and pencil. This is comparable to a calculator taking over computational tasks in a problem-solving situation, so the student can attend to the aspects requiring thought and creativity.

Students learn several important mathematical concepts while constructing such figures, such as the notion of a unit measure. The particular length of the Draw command is built into the program. This facilitates the creation of regular polygons. Similarly, the unit measure of the angle is built in. While most secondary school students may have a strong intuitive sense of a unit measure of length, they often do not have a similar notion of angle measurement. Because turns are drawn with discrete units, a small number of which are required for the familiar right angle, students can quickly develop an intuitive notion of angles, in particular, the useful 30- 60- 90- 120-degree angles. Finally, the one-to-one correspondence of text and graphics can help students grasp the notion of function at an intuitive level.

Exercise #2: Exploring Similarity and Congruence.   The combination of regular units of length and angle can facilitate learning about similarity and congruence. For example, the students will find early on that the shapes of their regular polygons do not change when 2D is substituted for D in drawing the sides. The only change is that the figure is bigger. This is, in fact, a precise definition of similarity, and would apply to any procedure for drawing a closed figure. Changing the number of turns, however, does produce a different result, in some cases a different polygon, and in others, a figure that is not a polygon at all.

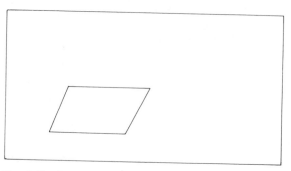

Fig. 4.10 [R DD RR DDD RRRR DD RR DDD]

Congruence might be investigated with the following activity. The teacher draws a figure and stores it on a disk. Students are instructed to load the program, display the figure, and make three copies of the figure: 1) in a different location, 2) so that it is oriented (pointed) at a different angle, 3) as a reflection of the original figure. The first two, translation and rotation, are quite straightforward with *Delta Drawing*, but the third, reflection, requires some student experimentation. for example, the parallelogram in Fig. 4.10 could be reflected as in Figs. 4.11 or 4.12.

The horizontal reflection in Fig. 4.11 is accomplished by replacing each of the R turns with an L turn, and the vertical reflection in Fig. 4.12 is done by turning Delta 180 degrees and then changing each R to L.

This approach to congruence and similarity of regular figures, although dealing with a traditional aspect of the curriculum, can lead students to some nontraditional insights. In fact, it might be argued that this procedural, manipulative approach is even more powerful than the usual axiomatic way of studying geometric forms, since it relies on skills and capacities, such as visual representation, which are most accessible to students and

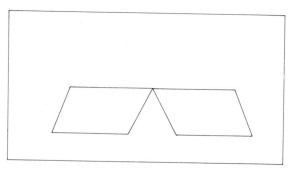

Fig. 4.11 [L DD LL DDD LLLL DD LL DDD]

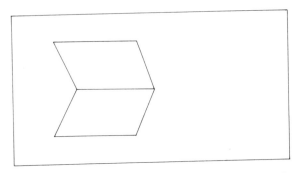

Fig. 4.12   [LLLLLL L DD LL DDD LLLL DD LL DDD]

adults. For many people, a picture may indeed be worth a thousand words. In any case, this approach offers another way of learning the same material, and thus helps students understand equivalent systems.

Exercise #3: Exploring External Angles.   The procedural approach to geometric figures can also help students understand more specific aspects of regular polygons, such as external angles. It is intuitively sensible, when drawing a regular polygon, to use a turn that is equivalent to the external angle of a polygon. Yet, if asked beforehand, "How many turn commands are required to draw the corner of an equilateral triangle, if each turn is 30 degrees?" most adults would probably respond, "two turns" because they remember that the interior angle in the triangle is 60 degrees!

The notion of exterior angles might be investigated in the following project:

1. Draw an equilateral triangle and define it as program #1. Now execute #1 several times in a row. What happens? (See Fig. 4.13.)

After the third triangle is drawn, Delta retraces its original path. No more than three triangles may be drawn. Define this as program #2.

2. Draw a square and define it as program #3. Execute #3 several times. What happens?

The students will find after four squares are drawn, Delta again starts to retrace its original path. Define this as program #4.

3. Draw a hexagon and define it as program #5. Execute #5 several times. What happens? (See Fig. 4.14.)

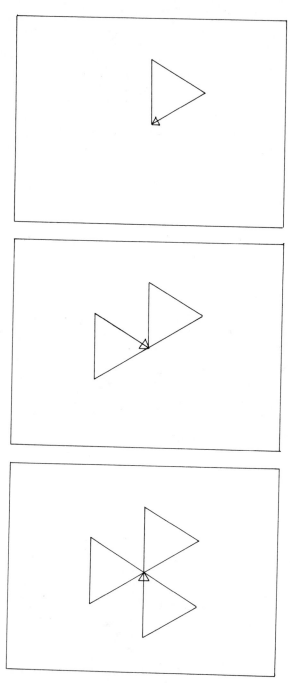

Fig. 4.13

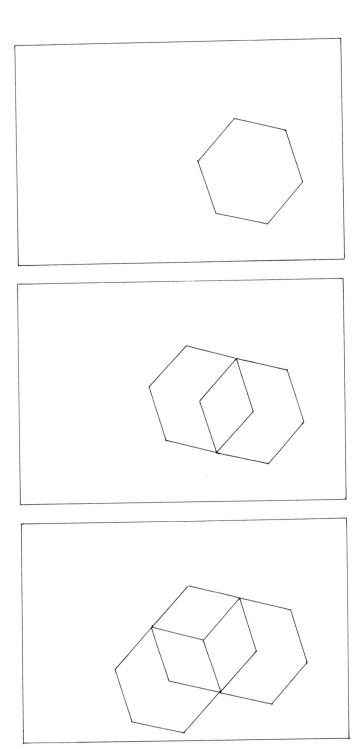

Fig. 4.14

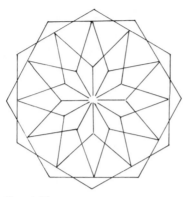

Fig. 4.15

As with the triangle and the square, Delta starts to retrace at a certain point, this time after drawing the sixth hexagon. However, because the exterior angle of the hexagon is smaller than its interior angle, which is not the case with the triangle or the square, the hexagons overlap when the program is executed repeatedly. Following this activity, students can engage in fruitful discussion of interior and exterior angles. For example, students could derive the number of degrees in the interior angles of a regular polygon, as a function of the number of sides in the polygon, or they might observe that regular polygons are much the same except for differences in their interior angles. Once again, the lesson begins with experiential exploration of procedures involved in drawing the figures; and from this, the formal rules are derived.

With regular polygons defined as programs, a concluding activity might have students create mosaics as in Fig. 4.15 by drawing a particular polygon, moving it to a new location, and drawing it again. But students will quickly discover that a more efficient system draws a larger unit (three hexagons for instance), and then moves to a new location and draws this larger unit again. To draw the larger units, students would first have to recognize the need to compensate for the smaller exterior angle. By this time, students are likely to be used to experimenting with *Delta Drawing* to discover such procedures.

A Turtle Graphics Language: Logo

All the graphics programming done in the preceding section can also be done with Logo. However, in contrast to *Delta Drawing*, which is primarily a graphics drawing tool, Logo is a complete, versatile and powerful programming language. Most versions of Logo contain an extensive set of graphics commands, each of which causes the turtle (cursor) to do something. Some of the commands available in Terrapin Logo, one of several versions available, are given below in Table 4.1.

Logo Command	Description
FORWARD x	Moves turtle ahead x screen units
BACKWARD x	Moves turtle back x screen units
RIGHT x	Turns turtle x degrees to the right
LEFT x	Turns turtle x degrees to the left
PENDOWN	Puts the turtle's pen down allowing it to trace its path
PENUP	Puts the turtle's pen up stopping it from tracing its path
REPEAT x (.....)	Causes the commands inside the parentheses to be repeated x times
SETXY A B	Moves the turtle to the screen location with coordinates x = A and y = B

Table 4.1   Logo Commands

Students can write elaborate programs, or procedures, as they are referred to in Logo, with these few commands. Logo has an editor that makes it very easy for students to enter procedures and to correct them when necessary. To define a new procedure named BOX, a student simply types "TO BOX" and presses return. This puts Logo in edit mode and the procedure can now be typed in. When the editor is being used the screen will look like this:

```
TO BOX
   FORWARD 50
   RIGHT 90
   FORWARD 50
 · RIGHT 90
   FORWARD 50
   RIGHT 90
   FORWARD 50
END
EDIT: CTRL = C to DEFINE, CTRL = G to ABORT
```

Fig. 4.16

Unlike with *Delta Drawing*, there is virtually no limit to the number of procedures that a student can define, and these procedures can be saved on a disk to be used at a later time. Following is a Logo procedure that will draw a hexagon:

```
TO HEX
  REPEAT 6 ( RIGHT 60 FORWARD 20)
END
```

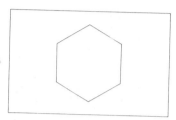

Fig. 4.17

This procedure will cause the turtle to turn 60 degrees to the right and then go forward 20 units, repeating this sequence of steps six times. Once the procedure HEX has been defined it can be used again in other procedures. For example, the procedure SUPERHEX, following, will draw the hexagonal design:

```
TO SUPERHEX
  REPEAT 6 ( HEX RT 60)
END
```

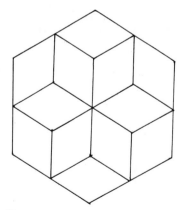

Fig. 4.18

Exercise #4: Using Logo to Introduce the Idea of a Variable. Another feature that distinguishes Logo from *Delta Drawing* is its use of variables. A procedure named SQUARE is defined following. Notice that the procedure is defined as SQUARE :SIDE instead of just SQUARE, and that :SIDE reappears in the definition. The colon signifies that SIDE is a variable and can take on any value assigned by the user.

```
TO SQUARE :SIDE
   REPEAT 4 ⟨ FD :SIDE RT 90⟩
END
```

Any time the student instructs the turtle to SQUARE, a value for SIDE must also be included. For example, the command SQUARE 50 will draw a square with sides 50 units long. The design shown in Fig. 4.19 was generated by the sequence of commands: SQUARE 10 SQUARE 20 SQUARE 30 SQUARE 40 SQUARE 50.

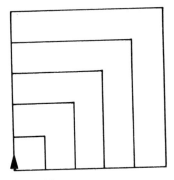

Fig. 4.19

After students have explored the SQUARE procedure for awhile, a teacher might suggest that they draw squares of different sizes and observe what the squares have in common and what is different about them. This exercise could be used to introduce young students to similar figures. Students could also make their own designs, using the same square many times or squares of different sizes. Two possibilities follow that use the REPEAT, PENUP, and PENDOWN commands.

```
TO DESIGN1
   REPEAT 10 (RIGHT 36 SQUARE 20)
END
```

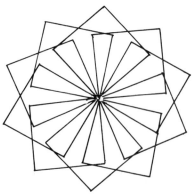

Fig. 4.20a

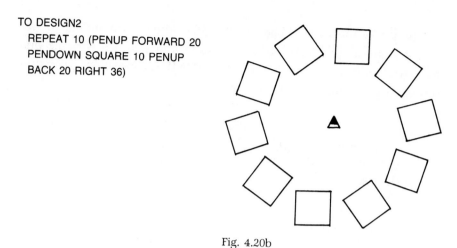

```
TO DESIGN2
  REPEAT 10 (PENUP FORWARD 20
  PENDOWN SQUARE 10 PENUP
  BACK 20 RIGHT 36)
```

Fig. 4.20b

The teacher now might ask the students to write a procedure that will draw a rectangle of length 50 and width 10. One possible procedure is given in Fig. 4.21.

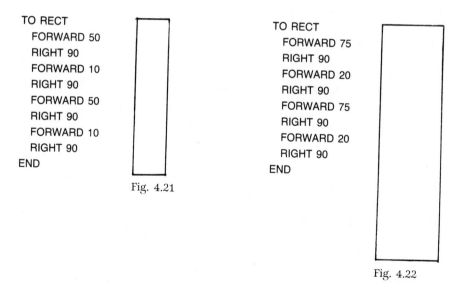

```
TO RECT
  FORWARD 50
  RIGHT 90
  FORWARD 10
  RIGHT 90
  FORWARD 50
  RIGHT 90
  FORWARD 10
  RIGHT 90
END
```

Fig. 4.21

```
TO RECT
  FORWARD 75
  RIGHT 90
  FORWARD 20
  RIGHT 90
  FORWARD 75
  RIGHT 90
  FORWARD 20
  RIGHT 90
END
```

Fig. 4.22

Once this is done successfully, the teacher could ask the students to change the procedure so that the rectangle would now be 75 × 20. (See Fig. 4.22.)

As the students write these programs, they should observe what is changing in the procedure to produce the different rectangles. Once they see that only the sizes of the length and width are changing, the teacher might suggest that they make the length and width a variable quantity by introducing variables :LENGTH and :WIDTH into their procedures. A modified procedure is given below:

```
TO RECT :LENGTH :WIDTH
   FORWARD :LENGTH
   RIGHT 90
   FORWARD :WIDTH
   RIGHT 90
   FORWARD :LENGTH
   RIGHT 90
   FORWARD :WIDTH
   RIGHT 90
END
```

or

```
TO RECT :LENGTH :WIDTH
   REPEAT 2 (FORWARD :LENGTH RIGHT 90 FORWARD :WIDTH RIGHT 90 )
END
```

The students could experiment with this procedure for awhile and again observe what all the figures have in common and how they are different. They could then use their RECT procedure to draw a series of similar rectangles.

These exercises help students see that a variable is a symbol in a procedure (or an equation for that matter) that stands for something that is going to change. Different values for :LENGTH and :WIDTH produce different rectangles. This process of using procedures with variable quantities as part of the procedure definition is very similar to giving students algebraic expressions containing a variable and asking them to evaluate the expression for some given value. For example, evaluate $4x - 5$ if $x = 2$. But with Logo, elementary school children can understand and use variables. Perhaps with such early exposure to variables, students may later experience greater success than is usually the case with the more abstract algebraic equations.

Exercise #5: Using Logo's Recursive Capabilities to Study Polygons. Logo can also be used by students to study the geometry of polygons in new ways. The following exercises may be given to students after they have written and used procedures such as SQUARE and HEX. The purpose of this exercise is to help students explore the relationship between the number of sides in a polygon and the measure of its angles. The exercise uses the following procedure:

```
TO POLY :ANGLE
   FD 50
   RT :ANGLE
   POLY :ANGLE
END
```

This procedure uses recursion, a powerful programming technique not available in some languages such as BASIC. Languages that use recursion allow the user to define procedures that use themselves. The last line of POLY :ANGLE is POLY :ANGLE, which causes POLY :ANGLE to be executed again. To see how recursion works, assume that the turtle has been instructed to POLY 120. The turtle will first move ahead 50 units and then turn right 120 degrees. Next, the turtle will POLY 120 again and then again and then again. . . . In fact the turtle will keep moving forward 50 and turning 120 (or marching around an equilateral triangle of side 50) until the user stops the procedure by typing Control/G on the keyboard. In this case, the effect is very similar to that caused by using the A command in *Delta Drawing*. To show students the power of recursion, a teacher might suggest that they try the following program:

```
TO NEW.POLY :ANGLE
   FORWARD 50
   RIGHT :ANGLE
   NEW.POLY :ANGLE + 10
END
```

After students understand how POLY works, a teacher might suggest they use this procedure to draw polygons of differing numbers of sides. They can do this by changing the value of :ANGLE and letting the turtle draw a polygon until it starts to repeat the figure, at which point it can be stopped with Control/G. Students might systematically explore the relationship between :ANGLE and number of sides of a polygon by making a table similar to the one in Table 4.2, as they vary the angle in their POLY procedure.

:ANGLE	TYPE OF POLYGON/NUMBER OF SIDES(N)
120	equilateral triangle (3 sides)
90	square (4 sides)
100	18 sided

Table 4.2

Once students have generated a variety of polygons, they should be able to distinguish polygons with intersecting sides from those with non-intersecting sides (regular polygons). Students could then use such a table to look for a relationship between the number of sides (:N) in a regular polygon and the value of :ANGLE used to generate it. Once the students begin to have some theories, the teacher might suggest that they test them by using the POLY procedure to draw polygons of N sides without retracing any side.

```
TO POLY :N :ANGLE
  REPEAT :N ( FORWARD 50 RIGHT :ANGLE)
END
```

Students would insert into this procedure the values of :N and :ANGLE suggested by their theory which, if correct, would cause the turtle to draw a polygon without retracing any side. At some point, most students will recognize the relationship between :N and :ANGLE in each case to be :N × :ANGLE = 360K OR 360K/:ANGLE = :N where K is a positive integer. At the appropriate time the teacher may wish to point out to the students that since :N has to be a positive integer, to get a regular polygon, :ANGLE must divide 360K an integral number of times.

Once students have mastered regular polygons, they can experiment with values of :ANGLE that do not divide 360 integrally. For example, what happens if a value of 100 is used for :ANGLE? What value of :N should be used to get a closed polygon (i.e., the turtle ends up where it started). In Fig. 4.23, the results are given for :N equal to 4, 8, 15, and 20. By the time :N equals 20, the turtle has started to retrace its path; so the correct value for :N must be less than 20.

Once students come up with a value for :N that yields a closed polygon, the teacher might ask if they think it is the smallest possible value and, if not, if they can find that. To do this, the students need to recognize that for the polygon to be closed, the turtle must have the same heading with which it began (0). This will occur when the total amount the turtle

Fig. 4.23

has turned in 100 degree segments is some multiple of 360. The first time this happens is when the turtle has turned a total angle equal to the least common multiple of 100 and 360, which is 1800 or (360 × 5). Then, using the relationship already derived between :N and :ANGLE, (360K/ :ANGLE = :N), students can show that :N = 18.

This example illustrates how a graphics language can be used to let students explore mathematical concepts by allowing them to develop and test their own theories and providing them with immediate feedback.

Exercise #6: Using Logo as a Coordinate Geometry Tool.   Logo can also be used to present traditional geometric concepts like theorems in new ways, as in the following example.

> The three medians of a triangle all intersect at the same point. This point is called the centroid of the triangle.

In the triangle in Fig. 4.24, L, M, and N are the three midpoints respectively of sides AC, AB, and BC. The medians AN, BL, and CM all intersect at the centroid G of the triangle.

A teacher could introduce this theorem to a class by providing them with, or asking them to develop, Logo procedures that would draw a triangle ABC given the coordinates A(X1,Y1), B(X2,Y2), and C(X3,Y3), and then draw in the three medians AN, BL, and CM. Students could then make up their own triangles, inputting their coordinates and having the program draw the medians, thereby verifying the theorem.

The Logo command SETXY is very useful for drawing objects on the screen when the coordinates of the vertices of the object are known. The command SETXY 5 20 will move the turtle from its current location to

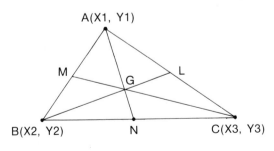

Fig. 4.24

the point on the screen with coordinates (5,20). But if the turtle's pen is down, a line segment will be drawn from wherever the turtle is to the point (5,20). The Logo commands PENUP and PENDOWN can be used to raise and lower the turtle's pen. The procedure LINE, following, raises the turtle's pen, moves it to the point with coordinates (:X1,:Y1), puts the pen down, moves the turtle to the point with coordinates (:X2,:Y2) and raises the pen again. This procedure will make the turtle draw a line segment from (:X1,:Y1) to (:X2,Y2) on the screen.

```
TO LINE :X1 :Y1 :X2 :Y2
  PENUP
  SETXY :X1 :Y1
  PENDOWN
  SETXY :X2 :Y2
  PENUP
END
```

A second procedure, DRAW.TRI, which will draw any triangle given the coordinates of the vertices, can now be written.

```
TO DRAW.TRI :X1 :Y1 :X2 :Y2 :X3 :Y3
  LINE :X1 :Y1 :X2 :Y2
  LINE :X2 :Y2 :X3 :Y3
  LINE :X3 :Y3 :X1 :Y1
END
```

Figure 4.25 shows two of the triangles that can be drawn using the procedure DRAW.TRI.

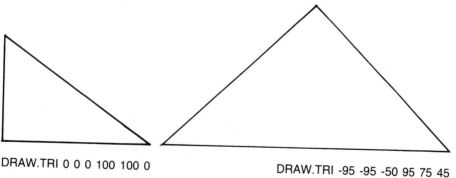

DRAW.TRI 0 0 0 100 100 0

DRAW.TRI -95 -95 -50 95 75 45

Fig. 4.25

A procedure is now needed that will draw the three medians, AN, BL, and CM, of triangle ABC. The coordinates of the three midpoints can be found using the coordinate geometry theorem, which states that the point $((x_1 + x_2)/2, (y_1 + y_2)/2)$ is the midpoint of the line segment with endpoints (x_1, y_1) and (x_2, y_2). Therefore, N, the midpoint of BC, has coordinates $((:X2 + :X3)/2, (:Y2 + :Y3)/2))$ and the Logo command

```
LINE :X1 :Y1 (:X2+:X3)/2 (:Y2+:Y3)/2
```

will draw median AN on the screen. In a similar fashion, commands can be written that will draw medians BL and CM. A procedure that will draw all three medians is given below.

```
TO DRAW.MEDIANS :X1 :Y1 :X2 :Y2 :X3 :Y3
    LINE :X1 :Y1 (:X2+:X3)/2 (:Y2+:Y3)/2
    LINE :X2 :Y2 (:X1+:X3)/2 (:Y1+:Y3)/2
    LINE :X3 :Y3 (:X1+:X2)/2 (:Y1+:Y2)/2
END
```

The procedures DRAW.TRI and DRAW.MEDIANS can be combined into the single procedure TRI.MEDIAN which will draw a triangle and its three medians.

```
TO TRI.MEDIAN :X1 :Y1 :X2 :Y2 :X3 :Y3
    DRAW.TRI :X1 :Y1 :X2 :Y2 :X3 :Y3
    DRAW.MEDIAN :X1 :Y1 :X2 :Y2 :X3 :Y3
END
```

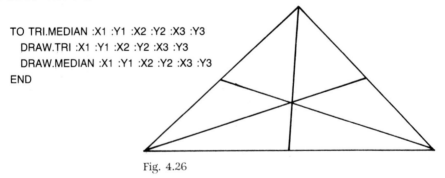

Fig. 4.26

One of the possible triangles that can be drawn using TRI.MEDIAN is shown in Fig. 4.26. Notice that the medians intersect at a single point, the centroid.

Students can use TRI.MEDIAN to find the centroids of a variety of different triangles. In addition, if a graphics printer is available, a teacher can use this procedure to prepare diagrams for tests and handouts. With one minor addition, this procedure can also be used to study a far more complicated theorem, as follows.

The triangle formed by the midpoints of the three sides of a triangle is called the medial triangle. TRI.MEDIAN1, a variation on TRI.MEDIAN, can be used to investigate the following: suppose a triangle and its medial triangle are drawn on the screen and then the medial triangle of the medial triangle, and then the medial triangle of the medial triangle of the medial triangle, and so on. A sequence of progressively smaller triangles is formed. What do all these medial triangles have in common? (Among other commonalities, they are similar and they all have the same centroid.) This problem makes a nice project for students to investigate. They will come up with all sorts of conjectures that they can test using TRI.MEDIAN1 which is identical to TRI.MEDIAN except for the final line which uses recursion to draw the next Medial triangle, and the next, and the next,

```
TO TRI.MEDIAN1 :X1 :Y1 :X2 :Y2 :X3 :Y3
   TRI.MEDIAN :X1 :Y1 :X2 :Y2 :X3 :Y3
   TRI.MEDIAN1 (:X1 + :X2)/2 (:Y1 + :Y2)/2 (:X2 + :X3)/2
   (:Y2 + :Y3)/2 (:X1 + :X3)/2 (:Y1 + :Y3)/2
END
```

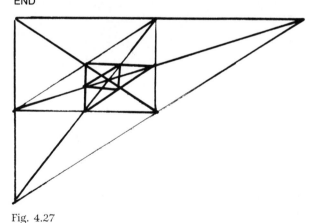

Fig. 4.27

These extended examples illustrate how students can use Logo to explore geometric concepts in new ways. They also show how the graphics capabilities of computers allow teachers and students to use them as electronic sketchpads to illustrate complex mathematical ideas.

THE MATHEMATICS OF
GRAPHICS PROGRAMMING

All microcomputers have the capacity for creating some form of graphic image. At the crudest level, pictures may be drawn on the screen, consisting only of characters that appear on the keyboard. This type of graphics, often referred to as character graphics, was widely used when teletypes were the only devices used for output. The graph in Fig. 4.28, produced by a MicroDYNAMO program, is an example of character graphics. Exercises using character graphics provide instant gratification to students just learning programming and can be used with students of all ages. But, today's computers have the capacity to do far more sophisticated graphics than this.

A series of exercises are provided in this section for students to explore computer graphics and the mathematics necessary to create images that move around the screen. In doing these exercises, students would write

```
URBAN GROWTH MODEL

    BUILD=B,CONST=C,DEMO=D

        0.0         250.0         500.0         750.0        1000.0  B
        0.000       20.000        40.000        60.000        80.000  CD
 0.0000 BC-------------------------------------------------------- BD
        DB           .             .             .            . BC
        DB           .             .             .            . BC
        DB           .             .             .            . BC
        D B          .             .             .            . BC
        .DBC         .             .             .            .
        .D BC        .             .             .            .
        .D   BC      .             .             .            .
        .D     BC    .             .             .            .
        . D      B C .             .             .            .
40.000  --D------B--C--------------------------------------------
        . D          .B C          .             .            .
        .  D         .    B C       .             .            .
        .   D        .       B C    .             .            .
        .     D      .          .  B       .            . BC
        .      D     .          .    C     B.            .
        .        D . C          .         B           .
        .         D. C          .             .     B     .
        .         DC            .             .    B    .
        .         C.            .             .    B  . CD
80.000  ----------C-----------------------------------B--- CD
        .         C.            .             .    B  . CD
        .         C.            .             .    B  . CD
        .         C.            .             .    B  . CD
        .         C.            .             .    B  . CD
        .         C.            .             .    B  . CD
```

Fig. 4.28

a large program that allows them to study many important mathematical concepts in ways impossible before computer graphics became available. These exercises are given in Applesoft BASIC, but in most cases, are easily translated into other forms of BASIC.

Plotting Two-Dimensional Shapes and Line Segments

Exercise 7: Creating an Image on the Screen.   The following exercise is a good one for making students use different cartesian coordinate systems and for introducing them to the concept of an array. The time spent in explaining arrays to students will be worth it because it will help them create a powerful graphics drawing tool for future use.

Before doing this exercise, the teacher should know the dimensions of the graphics screen to be used and the coordinates of the center of the screen. For example, on an Apple, the high resolution graphics screen is 280 × 192 and the origin is located in the upper left-hand corner. The center of the screen is located at the point with coordinates (140,96).

With the size of the screen known, students can draw on a piece of graph paper a simple design composed of line segments. This can then be put on the screen as in Fig. 4.29.

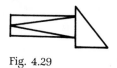

Fig. 4.29

Next, the students should label all the important points in the design as in Fig. 4.30 and make a table of these, as in Table 4.3.

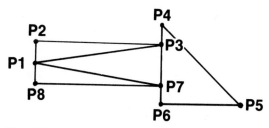

Fig. 4.30

POINT	X	Y
P1	0	0
P2	0	5
P3	30	5
P4	30	10
P5	45	-10
P6	30	-10
P7	30	-5
P8	0	-5

Table 4.3

This situation provides an ideal opportunity to introduce students to the concept of an array or matrix, if they are not yet familiar with it, because it makes the following work much easier. In this example, an array P is used. The element P(I, 1) contains the x-coordinate of the I-th point and P(I, 2) contains the y-coordinate of the I-th point. Students should translate the points in their table into elements in the array P, as in Table 4.4.

$$
P = \begin{bmatrix}
0 & 0 \\
0 & 5 \\
30 & 5 \\
30 & 10 \\
45 & -10 \\
30 & 10 \\
30 & -5 \\
0 & -5
\end{bmatrix}
$$

Table 4.4

Students can now write a **subroutine,** such as the following, that inputs the coordinates of the points using the READ and DATA commands in BASIC.

```
1000  REM ...THIS READS IN ORIGINAL DESIGN
1010  FOR I = 1 TO 8
1020  FOR J = 1 TO 2
1030  READ P(I,J)
1035  OD(I,J) = P(I,J)
1040  NEXT J
1050  NEXT I
1060  DATA  0,0,0,5,30,5,30,10,45,-10,30,-10,30,-10,30,-5,0,-5
1070  RETURN
```

Students can now write a subroutine to draw the design. To do this, they must find a path connecting all the points of the design in the proper order. The path P1 TO P2 TO P3 TO P4 TO P5 TO P6 TO P7 TO P8 TO P1 TO P3 TO P7 TO P1 defines the design in Fig. 4.29. Once the students determine a path, they make a list of the order of the points, which they enter into memory as a second array, called PA for path. For this example, the array PA consists of twelve numbers. The array element PA(10) would be 3 because the third point in the array P is the tenth point in the path. A READ statement can now be used to read the path into memory. The following subroutine performs two tasks: reads all the points in the design into memory and reads the order in which the points need to be read to plot the design.

```
2000  REM ...THIS READS IN DESIGN PATH
2015  FOR I = 1 TO 12
2020  READ PA(I)
2030  NEXT I
2040  DATA  1,2,3,4,5,6,7,8,1,3,7,1
2060  RETURN
```

Next, students write a subroutine that will draw the line segments connecting the points in the design. The specific commands that accomplish this are different for each machine, but they all have to accomplish the same task: connecting point 1 to point 2, point 2 to point 3, point 3 to point 4, point 4 to point 5, and so on. If the graphics screen of the computer being used does not use (0, 0) as the center of its screen, the teacher has a practical context in which to introduce the important topic of coordinate translations. Students are far more likely to be able to understand and be able to perform such translations when they appreciate their usefulness. For example, on the Apple II, the center of the screen is located at (140, 96) so the command HPLOT P(1, 1) + 140, 96-P(1, 2) TO P(2, 1) + 140, 96-P(2, 2) draws the line segment joining point 1 in array P to point 2. The following Applesoft subroutine draws the entire design given in Fig. 4.29.

```
3000   REM ...THIS PLOTS DESIGN
3010   FOR I = 1 TO 11
3020   HPLOT P(PA(I),1) + 140,96 - P(PA(I),2) TO P(PA(I + 1),1) + 140,96 -
       P(PA(I + 1),2)
3030   NEXT I
3040   RETURN
```

Once students have written a subroutine that will draw an image on the screen, they should be encouraged to experiment with different designs. An interesting programming project for students is to modify their programs so the coordinates of the points making up the design and their order in the path can be input as variable quantities. This can be accomplished using the BASIC INPUT command.

Transforming Objects on the Screen

Now that the students have developed a program for drawing a design on the screen, they are ready to learn how to move the design around on the screen. The concept of coordinate translations can be generalized to include all transformations associating one point in a plane with another. For example, the translation of the point (x, y) to the point (x + 20, y + 30) is a transformation. Transformations can be thought of as functions that move points, so to simplify the discussion we will use the notation T((x, y)) for transformations. The preceding transformation is defined as follows T((x, y)) = (x + 20, y + 30), which is read as follows: "T is the transformation that associates with each point (x, y) the point (x + 20, y + 30)". If the transformation T is applied to each point in the design in Fig. 4.29 and the translated points are joined by line segments the result is to move the design over 20 units and up 30 units, as shown in Fig. 4.31.

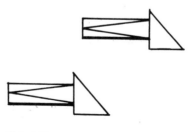

Fig. 4.31

The general translation in the plane is defined by T((x, y)) = (x + a, y + b) where a and b are any two fixed real numbers. This transformation is very useful for sliding objects around the screen.

Exercise #8: Translating Objects. Now students can apply translations to the designs they created in Exercise #7. The BASIC subroutine will perform the translation defined above to the points in array P. The INPUT command is used so different translations may be applied to the design.

```
4000  REM ...THIS IS TRANSLATION ROUTINE
4010  INPUT "VALUE FOR A?";A: INPUT "VALUE FOR B?";B
4020  FOR I = 1 TO 8
4030  P(I,1) = P(I,1) + A:P(I,2) = P(I,2) + B
4040  NEXT I
4050  RETURN
```

This subroutine will cause A to be added to the x-coordinate of each point in the design and B to be added to each y-coordinate. Using this translation subroutine, students can now be asked to create designs such as the one in Fig. 4.32.

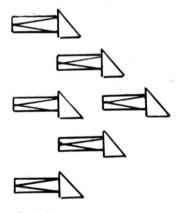

Fig. 4.32

After the students have created several designs, the teacher might ask what all the translated figures have in common. This provides an excellent introduction to the mathematical concept of invariance. In this case, students are being asked to find what properties of figures are invariant under translation.

Exercise #9: Making Objects Move: Simple Animation. Now, students can use their translation subroutines to achieve a very crude form of animation.

1. Plot the given object using white as a color.
2. Plot the given object using black as a color.
3. Apply a translation to the original set of points.
4. Plot the new set of points in white.
5. Plot the new set of points in black.
6. Apply a translation to the set of points defined in 3.
7. Plot this new set of points in white.
8. Plot this new set of points in black.
   etc.

Exercise #10: Making Objects Change Size. Another transformation makes shapes grow or shrink without changing the shape of the original object and is very useful for graphics purposes. These transformations are defined mathematically by $S((x, y)) = (cx, cy)$ where c is a positive real number. If $c > 1$, S will make an object get larger, while if $0 < c < 1$, S will make an object shrink. If the transformation $S(x, y)) = (3x, 3y)$ is applied to the design in Fig. 4.29, the result is a figure three times larger as shown in Fig. 4.33.

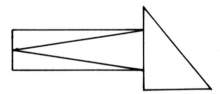

Fig. 4.33

Students can now add to their programs a subroutine similar to the one following that will change the size of the design. This subroutine can be used, in a similar manner to the sequence outlined in Exercise #9, to create some impressive animation effects.

```
5000  REM ...THIS CHANGES THE SIZE OF THE DESIGN
5010  INPUT "WHAT SCALE FACTOR?";SC
5020  FOR I = 1 TO 8
5030 P(I,1) = P(I,1) * SC:P(I,2) = P(I,2) * SC
5040  NEXT I
5060  RETURN
```

Exercise #11: Making Objects Rotate. A final, very useful transformation, called a rotation, rotates points about the origin through a fixed angle. Deriving the formula for this transformation provides the teacher with an opportunity to walk students through a trigonometric derivation in a motivating context.

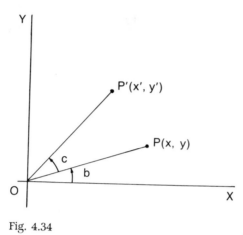

Fig. 4.34

In Fig. 4.34, the ray OP is rotated through an angle of c degrees resulting in the ray OP'. Letting r denote the length of OP and letting b denote the measure of angle XOP where X is any point on the positive x-axis, it can be shown that P has polar coordinates (r; b). Since P' was obtained by rotating P through c degrees about the origin, P' must have coordinates (r; b + c). Letting P have rectangular coordinates (x, y) and P' the coordinates (x', y') and applying the conversion formulas x = rcos(b) and y = rsin(b) we get that

$$x = rcos(b)$$
$$y = rsin(b)$$

and

$$x' = rcos(b+c)$$
$$y' = rsin(b+c)$$

Using the trigonometric addition formulas developed in high school trigonometry courses the expressions for x' and y' can then be rewritten as follows:

$$x' = r(\cos(b)\cos(c) - \sin(b)\sin(c))$$
$$x' = (r\cos(b))\cos(c) - (r\sin(b))\sin(c)$$
$$x' = x\cos(c) - y\sin(c)$$

and

$$y' = r(\sin(b)\cos(c) + \sin(c)\cos(b))$$
$$y' = (r\sin(b))\cos(c) + (r\cos(b))\sin(c)$$
$$y' = x\sin(c) + y\cos(c)$$

Letting $R((x, y)) = (x', y')$, the preceding demonstrates that the transformation $R((x, y)) = (x\cos(c) - y\sin(c), x\sin(c) + y\cos(c))$ will rotate an object about the origin through an angle of c degrees. If c is positive it will be a counterclockwise rotation and if c is negative it will be a clockwise rotation. If the student applies the rotation $R((x, y)) = (x\cos(45) - y\sin(45), x\sin(45) + y\cos(45))$ repeatedly to the design in Fig. 4.29 and plots each rotation of the figure, the result will look like Fig. 4.35.

Fig. 4.35

Once students have mastered the rotation formulas, they can be asked to modify their design plotting routines to rotate the original design through a given angle o.

The following is a BASIC subroutine that will rotate the design in Fig. 4.29.

```
6000   REM ...THIS IS ROTATION ROUTINE
6010   INPUT "WHAT IS THE ANGLE OF ROTATION? ";TT
6020 TT = TT * 3.14159 / 360
6030   FOR I = 1 TO 8
6040   FOR J = 1 TO 2
6050 R(I,1) = P(I,1) *  COS (TT) - P(I,2) *  SIN (TT)
6060 R(I,2) = P(I,1) *  SIN (TT) + P(I,2) *  COS (TT)
6070 P(I,1) = R(I,1):P(I,2) = R(I,2)
6080   NEXT J
6090   NEXT I
6100   RETURN
```

Exercise #12: Combining Transformations. Students can combine the transformations developed so far to produce some very sophisticated graphics. The design in Fig. 4.36 was produced using only rotations, slides, and enlargements.

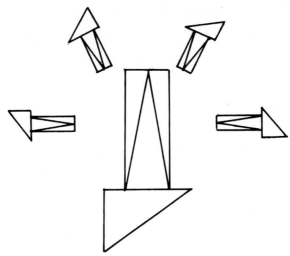

Fig. 4.36

Following is a listing of a BASIC program that combines all the subroutines developed so far in this section.

```
?SYNTAX ERROR
]LIST10-4050

10    REM ...TRANSFORMATION PLOTTING PROGRAM (JONATHAN CHOATE)
15    DIM P(8,2): DIM PA(20): DIM OD(8,2)
20    GOSUB 1000
30    GOSUB 2000
40    HGR : HCOLOR= 3
50    REM ...THIS ASKS FOR OPTIONS
60    INPUT "DO YOU WANT TO.(1)PLOT DESIGN.(2).TRANSLATE.(3)ENLARGE.(4)ROTAT
      E.(5)REFLECT.(6)ERASE.(7)RESTORE.(8)QUIT? ";CH
65    IF CH < 1 OR CH > 8 THEN 60
70    ON CH GOSUB 3000,4000,5000,6000,10000,7000,8000,9000
80    GOTO 60
100   END
1000   REM ...THIS READS IN ORIGINAL DESIGN
1010   FOR I = 1 TO 8
1020   FOR J = 1 TO 2
1030   READ P(I,J)
1035 OD(I,J) = P(I,J)
1040   NEXT J
1050   NEXT I
1060   DATA  0,0,0,5,30,5,30,10,45,-10,30,-10,30,-10,30,-5,0,-5
1070   RETURN
2000   REM ...THIS READS IN DESIGN PATH
```

```
2015   FOR I = 1 TO 12
2020   READ PA(I)
2030   NEXT I
2040   DATA   1,2,3,4,5,6,7,8,1,3,7,1
2060   RETURN
3000   REM ...THIS PLOTS DESIGN
3010   FOR I = 1 TO 11
3020   HPLOT P(PA(I),1) + 140,96 - P(PA(I),2) TO P(PA(I + 1),1) + 140,96 -
       P(PA(I + 1),2)
3030   NEXT I
3040   RETURN
4000   REM ...THIS IS TRANSLATION ROUTINE
4010   INPUT "VALUE FOR A?";A: INPUT "VALUE FOR B?";B
4020   FOR I = 1 TO 8
4030 P(I,1) = P(I,1) + A:P(I,2) = P(I,2) + B
4040   NEXT I
4050   RETURN


]LIST5000-12000

5000   REM ...THIS CHANGES THE SIZE OF THE DESIGN
5010   INPUT "WHAT SCALE FACTOR?";SC
5020   FOR I = 1 TO 8
5030 P(I,1) = P(I,1) * SC:P(I,2) = P(I,2) * SC
5040   NEXT I
5060   RETURN
6000   REM ...THIS IS ROTATION ROUTINE
6010   INPUT "WHAT IS THE ANGLE OF ROTATION? ";TT
6020 TT = TT * 3.14159 / 360
6030   FOR I = 1 TO 8
6040   FOR J = 1 TO 2
6050 R(I,1) = P(I,1) *  COS (TT) - P(I,2) *  SIN (TT)
6060 R(I,2) = P(I,1) *  SIN (TT) + P(I,2) *  COS (TT)
6070 P(I,1) = R(I,1):P(I,2) = R(I,2)
6080   NEXT J
6090   NEXT I
6100   RETURN
7000   REM ...THIS IS ERASE ROUTINE
7010   HCOLOR= 0
7020   GOSUB 3000
7030   HCOLOR= 3
7100   RETURN
8000   REM ...THIS RESTORES ARRAY P TO THE ORIGINAL DESIGN
8010   FOR I = 1 TO 8
8020   FOR J = 1 TO 2
8030 P(I,J) = OD(I,J)
8040   NEXT J
8050   NEXT I
8060   RETURN
9000   REM ...THIS IS END
9010   END
10000   REM ....THIS REFLECTS DESIGN AROUND THE Y-AXIS
10010   FOR I = 1 TO 8
10020 P(I,1) = ( - 1) * P(I,1)
10030   NEXT I
10040   RETURN
```

The program allows the students to do the following:

1. Plot the original design.
2. Translate the points in array P.

3. Enlarge the points in array P.
4. Rotate the points in array P.
5. Reflect the points in array P about the y-axis.
6. Erase the last figure plotted.
7. Restore array P to the original set of points.
8. Quit the program.

Teachers might ask students to use this program to study the mathematics of transformations. Below is a list of possible questions to investigate.

- Does each transformation have an inverse and, if so, what is it?
- Does it make any difference in what order the transformations are performed? Is the operation of combining transformations commutative?
- What properties of the design are preserved under each transformation? Which transformations produce congruent figures? Which produce similar figures?
- All of the transformations with the exception of translations are special cases of a more general transformation called a linear transformation. The general linear transformation $L((x,y))$ is defined by

$$L((x, y)) = (ax + by, cx + dy)$$

where a, b, c, and d are any real numbers. A teacher might ask students to add this transformation to their program and then to investigate what happens to the design for different values of a, b, c, and d. This provides an excellent introduction to many topics in the field of linear algebra, a very important mathematical field.

SPECIAL APPLICATIONS PACKAGES

There are now available a variety of graphics packages for special applications that are of interest to teachers and students of mathematics. All of these make it much easier to do a variety of mathematical tasks. Packages that display data easily on the screen and that graph mathematical functions can be used in a variety of ways in the mathematics classroom.

Data Display Devices

Students faced with making sense of a large collection of numbers can use one of the many histogram plotting packages now available. The typical program works as follows:

1. The student inputs the data into the computer.
2. The computer sorts the data and prints out a frequency distribution.
3. The student selects the number of frequency groupings, and the computer calculates the appropriate horizontal and vertical scales.
4. The program generates the appropriate histogram on the screen. A typical histogram output is given in Fig. 4.37.

Since these packages remove much of the tedious work from displaying data, students may now be asked to do exercises that focus on a variety of interesting data distributions. Here are a few.

Exercise #13: Using Histograms. Ask students to find the heights of all the students in their class or grade if possible. The more data the better. Once they have collected all the data, instruct them to divide it into boy data and girl data. Using a data display program, have them plot a histogram for the entire class, for the boys' data and for the girls' data. Once they have these plots, ask them to summarize each set in words using the histograms.

Next, have them repeat the above exercise, but now collect the weights of the class. Ask them to compare the two sets and to make a list of the differences and the similarities between them.

Finally, have the students collect the average daily temperature for their town for a year. Ask them to make a histogram of these data and

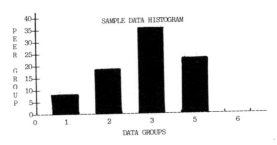

Fig. 4.37

to compare this with the height histogram. Ask them which is more variable and why.

This type of exercise can be repeated in a variety of ways. In each case, by making the display of data easy, the computer has allowed students to focus on what the collection of numbers is telling them and not on a lot of tedious computation and plotting. Data display packages make the study of data analysis far easier for students.

Besides making it easy for students to create histograms, many data display packages also can be used to plot a series of points, given the coordinates of the points. These point-plotting routines will draw the appropriate axes and then plot each given point in its proper place. The graph in Fig. 4.38 is a sample output of a typical point-plotting routine.

Exercise #14: Using Point-Plotting Routines. Point-plotting programs can be very useful for studying how different quantities vary over time. Students can be asked to keep track of how many hours of sleep they got during a specific period. This set of data can be put into graphic form using a point-plotting routine. After they have done this, ask them to collect a set of data that possesses a similar oscillating pattern. After they do this, ask them to collect data about a quantity that grows steadily over a period of time. Next, they can be asked to find a quantity that decays over time.

```
RANGE OF X = 1 TO 5.8
RANGE OF Y = 1 TO 33.8


  y
  +
  +                                                      *
  +
  +
  +
  +
  +
  +
  +               *     *
  +            *
  + *      *
  +++++++++++++++++++++++++++++++++++++++++++++++++++++++++ x
```
Fig. 4.38

This collection of graphs can be used to show students many of the common ways phenomena vary over time and can help pave the way for the study of the more common mathematical functions, such as the trigonometric functions and the exponential functions. The point-plotting programs make it very easy for students to display data about the world around them and help them to relate mathematics to their own reality.

Function Plotting Programs

There are other types of graphics packages available for the study of mathematics that do more specific tasks than either of the graphics tools mentioned so far. One of these types allows the user to graph mathematical functions of the form $y = f(x)$ such as $y = 3x + 4$ or $y = \sin(3x + 12)$. These function-plotting packages make it very easy to input the function to be graphed, to graph several functions together, and to change the x and y scales. These programs can be used to: introduce younger students to simple linear graphs, help students develop general graphing skills, and allow students to solve equations which do not have algebraic solutions. In what follows, only some of the options available with these packages are used: changing the current function, changing the x-scales, and changing the y-scales.

This program can be used in an algebra I class when the graphs of linear functions are first studied. A teacher might do the following.

Exercise #15: Using a Function Plotter.   At the start of the class, use a function plotter to display the graph of $y = x$, and then ask the students to sketch the graph of $y = 2x$. When most of the students have made their sketches, display the graph of $y = 2x$ on the screen. Repeat this process until the students can predict quickly what any graph of the form $y = mx$, where m could be any real number, would look like. Once the students have mastered this type of linear graph, display the graph of $y = 3x + 5$ and ask the students to sketch the graph of $y = 3x - 4$. Then display this new function so the students can check their sketch graphs. This process can be continued until the students feel comfortable graphing any function of the form $y = mx + b$ where m and b are any real numbers. The computer is being used here to draw graphs without the tedium of plotting a lot of points, so that students can concentrate more on the graphing and less on the computation.

Exercise #16: More Function Plotting.   This series of exercises can be used with students who are studying the elementary functions. It is designed to help them develop general graphing skills. Students should be asked to select a function they are interested in such as cos(x), log(x), or 2x. Students then should be asked to plot the following graphs for their choice of $y = f(x)$.

1. $y = f(x)$
2. $y = 2f(x)$
3. $y = f(x - 2)$
4. $y = f(x + 3)$
5. $y = f(x) + 4$
6. $y = f(x) - 6$
7. $y = f(2x)$
8. $y = f(-x)$
9. $y = 2(f(x - 1)) + 4$

As each new graph is completed, the students should be asked to compare the graph to the graph of $y = f(x)$. For example, they might observe that the graph of $y = f(x - 2)$ has the same shape as $y = f(x)$ but has been shifted 2 units to the right. Likewise, the graph of $y = f(2x)$ has the same shape as $y = f(x)$ but the horizontal scale has been compressed by a factor of 2. After a little practice, students can draw an accurate sketch graph of complex functions such as $y = 2\log(2(x + 2)) - 3$ very quickly. Function-plotting packages can be used by students to greatly improve their graphing skills.

These packages can also be used to graph functions quickly by a teacher in a class setting. Teachers can use far more graphs in their day-to-day teaching when they are done so quickly on a microcomputer.

Exercise #17: Solving Quintic Equations.   Function-plotting routines can be used to locate the solutions of any equation of the form $f(x) - 0$ for which the computer can compute the value of $f(x)$. This includes equations for which there exist no formulas for exact solutions such as quintic

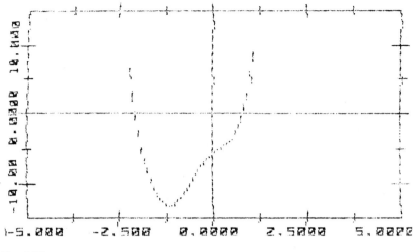

Fig. 4.39

equations. A typical quintic equation is $x^5 + 5x^4 + 2x^3 - 4x^2 + 5x - 6 = 0$. Ask students to solve this by having the computer draw its graph and then looking for the x-intercepts of the graph. By changing the x scale, they can find very good approximate solutions. (See Fig. 4.39.)

THE FUTURE

There already exist graphics tools that make the ones discussed in this chapter seem trivial. One type in particular, computer aided design packages, allow the user to create three-dimensional objects on the screen that are almost lifelike. These objects can be rotated, colored, expanded, and deformed in a variety of ways. Some packages allow the user to create objects by combining a variety of different solids. For example, surfaces can be formed that are the intersection of a cone with a cube. These packages could be used by students to learn and explore three-dimensional geometry in ways unimagined five years ago.

In the years to come, as the cost of computer memory goes down and the quality of resolution on the video screen goes up, computer graphics will become a far more powerful tool for educators. Improvements in light pens, graphics tablets, and three-dimensional digitizers will make it much easier to enter the points making up objects into the computer.

New color printers will permit full-color printouts of the objects students design. Video discs will allow students and teachers to access visual information in new and exciting ways. Improvements in holographic technology will permit the use of true three-dimensional images on the graphics screen.

All of the coming graphics tools will help make the study of mathematics an increasingly visual, interactive, personal, and exciting experience for both students and teachers.

Applied Mathematics: **5**
Transforming Content

During the past thirty years, there have been on-going efforts to transform the mathematics curriculum. The most famous, and to some, infamous, of the curriculum reforms was the so-called new math. The outgrowth of a massive federally funded project (School Mathematics Study Group), the goal of the new math was for students to see mathematics much as mathematicians do. It was believed that when students were taught the underlying structures of mathematics, they would better understand and be better able to perform mathematical skills.

On the whole the new math was a failure, not necessarily because its premise was wrong, but because its politics were naive. Most parents were bewildered by the new math homework their children brought home. Many elementary school teachers, just barely comfortable with the "old math," were so afraid of these new approaches they consciously and unconsciously subverted them. Even high school mathematics teachers who were familiar with the new math approach from their college mathematics courses weren't always confident in their ability to teach it.

But the new math curriculum developers were undaunted. They established in-service training workshops, summer institutes, and even evening courses on the new math for anxious parents. These efforts were to little avail. They were too few and too late. The backlash was formidable and came from many quarters: minority parents complained that their children weren't being taught the real-world mathematics skills they needed; business leaders lamented the decline in workers with adequate computational skills; some proponents of the "Back to Basics" movement viewed the new math as a conspiracy on the part of university intellectuals to deprive children of a basic American education; and even the various teacher's organizations had little praise for the new math.

The developers and proponents of the new math made several crucial errors that doomed their efforts from the start. First, theirs was a "top–down" reform, originating with university mathematicians and a hand-picked elite of secondary school mathematics teachers operating under federal funding, mostly from the National Science Foundation. There was never much grass-roots involvement, either during the planning stage or during implementation. Second, the new math was simply too much of a departure from what parents, students, and many teachers were used to. It didn't begin where they were and move them along from there; it began with ideas, concepts, and methods that were alien and that only got stranger as they were developed. Third, the new math demanded too much of teachers. It required them to learn new content and new methods, to become accustomed to new texts, new problem sets, and new types of test questions. Teachers were pressured to attend workshops and summer institutes, just so they could keep up with the changing curriculum. Fourth, the excesses of some of the new math approaches opened the entire effort up for ridicule in the public press, where new math jokes became commonplace. Fifth, the new math ran afoul of a growing political conservatism in this country, which focused its wrath on the new schools and the "effete intellectuals" from universities who were "destroying" basic education. And sixth, the proponents of the new math failed to keep up with the other changes in society that impacted all of education, including mathematics.

The new math was born in the late 1950s as a reaction to Sputnik. In the meantime, an increasingly militant civil rights movement in the 1960s, a brief flurry of political and educational progressivism in the early 1970s, the emergence of neo-conservatism in the late 1970s, and the deepening world economic crises of the early 1980s all made themselves felt in the schools. The new math was inconsistent with virtually every political development and educational philosophy that was influential in the past twenty-five years.

The political failure of the new math is not unique among educational reform efforts. In his book, *Transformation of the School*, educational historian Robert Cremin traces the collapse of the progressive education movement to virtually identical factors. Others have suggested the same explanations for the decline of the free school movement of the 1960s, the open-school movement of the 1970s, and all the other various new curriculum efforts of the past twenty-five years: PSSC and Project Physics, CHEM Study and CBA, BSCS, ESCP, ECCP, SCIS, ESS, Man A Course of Study, and others. Might not the educational computing revolution experience a similar failure?

Indeed, it might. It is incumbent upon those who wish to see computers transform the processes and content of education to be aware of these past failures and to learn from them. There are signs that this is happening to an extent in the small but growing ranks of educational computing advocates. The best sign is that educational computing is, in many ways, a grass-roots movement. It has grown out of, and has been nurtured by, personal computer enthusiasts: parents, teachers, and students. It has received almost no support from the federal government or the elite funding foundations. And few of the real successes of educational computing have come out of the universities, PLATO and Patrick Suppes notwithstanding.

Perhaps as important to its success is the almost inherently up-to-date nature of educational computing. Because computers promise to be a dominant feature of western civilization for some time to come, educational computing is unlikely to fail to keep up with important sociopolitical developments.

However, educational computing does contain some seeds of failure. It can be very demanding of teachers, requiring retraining, changes in pedagogical practices, and an entirely new body of knowledge to master. The most exciting uses of computers in education are a radical departure from current educational practices and could be threatening to educators and parents alike. These same uses, as well as some of the least exciting applications, such as drill, are perfect targets for media attention and ridicule.

Nevertheless, the signs of a successful curriculum reform movement are prevalent, particularly in mathematics education where innovative teachers are slowly infusing computer activities into their lessons and courses. These pioneering efforts are largely self-supported, with a little help from friends and colleagues in the new computer culture. No national curriculum projects or funding measures are helping them. These teachers read avidly, experiment with their computers in their classes, and attend workshops sponsored by the growing number of educational computing consortia or organizations. Occasionally, they may take a college course, but when they do, it is more likely to be offered by the education department than by the mathematics or computer science department, and it is more likely to be taught by an adjunct instructor who is also an elementary or high school teacher than by a college faculty member.

The transformation of content in mathematics is likely to be a slow process, as indeed it should be. Students, parents, and teachers need to get used to new and different ways of understanding mathematics. The new content should emerge naturally from the old. With computers, traditional mathematics problems can be recast in more realistic and complex forms. Problems from the real world can be introduced and problems from other disciplines considered. Such approaches are likely to find favor with both the progressively minded and advocates of the basics. Students will learn and use the skills they will need while solving problems of genuine relevance to their current interests and emotional maturity. As the computer becomes a more accepted and familiar feature in a given school or classroom, the transformation of content may become more rapid and more radical. With computers, students may consider problems heretofore the province of mathematicians. Sophisticated concepts in computer science and programming may become quite accessible to even elementary school children. Some of the goals of the new math may yet be realized.

TRANSFORMING ELEMENTARY SCHOOL MATHEMATICS

It would be inappropriate and counter-productive to prescribe the computer content for an elementary school mathematics program. Instead, we offer a long vignette that suggests one way in which computer activities can play a role in the elementary school curriculum and hope that others may add their stories to this one as a way of spreading the educational computing culture. The people and events in this story are fictional; the computer activities described and program listings provided are real. This is a story waiting to be made real by an educational computing pioneer in the elementary school.

A Computer-Based Ecology Unit

"Save the Bay!" "The Chesapeake is dying!" "Where have all the grasses gone?" These signs lined the walls of Sally Peach's sixth-grade classroom at Bayview Elementary School on the eastern shore of Maryland. Sally's class was in the midst of a five-week ecology unit she had designed, which involved objectives from science, mathematics, social studies, reading, and language arts. To enrich the unit, Sally had arranged for the school's single microcomputer to be available to her class for one hour during the first day of the unit and for an hour a day toward the last week of the unit.

Sally began the unit by showing a documentary depicting the tremendous changes in the ecology of the Chesapeake Bay that had occurred over the last thirty years. The students were greatly surprised at the changes. Most of them spent time on the Bay and were familiar with its appearance today. They were shocked when they saw footage taken of it in the early 1950s. Then, plentiful tidal grasses grew out of the clear waters, which were filled with crabs and rockfish. Today, the crabs and rockfish are gone, replaced by menhaden and bluefish, and very little grass grows in the murky, algae-filled waters of the Bay. After the documentary, Sally wheeled in the microcomputer and plugged it in. She explained to the students that they could begin to understand how and why the Bay was changing by first looking at a simple computer simulation of water pollution. The students knew what a simulation was because they had used a computer simulation last year to search for The Lost City of Gold with their fifth-grade teacher.

Sally loaded the disk *Pollute* into the micro. As the program unfolded, Sally typed in the responses called for, usually after consulting with the class. The class interacted with the program, as follows:

]RUN POLUT
    WATER POLLUTION STUDY
DO YOU WANT INSTRUCTIONS? **Y**
IN THIS STUDY YOU CAN SPECIFY THE FOLLOWING CHARACTERISTICS:
A. THE KIND OF BODY OF WATER: LARGE POND, LARGE LAKE, SLOW-MOVING RIVER, OR FAST-MOVING RIVER
B. THE WATER TEMPERATURE IN DEGREES FAHRENHEIT
C. THE KIND OF WASTE DUMPED INTO THE WATER: INDUSTRIAL OR SEWAGE
PRESS ANY KEY TO CONTINUE
D. THE RATE OF DUMPING OF WASTE IN PARTS PER MILLION (PPM)/DAY.
E. THE TYPE OF TREATMENT OF THE WASTE:
    NONE

PRIMARY (SEDIMENTATION OR PASSAGE THROUGH FINE SCREENS TO REMOVE GROSS SOLIDS)
SECONDARY (SAND FILTERS OR ACTIVATED SLUDGE METHOD TO REMOVE DISSOLVED AND COLLOIDAL ORGANIC MATTER)
PRESS ANY KEY TO CONTINUE
PLEASE SPECIFY THE KIND OF BODY OF WATER USING THE FOLLOWING CODE:
  LP = LARGE POND
  LL = LARGE LAKE
  SR = SLOW-MOVING RIVER
  FR = FAST-MOVING RIVER
BODY OF WATER = **SR**
WATER TEMPERATURE (FAHRENHEIT)?**40**
KIND OF WASTE? I = INDUSTRIAL S = SEWAGE?**S**
PLEASE ENTER THE DUMPING RATE (PPM)**9**
PLEASE SPECIFY THE KIND OF TREATMENT USING THE FOLLOWING CODE:
  N = NONE
  P = PRIMARY
  S = SECONDARY
KIND OF TREATMENT = **P**
LET ME THINK ABOUT THAT............WHICH DO YOU WANT?
  G = GRAPH
  T = TABLE
  B = BOTH
  B

Time Days	Oxy. Content PPM	Waste Cont. PPM
0	11.89	2.67
1	11.05	5.92
2	10.03	7.4
3	9.44	8.09
4	9.15	8.4
5	9.01	8.54
6	8.94	8.61
7	8.91	8.64
8	8.9	8.65
9	8.89	8.66
10	8.89	8.66
11	8.89	8.67
12	8.89	8.67
13	8.89	8.67
14	8.89	8.67
15	8.89	8.67

PRESS 'C' THEN 'RETURN' TO CONTINUE TABLE. ENTER 'S' TO STOP. **S**
PRESS 'RETURN' TO CONTINUE

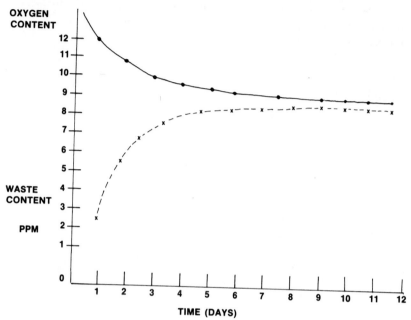

Fig. 5.1

The students told Sally to stop the program because it was clear to them that some sort of steady state had been reached. But why? The students bombarded Sally with questions. "Why do the numbers keep repeating themselves?" How does the computer know what the numbers should be?" "What do the numbers mean?" "Now that we know the numbers, what can we do with them?" "How can you reduce waste and increase oxygen content?" "Would the results be different for a different type of body of water, or a different temperature, or a different kind of waste, or a different dumping rate?" "What if there were a lot of rain and the river ran more quickly?" "What if the waste were from agricultural runoff or erosion?"

Sally was surprised and pleased at the quantity and quality of the questions being asked. She'd hoped for some of that, but hadn't expected so many different students to raise questions that would reveal the limits of the simulation model. Sally started by calming the class down. She told them she'd try to answer some of their questions and that they would have the chance themselves to answer many of the rest of them. Sally told the class that the computer "knew" what the numbers should be because a computer programmer had written the program for *Pollute* to include formulas that yielded such tables and graphs when various conditions were entered in it, such as those she and the class had typed in. Sally asked if the class would like to see what the program looked like. Excitement rippled through the room. Yes, of course they would. Sally typed in the command: LIST.

```
5   TEXT : HOME
10  GOSUB 3005
35  SPEED= 255: GOTO 135
60  FOR XX = 1 TO 500: NEXT XX: RETURN
70  VTAB 22: INVERSE : PRINT " PRESS ANY KEY TO CONTINUE ";: NORMAL : GET
    Q$: PRINT Q$: HOME : VTAB 4: RETURN
135 DIM  X(51),W(51),Q$(15),A$(4)
140 POKE  37,9: PRINT    TAB( 10) "WATER POLLUTION STUDY": PRINT
150 POKE  37,14: INPUT  "DO YOU WANT INSTRUCTIONS? ";Q$
160 IF   LEN (Q$) = 0  THEN  170
162 IF   LEFT$ (Q$,1) = "N"  THEN  310
164 IF   LEFT$ (Q$,1) = "Y"  THEN  180
170 PRINT : PRINT  "PLEASE ANSWER YES OR NO.": GOTO  150
180 HOME
185 PRINT "IN THIS STUDY YOU CAN SPECIFY"
190 PRINT  "THE FOLLOWING CHARACTERISTICS:": PRINT
200 PRINT  "A. THE KIND OF BODY OF WATER:"
210 PRINT  "  LARGE POND, LARGE LAKE, SLOW-MOVING      RIVER, OR FAST-MOV
    ING RIVER.": PRINT
230 PRINT "B. THE WATER TEMPERATURE IN DEGREES        FAHRENHEIT": PRINT

240 PRINT  "C. THE KIND OF WASTE DUMPED INTO THE      WATER:"
250 PRINT  "   INDUSTRIAL OR SEWAGE": PRINT
255 GOSUB 70
260 PRINT  "D. THE RATE OF DUMPING OF WASTE IN        PARTS PER MILLION
    (PPM)/DAY.": PRINT
270 PRINT  "E. THE TYPE OF TREATMENT OF THE WASTE:    NONE"
280 PRINT  "   PRIMARY (SEDIMENTATION OR PASSAGE      THROUGH FINE SCR
    EENS TO REMOVE            GROSS SOLIDS)"
290 PRINT  "   SECONDARY (SAND FILTERS OR ACTIVATED     SLUDGE METHOD TO
    REMOVE DISSOLVED       AND COLLOIDAL ORGANIC MATTER)"
300 GOSUB 70
310 HOME
320 PRINT : PRINT "PLEASE SPECIFY THE KIND OF BODY OF WATERUSING THE FOLL
    OWING CODE:": PRINT
330 PRINT  " LP = LARGE POND": PRINT  " LL = LARGE LAKE"
340 PRINT  " SR = SLOW-MOVING RIVER": PRINT  " FR = FAST-MOVING RIVER"
350 PRINT : INPUT  "BODY OF WATER = ";Q$
360 D1 = 2:N = .75
370 IF   LEN (Q$) = 0  THEN  420
380 IF   Q$ = "FR"  THEN  C = 3: GOTO  425
390 IF   Q$ = "SR"  THEN  C = 1.5: GOTO  425
400 IF   Q$ = "LL"  THEN  C = 1: GOTO  425
410 IF   Q$ = "LP"  THEN  C = .4: GOTO  425
420 PRINT : PRINT  "PLEASE ANSWER LP, LL, SR, OR FR.": GOTO  350
425 HOME : VTAB (10): PRINT "WATER TEMPERATURE (FAHRENHEIT)": INPUT T
435 IF T > 90 THEN 1055
440 IF T < = 32 THEN 1070
445 IF T > 50 THEN 465
455 X9 = 15 - 2 * (T - 32) / 9: GOTO 470
465 X9 = 11 - (T - 50) / 9
470 HOME : VTAB (10)
```

Program 1.

Sally stopped the listing at line 470. She saw the looks of bewildered disappointment on her students' faces. She'd expected that. She and the students agreed that seeing the BASIC listing didn't give them the vaguest idea of why the oxygen and waste content changed as they did. Tomorrow, Sally promised, the class would start an activity that, over time, would show them more realistic and more complicated effects of pollution on a body of water in a way they would be able to understand. She also suggested that this approach would answer many of the other questions they had raised.

The next day, the students pleaded with Sally to start the ecology lesson earlier than scheduled, but Sally insisted that first they do their reading assignment, which the students soon discovered was an article on the ecology of Chesapeake Bay, adapted by Sally for readability level from an article she'd read in a newspaper.

When it came time for the ecology lesson, Sally went to the chalkboard and asked the students questions about what they'd read. Every time a student mentioned a factor in the Chesapeake ecosystem, Sally wrote it on the board. After ten minutes, she had over a dozen different words or phrases spread around the board. She told the class they needed to draw the connections between these factors if they wanted to know how pollution affects the Chesapeake Bay ecosystem. As a first approximation, she suggested drawing simple one-way arrows to indicate that a particular factor leads to or has an effect on another factor. As students proposed various connecting arrows, Sally moved certain words or phrases on the board to avoid arrows criss-crossing. After three-quarters of an hour of frenzied discussion, the diagram in Fig. 5.2 emerged on the chalkboard.

Sally told the class that, as part of her course on system dynamics at a nearby university, she would write a program of the model they had just created, using MicroDYNAMO, a computer language created specifically to allow the simulation of systems such as this one. She promised to bring it in for them to use when she finished writing the program.

During the next several weeks, the students carried out a variety of activities and research in the library, on a specimen-gathering field trip to the marshlands of the Bay, in their classroom laboratory, and through interviews of scientists at the U.S. Naval Academy, the Johns Hopkins University Chesapeake Bay Institute, the U.S. Army Corps of Engineers, and even the Environmental Protection Agency in Washington, D.C. Also during that time, Sally arranged for a speaker from the Chesapeake Bay Foundation to come to class to speak about the ecology of the Bay; she showed several films on water pollution; and she and the students spent some time brainstorming possible solutions to the problems described by their model. They added these possible solutions to the diagram they'd

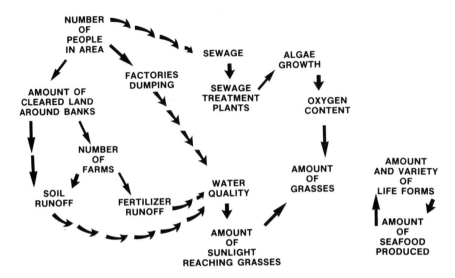

Fig. 5.2

drawn, and Sally promised that she would add these to the program she was working on so the class would be able to see the effects, if any, of their proposed solutions.

Finally, the big day arrived. Sally brought in the MicroDYNAMO disk on which she had programmed the Chesapeake Bay ecosystem model the class had developed. She asked with a grin if the class would like to see the program listing she had written for their model. The class groaned in unison, remembering the obscure program listing of *Pollute*. Sally just smiled and loaded the disk into the computer. The title screen came on.

Chesapeake Bay Ecosystem

Authors: Ms. Sally Peach's Sixth-Grade
Bayview Elementary School

The program then listed all the variables the students had identified, along with their abbreviations. The students stared in disbelief. Was that the whole program? Sally could hardly contain her excitement and amusement. She asked the class what they wanted to find out about it. The students chose the relationship between the amount of nutrients in the water and the amount of seafood harvested. They wanted to know what would happen if people kept dumping things in the water, causing the amount of nutrients to rise unchecked.

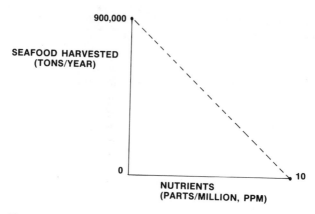

Fig. 5.3

On the board, Sally drew axes for a graph of tons of seafood harvested versus parts per million of nutrients. She asked the students to suggest what they thought the relationship would be between the amount of nutrients and seafood. The students suggested the relationship shown in Fig. 5.3, which Sally drew on the board.

Sally told them they could test this predicted relationship by entering data from the graph into two equations she had written for their model. She drew a table on the board to record the tons of seafood harvested for each part per million nutrients and asked the students to read these values from the graph. After it was filled out, the table looked like Fig. 5.4.

Seafood Harvested (thousand tons/year)	Nutrients (PPM)
900	0
810	1
720	2
630	3
540	4
450	5
360	6
270	7
180	8
90	9
0	10

Fig. 5.4

She entered these values on the computer into the rate (R) and table (T) equations she had developed, as follows:

R SEAFD.KL = TABLE(TSEAFD,NUTR.K,0,10,1)
T TSEAFD = 900/810/720/630/540/450/360/270/180/90/0

where:

R SEAFD.KL = TABLE(TSEAFD,NUTR.K,0,10,1)

is an equation indicating that the Rate of seafood harvested (SEAFD) over time (.KL)(in units of 1000 tons/year), is determined by a TABLE, called TSEAFD, whose independent variable is the nutrient level, NUTR., which has values from 0 to 10 ppm in increments of 1 unit.

T TSEAFD = 900/810/720/630/540/450/360/270/180/90/0

gives the values for the dependent variable, seafood harvested (TSEAFD) as determined from the students' graph.

Sally then ran the model on the computer to look at the effect of this assumption about nutrients on the production of seafood in the Bay area over the last eighty years. The computer graphed the results as in Fig. 5.5.

The computer output showed that the model was not producing the behavior the data suggested. Actual seafood production in the Chesapeake did not die out by 1930. In fact, it has only recently started to decline appreciably.

With Sally's help, the students decided to try a different assumption

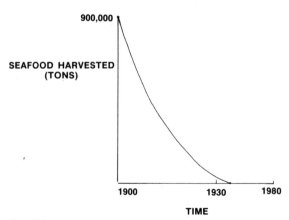

Fig. 5.5

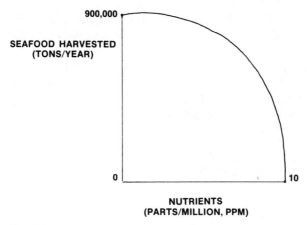

Fig. 5.6

about the effect of nutrients on seafood harvested. This time the table function they chose looked like Fig. 5.6.

When these new data were entered into the model, the output was as shown in Fig. 5.7.

The students thought the production shown for 1950 was still lower than it had really been. Sally suggested that a closer look at other parts of the model might be appropriate at this point. The students went back to the causal-loop diagram to see what else affects the seafood harvest.

For the rest of the unit, Sally explained each part of the model to her class, encouraging them to question each assumption as she went along. The interaction between teacher and students produced a "better" model by the end of the unit, but still left many relationships unclear.

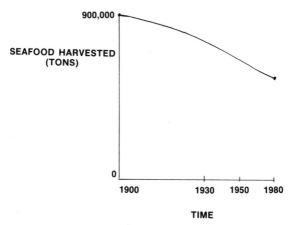

Fig. 5.7

However, the depth of understanding of the issues involved, and the appreciation of the need for more study, by both Sally and the students, were apparent.

At the end of five weeks, the signs for the ecology unit came down, the scale model of the Bay was taken home by the boy who'd built it, and the computer was sent down the hall where the fifth grade was about to begin their search for the Lost City of Gold.

TRANSFORMING HIGH SCHOOL MATHEMATICS

Again, rather than prescribing the computer content for the high school mathematics curriculum, we offer a story of one way it may be done. Only, this time the story is real. It is about a computer-based course currently being taught at Groton School, a private secondary school located in Groton, Massachusetts.

Overview of an Applied Mathematics Course

In 1980, a mathematics teacher and a science teacher at Groton School began integrating computers into their teaching in a major way. They developed a two-year course, which they call applied mathematics. It meets six times a week, allowing interested students to spend a good deal of time concentrating on mathematics. To be eligible, students must have completed a course in algebra II and preferably a course in pre-calculus. The course is an alternative to the advanced placement program in calculus. Calculus is included in the applied mathematics course, but the students are not trained to take the advanced placement examination.

Since Groton uses a trimester system, the course lasts six terms and includes the following topics.

Term	Content
1	computer programming, system dynamics
2	differential calculus, probability, and statistics
3	integral calculus
4	linear algebra
5	differential equations
6	individual projects

Programming and Problem Solving

Since computers can be used in creative ways to teach problem-solving skills, problem solving and computer programming are often taught together. While studying Grogono and Nelson's book *Problem Solving and Computer Programming*, students use Logo. As they learn to break problems into parts, they also learn to write procedures in Logo. Because of the nature of Logo and the ease with which it can be used to do graphics, they work on many visual design problems. One of these problems is to write a program that creates the design in Fig. 5.8. The key to this program is creating the highlighted seven motif and transforming it in a variety of ways.

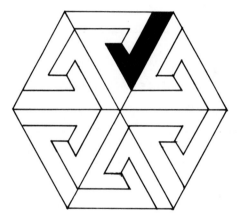

Fig. 5.8

In the applied mathematics course, students apply various programming skills as soon as they learn them. In many cases, the students' programming is motivated by the problems they encounter; students develop programming skills in different languages as they need these skills to solve particular problems. As a result, students solve types of problems rarely found in high school mathematics courses. Early in the course the students are given the following problem.

PROBLEM #1

Write a Logo procedure that makes the turtle move in such a way that the angle between a given fixed point, the turtle, and a second fixed point remains constant. For example, in Fig. 5.9, the turtle at point T moves so that the angle ATB remains constant.

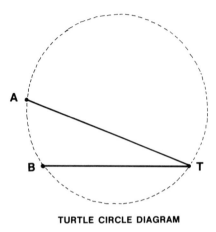

TURTLE CIRCLE DIAGRAM

Fig. 5.9

A plane geometry theorem governing inscribed angles in circles suggests that the turtle should move in a circle passing through points A and B. Students must write a procedure that makes the turtle move in a circle without giving the turtle a predetermined path. This type of problem arises often in the design of automatic guidance systems and its solution has a variety of applications. In one solution, the turtle measures the angle ATB and heads back towards the circle when the measured angle is smaller than the given angle, or away from the circle when the measured angle is larger than the given angle. To get a smooth circle, the turtle adjusts the amount it turns based on where it is in relation to the two given points. This means that its new position is defined in terms of its old position, a feedback loop. To solve this problem, students use the system dynamics they have begun to study.

System Dynamics

Mathematical modeling in general, and system dynamics in particular, are key elements in the applied mathematics course. System dynamics, through causal loop diagrams, allows students to break a problem down into its component parts and is a powerful tool for analyzing the underlying structure of a problem. Because system dynamics has so many applications, it is a truly interdisciplinary tool. In system dynamics, the user can model situations in which simple closed-form functions are inadequate to describe a given behavior. For example, trigonometric functions can be used to model the oscillations produced when a weight on a spring is pulled down, but more sophisticated mathematical functions are needed to describe the behavior of more complex oscillations.

As we have seen in this book, system dynamics models can be tested by writing them in MicroDYNAMO, which calculates a series of primarily linear finite difference equations. In this way, MicroDYNAMO approximates a continuous process with a finite, discrete process. Recall the coffee cooling problem from Chapter 3.

PROBLEM #2

I have just poured myself a cup of coffee which is very hot (190 degrees to be exact). I know that I can enjoy my coffee when it is 104 degrees. How long will I have to wait before I can drink my coffee?

This problem could be solved using differential equations, which require at least one year of calculus to understand, not to mention the existence of an exact solution. But as shown in Chapter 3, a MicroDYNAMO system dynamics model offers a perfectly acceptable approximate solution.

System dynamics and the MicroDYNAMO language can be used to solve far more complex problems than this, but which have a similar feedback structure. When students use a system dynamics modeling approach to such problems, the difficulties they encounter are not computational but conceptual. Arriving at the correct equations for the MicroDYNAMO model takes skill, time, and effort but all of these are focused on the structure of the problem rather than on tedious computation.

In the course, students examine models of well-known systems in some detail, using system dynamics methods to learn about the general behavior of systems. Early in the course, students construct a model of how the school cafeteria operates. Before doing this, they observe several lunch periods, counting the number of arrivals and departures per five-minute period. Fig. 5.10 shows a graph of the data one group of students obtained. The goal of the exercise is to construct a model that predicts the behavior observed.

On the basis of this data, the students extrapolate how many people are in the dining hall at any given time and how many people have eaten at any given time. Without knowing it, the students are studying derivatives and integrals, since the arrivals graph tells the rate of change of the total number of people who have eaten. They will study the concepts of derivatives and integrals more formally later in the course.

Model building is often best done in groups so when the students work on major models, they do so in groups of two or three. The students learn from each other and get far more from the exercises than they would if working alone. Because many models used in the course are open-ended and have no single right answer, students become used to working on

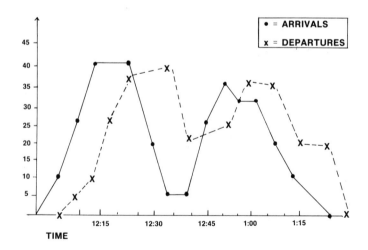

Fig. 5.10

problems that have no easy solution. Many of the computer programs assigned are completed over a long period of time, during which the students keep working at the problem until they have an answer they can accept. This makes them critical of their own work.

Differential Calculus

Differential calculus deals with the mathematics of change in a different way than system dynamics. It provides students with methods for solving problems that require finding the maximum and/or minimum value of a function. While studying differential calculus, students write computer programs to find approximations for derivatives of functions, particularly ones that are hard to differentiate using standard techniques. Students are also given several maximum and minimum problems that arise from specific applications. In each of these, the function derived is very complex and hard to differentiate. In each case, the students use the function

---

PROBLEM #3   6. ARTERIAL BRANCHING

6.1   A Surgeon's Dilemma

   A surgeon must attach a blood vessel to an artery AB, which will lead to a point C. (See figure.) The surgeon wishes to attach the vessel

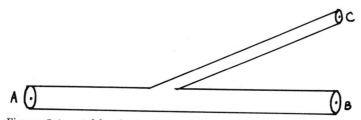

Figure 6-1.   A blood vessel connecting artery AB to a point C.

so as to minimize resistance to the flow of blood from point A to point C. This will minimize strain on the heart.

Fig. 5.11   Five applications of maximum/minimum theory from calculus. W. Thurmon Whitley, UMAP Unit 341. With permission from COMAP, Inc., Lexington, MA © 1980.

graphing routine, mentioned in Chapter 4, to graph the function and then search for its maximum and minimum points. An example of the type of problem that leads to a complicated function follows.

Probability and Statistics

Probability and statistics are included in the course because basic counting skills, the construction of probabilistic models, and the collection, sorting, and interpretation of data are all useful real-world skills. The students are trained to deal with three questions: what should happen in an experiment, what actually did happen, and are the results surprising?

While learning probability and statistics, the students write an extensive program that:

1. Loads and stores data.
2. Finds the mean, mode, and standard deviation of a set of data.
3. Finds the correlation coefficient and line of best fit for two sets of data.

The students use Monte Carlo methods on the computer to simulate situations that are hard to do using other methods. Some of these situations are: lotteries, waiting lines in a supermarket, and the long-range effectiveness of differing dosages of a drug.

Integral Calculus

Integral calculus, a natural sequel to differential calculus, gives students the theoretical background they need to study differential equations. Students can also use it to find areas enclosed by curves, volumes and surface areas of solids with regular cross sections, and the length of curves. The students write computer programs that find approximations for the area under a curve (with special emphasis on the area under $f(x) = 1/x$ when the natural logarithm function is studied). For example, the students use programs that find the area under a curve to study a technique used by heart specialists to measure cardiac output.

Linear Algebra

Linear algebra is the last major component of the course. It is included because of its wide range of applications, and because this is the area of mathematics that has grown and blossomed with the arrival of computers. Much of the computer time used today in business, industry, and basic research involves solving systems of linear equations and making use of linear algebra techniques. Linear algebra is the study of systems of linear equations and linear transformations using vectors and matrices. The arithmetic of vectors and matrices is defined in terms of the arithmetic of the real numbers and contains conceptually simple algorithms that require many routine arithmetic computations.

Although students in first-year algebra are taught how to solve two equations in two unknowns, they are rarely asked to solve larger systems because the number of computations becomes prohibitive. However, the method students learn can be easily generalized to solve any number of equations in any number of unknowns, provided a computer is available for performing the calculations.

Matrix multiplication, another useful technique, requires only simple arithmetic and the ability to use a complicated algorithm. The algorithm is not conceptually difficult, but requires a great deal of computation. By using a computer, students can focus their attention on the uses of matrices instead of wasting time on repetitive computations.

The concept of a linear transformation, one of the most important in linear algebra, has many applications. A transformation is a function that associates points in one set with those in another. The Dymaxion projection mentioned in Chapter 1 uses a transformation that associates points on a sphere with those on the surface of an icosahedron. A transformation is said to be linear when it associates straight lines through the origin in one set with straight lines through the origin in the second set. This concept is useful in many areas of mathematical study, and it is central to defining the mathematical concept of symmetry.

Rotations about a point can be expressed as linear transformations. The design in Fig. 5.12 has rotational symmetry because it can be rotated 45 degrees around the point 0 and still look the same.

Symmetry is a key concept in the mathematical study of art; linear transformations are also important in the field of computer graphics. One of the reasons Logo is such a powerful language is the ease with which it permits the use of certain linear transformations. Fig. 4.37 in Chapter 4 demonstrates how Logo uses linear transformations to create new figures. Linear transformations convert complicated problems into simpler ones.

Fig. 5.12

For example, the points of intersection of the hyperbola and the circle in Fig. 5.13 are very difficult to find when the equations of the conics are expressed in terms of the standard X-Y coordinate system, since they require the solution of a 4-th degree polynomial, as follows:

$$(x + 4)^2 + (y + 4)^2 = 256$$
$$xy = 16$$

The solution is easier when the equations are expressed in terms of a coordinate system rotated 45 degrees counterclockwise such as the U-V system below. The linear transformation following can be used to transform the equations from the X-Y system to the U-V system.

$$x = (\sqrt{2}/2)u - (\sqrt{2}/2)v$$
$$y = (\sqrt{2}/2)u + (\sqrt{2}/2)v$$

To solve the problem, the student expresses x and y in terms of u and v and solves the resulting equations for u and v:

$$u^2 - v^2 = 32$$
$$(u + 4\sqrt{2})^2 + v^2 = 256$$

The same transformation used to simplify this problem can be used to rotate a figure through an angle of 45 degrees around the origin. Most

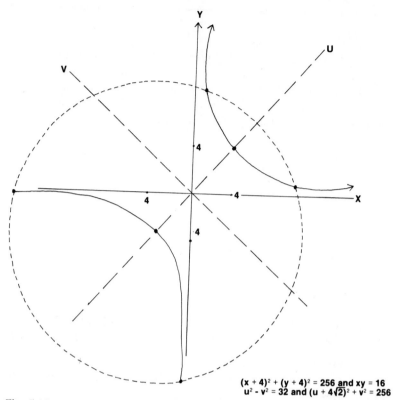

$(x + 4)^2 + (y + 4)^2 = 256$ and $xy = 16$
$u^2 - v^2 = 32$ and $(u + 4\sqrt{2})^2 + v^2 = 256$

Fig. 5.13

plane geometry textbooks now include a chapter on linear transformations, and a great deal of plane geometry theory can be developed using linear transformations, as Arthur Coxford and Zalman Usiskin have done in *Geometry: A Transformation Approach*. The linear transformation concept becomes very important in higher-level mathematics, where it is used in the development of such topics as linear differential equations and the theory of coordinate systems.

Computers are used extensively in the study of linear algebra in the applied mathematics course. As the students study the theory of linear algebra, they write a major utility program that allows them to perform matrix arithmetic, to solve systems of equations, and to evaluate determinants. Using this program, they explore a variety of applications. Below is a typical problem that can be solved using matrix multiplication.

PROBLEM #4

The Bucket of Bolts car rental agency has three rental locations: 1, 2, and 3. A customer may rent a car for a month from any of the three locations and return the car to any of the three locations. The manager finds that the customers return the cars at the end of each month to the various locations according to the following probabilities:

rented from location

1	2	3	
.8	.1	.1	*1* returned
.3	.2	.5	2 to
.2	.6	.2	*3* location

If, at the beginning of the year, there are 100 cars at each location, how many will there be at the end of 24 months?

The applied mathematics students can solve this problem quickly by using their program. In the process they learn about Markov chains, an area of mathematics useful in solving problems such as this. The computer thus frees the students from repetitive computation and allows them to focus their attention on the concepts involved.

Differential Equations

The last formal topic in the course is a study of differential equations because system dynamics, the core of the course, is a method of finding approximate solutions to a system of differential equations. The course thus ends with a mathematical explanation of the principles of systems studied earlier. Some of the models formulated earlier are redone using differential equations at the end of the course. While studying differential equations, students construct a model of a flu epidemic using MicroDYNAMO as discussed in Chapter 3. They then construct another model using differential equations. These models are particularly interesting both because of the different approaches employed and because flu epidemics are a regular feature of winter at the school. Students are thus able to check their models against what actually happens.

Student Projects

At the conclusion of the course, students do extensive projects. One student, at the request of his chemistry teacher, wrote a series of programs for displaying models of molecules on a computer monitor (see Fig. 5.14). The program also allowed the user to rotate the model in three dimensions.

Another student built a model of the natural gas economy which clearly showed price fluctuations. A third student wrote a graphics program that demonstrated some of the principles of Origami, the art of paper folding.

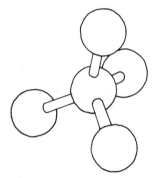

Fig. 5.14

The Results of the Applied Course

The originators of the applied mathematics course learned some important lessons. First, computers make applications of mathematics far more accessible to students, allowing them to do more with the mathematics they learn in the course. Second, computers remove the necessity of learning complicated computational techniques and free the students for developing and applying concepts. This aspect of computer use has numerous ramifications for the mathematics education of younger students as well. Finally, computers give students a new set of problem-solving tools to use in studying the world around them. The end result is that the applied mathematics students have a better understanding of their complex world.

Computer Science: Mathematics in the Computer

6

The availability of high-powered, low-cost, computers is likely to radically alter the high school curriculum. The computer introduces new approaches in old courses, it introduces exciting new courses, and it has created a whole new discipline: computer science. Even at the high school level, a computer science curriculum can include much more than introductory and advanced courses on high-level computer languages. Computer science is a whole discipline, with programming representing only the tip of the iceberg.

The computer adds variety to the high school curriculum, and ties theory to practice in a variety of fields:

- Logic. Boolean algebra, logical design, language and reasoning, arguments and representation (computers are the ultimate logic machines).
- Art. Graphics and animation.
- Physics. Electricity and circuitry, building computer peripherals.
- Philosophy. Artificial intelligence, superficial intelligence, and ethics.
- English. Formal languages, syntax, and semantics.
- Social Science. Cottage industry and the "Third Wave," the social structure of a dungeon.
- Music. Computer music, theory and practice.
- Robotics. Uses and abuses, control theory, computer vision, Asimov's Laws.

And mathematics . . . If there were no computers, mathematics teachers would have to invent them, for they are an unbelievably rich source of mathematics problems and topics. Computers use number systems other than base 10 extensively. Calculating and reasoning are integral parts of the simplest programming, and, in the programming environment—conceptually, the inside of the machine—numbers are everywhere. There are a variety of mathematically oriented topics and courses possible in this new computer science discipline:

- Structured programming.
- Systems theory.
- Data structures.
- Arrays and lists.
- Sorting (alphabetizing) and searching methods.
- Formal languages.
- Recursion and trees.
- Organizing data bases.

. . . and these are only the beginning. Wherever we look, the computer alters our way of looking. And a computer fosters the true spirit of scientific investigation, because looking further is rewarded.

Most courses about the computer are inherently about mathematics and problem solving. In this chapter we present a "short course," complete with mathematics exercises, on the way the computer places the word "HI" in the top left corner of the screen. This course teaches how to talk about what is going on in a computer from a programming perspective, and it is an example of how the computer provides a practical foundation for a wide variety of mathematics. It is intended for the teacher who already knows BASIC, or some other programming language, and wants to fit this knowledge into a wider understanding of computing. It could be the core of a new sort of programming course for students that focuses on the context within which programming occurs. It has an essential mathematics component that mathematics teachers could use in teaching students computer science.

HIERARCHIES

Humans would be at a supreme disadvantage if we had to programs as in Fig. 6.1.

1010100111001000100011010000000000000100
1010100111001001100011010000000100000100

Fig. 6.1　Bunches of 1s and 0s.

To avoid this mess, computer scientists created hierarchies, which, at each level, allow a better understanding of the previous level. Some of these hierarchies are established by a single convention, such as, "Group the above collection of 1's and 0's into subgroups of 8". Some of them are full-blown languages. But all of these hierarchies, from the simplest to the most complex, share the following feature:

> Hierarchies allow the programmer to take what are, at a lower level, many small steps and consider them as a single step—a "chunk."

This "chunking" occurs at many different levels when a programmer thinks about computers or their languages. The nature of these different hierarchies affects our understanding at each level and of the computer overall. Taking advantage of this understanding, and the process of chunking, is at the heart of good programming.

Warehouses, Minds, and Machines

The jargon used to talk about computers is a mix of several different metaphors: "**storing** information," "**loading** information," "**memory**," and "**memory locations**" or "**addresses**." The mixed metaphors come from thinking of the mind as a warehouse, and thinking of the computer as having mental capacity. (Neither are viable assumptions, but they get the language going.) Information is stored in certain locations in the warehouse. These locations are numbered. The numbers serve as the name, or address, of the location. Information can be moved to other locations, changed, put back, or sent to an **output device.** New information can be brought in through an **input device.**

A **digital computer** works with numbers expressed as digits in a decimal, binary, or other number system. The enormous power of these machines derives from the possibility of these digits serving multiple functions. The digits can represent numbers (integers, signed numbers, or decimals); **alphanumeric characters** (numerals, letters, punctuation marks); logical values; names of locations in memory (addresses); operations on numbers, letters, or logical values; or operations on operations, sounds, or even colors.

To channel this power it is only necessary, from an engineering perspective, to copy and move the digits. Claude Shannon, one of the founders of information science, in his book, *The Mathematical Theory of Communication*, calls this the fundamental problem of communication. This problem is to reproduce at one point either exactly or approximately a message selected at another point. The semantic aspects of communication—the *meaning* of the messages—are irrelevant to the engineering problem.

The engineer need not know how these digits will be used in a particular situation. He or she must simply make it possible for the programmer to store a pattern of digits at a specific location, to return to that location, and to find the same pattern of digits there. It is up to the programmer to define these digits as representing a number or a letter or an instruction, that is, to devise, or use, a conventional system to give these messages meaning. When digits are moved from one location to another, the engineer must make sure they can be reliably replicated. The programmer must remember what these digits represent.

To the computer engineer, programmers are simply moving digits around. To the programmer, on the other hand, these digits stand for different semantic entities. The new programmer's task is to learn the conventional semantic systems by which these digits are accorded meaning.

A small, but not the smallest possible, way to think about computers is in terms of **bits** and **bytes.** Ascending the hierarchy lets us think of larger and larger combinations: machine language, assembly language, and finally high-level programming languages.

STORAGE

Digital computer circuits are designed to carry one of two possible signals, either a high or low voltage. Each signal is equal to one or the other of these voltages. Computer memory is made possible by a device called a **"flip-flop**." A flip-flop can only be in one of two states, and it always stays in the last state it was in. So, if the last signal was a high-voltage signal, the circuit is "flopped." Several moments later it will still be flopped. If a low-voltage signal is sent through, the circuit is flipped and it will stay flipped.

The flip-flop has one of two values. The two-valued, or binary, signals are represented by the digits 1 and 0. Each signal is called a bit—a contraction of Binary digIT—as in "just a little bit."

Fig. 6.2   A bit.

Programs are, at one level, nothing more than an ordered sequence of bits. For example, the list of 1s and 0s at the beginning of the chapter (Fig. 6.1) prints "HI" in the upper left-hand corner of the Apple II microcomputer screen. While this sequence may accomplish the task, it is incomprehensible to humans. The first step on the road to intelligibility is to consider the bits in groups.

Four bits are a **nibble** (sorry, but that is really what they call it). This is one of the first cases where chunking plays a role. It is easier to recognize, and see patterns in, four bits together. As each of the bits (going from right to left "bit 0," "bit 1," "bit 2," and "bit 3") changes value from 0 to 1, the nibble changes to the various patterns from 0000 to 1111.

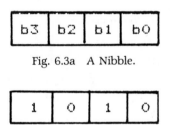

Fig. 6.3a   A Nibble.

Fig. 6.3b   A particular nibble (the first four bits from Fig. 6.1).

If a bit is thought of as a letter, a byte can be considered a word. A byte is the smallest addressable unit in a computer. Most personal computers use eight-bit bytes. Therefore, two nibbles together form a byte (computer theory parallels gastronomic practice). Each byte is composed of eight binary digits, which we designate (going right to left) as "bit 0," "bit 1," . . ., "bit 7."

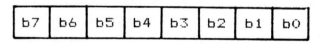

Fig. 6.4   A byte.

If one spends a great deal of time staring at bytes, one needs a sandwich. A sandwich is what programmers often eat for lunch—or very late at night when a **bug** has crept into a program. It is essential when removing bugs not to let them get into sandwiches.

‗‗‗‗‗‗‗‗‗‗‗‗‗

✴✴✴✴✴✴✴✴✴✴✴

‗‗‗‗‗‗‗‗‗‗‗‗‗

Fig. 6.5   A sandwich.

The sequence of bits writing "HI" are structured as bytes. This, again, makes them more manageable. Note that the bytes are also broken up into nibbles.

1010 1001   1100 1000   1000 1101   0000 0000   0000 0100

1010 1001   1100 1001   1000 1101   0000 0001   0000 0100

Fig. 6.6   Bytes to print "HI" on the Apple screen.

All information handled by a computer must be stored in the same manner—as a pattern of bits in one or more bytes. However, although data all has the same form, the nature of the information stored varies tremendously, and the computer must interpret each message appropriately. A byte can represent quite different things, depending on what the computer expects at a particular location. The digits can be used in a binary number system to represent numbers; to represent logical values (either true (1) or false (0)); to represent letters (0100 0001 is the code for "A"); and to name locations in memory (0000 0100 0000 0001 is a specific memory location).

A byte can also be used to represent **operations.** The specific operations a computer can perform are determined by the particular **central processing unit** (CPU) of the machine in question. The Apple II, Atari 800, and Commodore Pet computers all have the same CPU, the "6502." In the 6502 central processing unit, "1000 1101" is an **operation code**—a numerical code that stands for an operation. When this particular operation is carried out, the 6502 takes a value stored in a special location, called the **accumulator,** and copies it into another specified location in memory.

These numerical codes constitute the **machine language** of a computer. The computer interprets a particular byte as an operation, or as a type of data, entirely by its location in a program. When a program begins, the **program counter** is set to the address of the first byte of the program. The computer starts by looking for an operation at this address. The first byte it finds must be a number standing for an operation, because the computer interprets it that way. The particular operation then determines how the computer interprets the next byte. It may be part of an address, a value, or a new operation.

NUMBERS

Computers calculate in a binary, as opposed to a decimal, number system. If a programmer enters a decimal number, the computer must translate it to binary to perform any calculations and then translate it back to decimal to print out the answer (this is a biological accident, early computers only had two fingers). In the computer a byte represents a binary number by giving each bit a different place value. If a bit is 0, its value is 0. If a bit is 1, its value is equal to the decimal value equivalent of two to the power indicated by the bit position. The total value of the byte is equal to the sum of the bit values. Following the rules for binary arithmetic (imagine a real application for binary arithmetic!), the decimal value of a byte can range from 0 (0000 0000) to 255 (1111 1111).

The way a byte represents a number is shown in Fig. 6.7. Bit 7 (b7) is the **most significant bit** (MSB) or the **high bit,** because it has the most significance in determining the size of the number (if the high bit is 1 the number is increased by 128). Correspondingly, bit 0 (b0) is the **least significant bit** (LSB) or the **low bit,** because it has the least significance in determining the size of the number (if the low bit is 1 the number is increased by 1).

It can get very difficult for humans, as opposed to computers, to recognize and keep track of all the 0s and 1s. To make this easier, machine

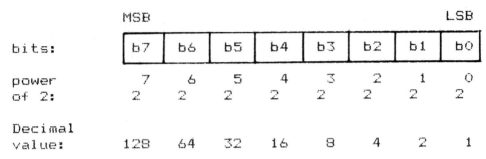

Fig. 6.7   A byte representing a number in binary.

language programming uses other number systems—typically either base 8 **octal** or base 16 **hexadecimal,** depending on the type of computer.

Converting from the binary to the octal (base 8) number system can be done by using Table 6.1, and by applying a simple algorithm: separate the bits into groups of three (starting at the right) and convert these to their octal equivalent (0 through 7).

PROBLEM #1

Convert the following to Octal:

1111 0101 1000 0011 0001

ANSWER

First, separate into groups of three bits:

11 110 101 100 000 110 001

Second, assign values (0–7) to each group:

3   6   5   4   0   6   1
11 110 101 100 000 110 001

So the answer is:

3654061

In nibbles, the decimal values range from 0 (0000) to 15 (1111). This is valuable in translating from binary to the base 16 number system

Decimal	Binary	Octal
0	0000	0
1	0001	1
2	0010	2
3	0011	3
4	0100	4
5	0101	5
6	0110	6
7	0111	7
8	1000	10
9	1001	11
10	1010	12
11	1011	13
12	1100	14
13	1101	15
14	1110	16
15	1111	17

Table 6.1   Numbers in decimal, binary, and octal.

(hexadecimal). Hexadecimal uses the numerals 0 through 9 and the letters A through F. To translate from binary (base 2) to hexadecimal (base 16— or base 2^4), chunk the sequence by nibbles and then rewrite each binary nibble (each four bits) as the corresponding hexadecimal number. Table 6.2 shows the representation of the numbers from 0 to 15 in decimal, binary, and hexadecimal systems. A dollar sign ($) appears in front of hexadecimal number to eliminate confusion.

PROBLEM #2

Translate 0100 1100 1001 to hexadecimal.

ANSWER

Look up the bit patterns in Table 6.2: 0100 is $4; 1100 is $C; and 1001 is $9. The hexadecimal number is derived as follows:

```
0100 1100 1001
 4    C    9
```

or $4C9.

Decimal	Binary	Hexadecimal
0	0 0 0 0	$0
1	0 0 0 1	$1
2	0 0 1 0	$2
3	0 0 1 1	$3
4	0 1 0 0	$4
5	0 1 0 1	$5
6	0 1 1 0	$6
7	0 1 1 1	$7
8	1 0 0 0	$8
9	1 0 0 1	$9
10	1 0 1 0	$A
11	1 0 1 1	$B
12	1 1 0 0	$C
13	1 1 0 1	$D
14	1 1 1 0	$E
15	1 1 1 1	$F

Table 6.2   Numbers in decimal, binary, and hexadecimal.

To rewrite a hexadecimal number as a decimal, expand by using place-value notation.

PROBLEM #3

Translate $4C9 back to decimal.

ANSWER

$$\$4C9 = (4 \times 16^2) + (C \times 16^1) + (9 \times 16^0)$$
$$= (4 \times 256) + (12 \times 16) + (9 \times 1)$$
$$= 1,225$$

PROBLEM #4

Take the program from Fig. 6.6 to print "HI" on the screen and write it in hexadecimal.

ANSWER

See Fig. 6.8.

By looking up the patterns in Table 6.2:

1010 1001	1100 1000	1000 1101	0000 0000	0000 0100
A 9	C 8	8 D	0 0	0 4

1010 1001	1100 1001	1000 1101	0000 0001	0000 0100
A 9	C 9	8 D	0 1	0 4

or more simply:

| $A 9 | $C 8 | $8 D | $0 0 | $0 4 |
| $A 9 | $C 9 | $8 D | $0 1 | $0 4 |

Fig. 6.8   Hexadecimal to print "HI" on the Apple screen.

This program, written as hexadecimal numbers, is machine language, the lowest level that is considered to be a programming language.

If something evil happens to your computer, you might see a display like Fig. 6.9 on your screen. This is the hexadecimal value of some memory locations. The display in Fig. 6.9 shows the contents of memory locations $B800 to $B807. When this occurs, programmers say you have "crashed into the monitor." If this happens, just apologize to the monitor and lift him or her carefully off the floor.

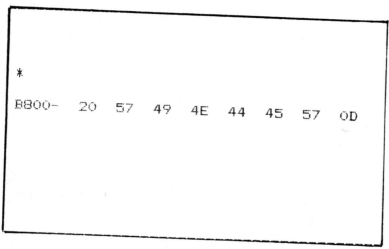

Fig. 6.9   A crash into the monitor.

PROBLEM #5

What is the largest decimal number that can be represented in four bits, six bits, eight bits, ten bits? If n is the number of bits, what formula will express the largest number that can be represented in n bits?

ANSWER

Left for homework.

ALPHANUMERICS

From this point on we will focus on how the computer can print the word "HI." To do so, we need to know how the computer handles letters. The alphanumeric characters—letters, numerals (the symbols used to represent numbers), punctuation marks—are also represented by bytes. There is no natural interpretation of digits for alphanumerics, so it is necessary to set up an arbitrary code, assigning a bit pattern to each letter, numeral, and mark. An industry-wide standard code for these characters was developed by the American National Standards Institute (ANSI). This code, the *American Standard Code for Information Interchange*, **ASCII** (pronounced as-key), uses seven bits (b0–b6). The most significant bit, b7, is generally used to check the accuracy of the signal, and for different purposes by different machines. In this chapter we will assume it is always 0. Table 6.3 shows the alphanumeric characters and their ASCII codes, in decimal and hexadecimal.

In ASCII the word "CAT" is,

in binary:	0100 0011	0100 0001	0101 0100
in hexadecimal:	$4 3	$4 1	$5 4.
letter represented:	C	A	T

There is a difference between the decimal number 5, represented by 0000 0101, and the numeral "5", represented by 0011 0101 (the former stands for a number, the latter stands for an alphanumeric character).

In ASCII the word "HI" would be,

in binary:	0100 1000	0100 1001
in hexadecimal:	$4 8	$4 9
letter represented:	H	I

DEC	HEX	CHAR	DEC	HEX	CHAR	DEC	HEX	CHAR	DEC	HEX	CHAR
0	$00	ctrl "at"	32	$20	SPACE	64	$40	"at"	96	60	--
1	$01	ctrl A	33	$21	!	65	$41	A	97	61	a
2	$02	ctrl B	34	$22	"	66	$42	B	98	62	b
3	$03	ctrl C	35	$23	#	67	$43	C	99	63	c
4	$04	ctrl D	36	$24	$	68	$44	D	100	64	d
5	$05	ctrl E	37	$25	%	69	$45	E	101	65	e
6	$06	ctrl F	38	$26	&	70	$46	F	102	66	f
7	$07	ctrl G	39	$27	'	71	$47	G	103	67	g
8	$08	ctrl H or <--	40	$28	(	72	$48	H	104	68	h
9	$09	ctrl I	41	$29	)	73	$49	I	105	69	i
10	$0A	ctrl J	42	$2A	*	74	$4A	J	106	6A	j
11	$0B	ctrl K	43	$2B	+	75	$4B	K	107	6B	k
12	$0C	ctrl L	44	$2C	,	76	$4C	L	108	6C	l
13	$0D	ctrl M or <ret>	45	$2D	-	77	$4D	M	109	6D	m
14	$0E	ctrl N	46	$2E	.	78	$4E	N	110	6E	n
15	$0F	ctrl O	47	$2F	/	79	$4F	O	111	6F	o
16	$10	ctrl P	48	$30	0	80	$50	P	112	70	p
17	$11	ctrl Q	49	$31	1	81	$51	Q	113	71	q
18	$12	ctrl R	50	$32	2	82	$52	R	114	72	r
19	$13	ctrl S	51	$33	3	83	$53	S	115	73	s
20	$14	ctrl T	52	$34	4	84	$54	T	116	74	t
21	$15	ctrl U or -->	53	$35	5	85	$55	U	117	75	u
22	$16	ctrl V	54	$36	6	86	$56	V	118	76	v
23	$17	ctrl W	55	$37	7	87	$57	W	119	77	w
24	$18	ctrl X	56	$38	8	88	$58	X	120	78	x
25	$19	ctrl Y	57	$39	9	89	$59	Y	121	79	y
26	$1A	ctrl Z	58	$3A	:	90	$5A	Z	122	7A	z
27	$1B	ESC	59	$3B	;	91	$5B	ctrl-n	123	7B	n/a
28	$1C	n/a	60	$3C	<	92	$5C	n/a	124	7C	n/a
29	$1D	ctrl Shift-M	61	$3D	=	93	$5D	Shift-M	125	7D	n/a
30	$1E	ctrl Shift-N	62	$3E	>	94	$5E	Shift-N	126	7E	n/a
31	$1F	n/a	63	$3F	?	95	$5F	n/a	127	7F	n/a

Table 6.3 The American Standard Code for Information Interchange.

Note that the high bit is 0. When writing to the Apple screen, the high bit determines whether the character appears normally (set to 1), or is flashing or inversed (set to 0). This convention is peculiar to the Apple.

In Fig. 6.8 we have calculated the hexadecimal code to print "HI" on the screen. Problem #6, following, shows us that the second byte, "$C 8", is the letter "H", and the sixth byte, "$C 9", is the letter "I". As we proceed in the chapter we will provide an explanation for each of the rest of the bytes in this program.

PROBLEM #6

The ASCII codes for "H" and "I" in hex are $48 and $49, respectively (with the high bit set to 0). What are the new ASCII codes, in hex, if the high bit is set to 1? (Extra credit: What is so special about the number 128 in decimal)?

ANSWER

With the high bit set to 1, "H" and "I" become:

in binary:	1100 1000	1100 1001
in hexadecimal:	$C 8	$C 9
letter represented:	H	I

ADDRESSES AND PHONE NUMBERS

Computers use phone numbers much like the rest of us—to make phone calls to friends and relatives. **Memory addresses** refer, in contrast, to locations inside the computer memory. Addresses, in most cases, require two bytes to name a location, because one byte can name only 256 locations (including 0). With two bytes it is possible to have much larger numbers, and therefore more memory locations.

PROBLEM #7

Compute the number of addressable locations using two bytes.

ANSWER

In each byte, each bit position can be thought of as a power of two.

```
        BYTE 2      BYTE 1

        1111 1111   1111 1111

    BYTE 1

              7   6   5   4   3   2   1   0
1111 1111 =   2 + 2 + 2 + 2 + 2 + 2 + 2 + 2

          = 128 + 64 + 32 + 16 + 8 + 4 + 2 + 1

          = 255
```

BYTE 2

$$1111\ 1111 = \overset{15}{2} + \overset{14}{2} + \overset{13}{2} + \overset{12}{2} + \overset{11}{2} + \overset{10}{2} + \overset{9}{2} + \overset{8}{2}$$

$$= 32,768 + 16,384 + 8,192 + 4,096 + 2,048 + 1,024 + 512 + 256$$

$$= 65,280$$

and BYTE 1 + BYTE 2 = 255 + 65,280

$$= 65,535.$$

So, the highest possible number with two bytes is 65,535, which means that, including 0, there are a possible 65,536 locations.

EXTRA CREDIT

Explain why $2^n = 2^{n-1} + 2^{n-2} + \ldots + 2^0$

There are 1,024 bytes (2^{10}) in a K of memory.

PROBLEM #8

How many K of memory can be addressed with two bytes?

ANSWER

Two bytes can address 65,536 locations, so:
65,536 / 1024 = 64 or
$2^{16} / 2^{10} = 2^6 = 64$

Byte 2 (worth a maximum of 65,280) is called the **high order byte.** Byte 1, which pales in comparison (worth a paltry maximum of 255), is called the **low order byte.** In machine language, hexadecimal values are always used to specify addresses, and the low order byte is presented first.

Various locations in memory are reserved for special purposes: for making sounds, for communicating with input/output devices and, in particular, for placing characters on the screen. If we are running the "HI" program on an Apple, it is necessary to look at the Apple reference manual to find the memory locations for the text screen. The text screen locations for the Apple are a 24 × 40 matrix (see Fig. 6.10).

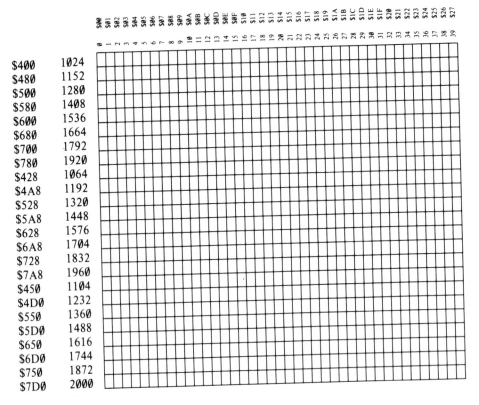

Fig. 6.10

The top-left position in the Apple screen is, in hexadecimal, location $400 in memory. When something is placed in location $400, something appears on the screen in the top-left corner. In particular, when you put the ASCII value of "H" ($C 8) in location $400, an "H" appears in the top-left corner of the screen.

In the program to print "HI" on the Apple screen (see Fig. 6.8), bytes four and five are the top-left screen address. Thus, byte four (the low order byte) is "$0 0" and byte five (the high order byte) is "$0 4". Reading them from right to left (putting the high order byte first) gives you $0400, or, location $400, as just indicated.

To print the "I" next to the "H" its ASCII value must be put into location $401. Thus, in the "HI" program, byte nine is "$0 1" and byte ten is "$0 4". Again, reading from right to left gives you $0401.

OPERATIONS

But memory, and remembering, is not enough. For computers to compute they must act so as to change memory: move it, alter it, put it back again, erase it, create it, and move it again. Each central processing unit has its own set of operations by which it accomplishes these tasks. On the whole, though, CPUs are remarkably similar.

The 6502 CPU has three temporary memory locations, called **registers.** Like other memory locations, these are eight bits long and maintain their value until deliberately changed. On the other hand, they are very special. Most of the instructions in machine language refer to these registers. To do anything with a piece of information, the computer must move it from memory into one of the registers. Once it is in a register, the computer can alter it and then move it back into memory. To move from any memory location to another, a piece of information must go through a register. That is, to move the contents of memory location $C7A1 to memory location $0320 the information must first be loaded from $C7A1 into a register, and then moved from the register into memory location $0320.

One register—the accumulator, or "A" register—is used for all arithmetic functions. The other two registers, called "X" and "Y", are used for temporary storage and as indices. Any binary number expressible in one byte can be added to, or subtracted from, the accumulator. The X and Y registers can only be incremented or decremented by one, that is, you can only add one to them or take one away, which is why they are ideal for keeping count, what programmers call **indexing** (for example, in "FOR-NEXT" loops).

Machine language uses hexadecimal codes for each instruction. This is fine for machines, but humans require something easier to remember and use. To do machine level programming, a programmer loads a program, called an **assembler,** into the machine. The programmer then writes in **assembly language,** instead of machine language. The assembler translates the program from assembly language into machine language so the computer can execute the programmer's instructions.

All of the computer's instructions have hexadecimal numbers, called their **operation codes**, or **op codes**. That is their machine language code. They also have a three-letter mnemonic code, which is their assembly language code. The instructions are of several types: memory moves, arithmetic operations, flow of control operations, and logical operations.

Move Memory

These instructions can move the contents of a register into memory, load the contents of a memory location into a register, or transfer the contents from one register to another.

Arithmetic Operations

Instructions for arithmetic operations allow you to increment the X or Y register, or a memory location, by 1; decrement the X or Y register, or a memory location, by 1; add to the accumulator; and subtract from the accumulator.

Flow of Control Operations

Instructions that control the flow of operations allow you to branch on some condition to a specific memory location; compare some memory location with a register; jump to a new location; jump to a subroutine; and return from a subroutine.

Logical Operations

Instructions for logical operations allow the normal logical operations of *and, or, exclusive or* (meaning: A or B, but not both A and B). These use the accumulator and some specified address.

Two of the Memory move instructions are Store and Load.

Store.   Store instructions take the contents of a register and store them in a memory location. The assembly language mnemonic for "store" is ST followed by the name of the register (A, X, or Y). STA $0401 stores the contents of the accumulator in hexadecimal address $0401. In machine code, STA is $8D. The programmer stores the contents of the accumulator in $401 by entering $8D $01 $04 (remember low byte first for the address).

Load.   Load instructions put something into a register, either a constant or the contents of a memory location, or the contents of another register.

The assembly language mnemonic for "load" is LD followed by the name of the register. For example, to load the constant $C8 into the accumulator the programmer enters: LDA $C8. In machine code, LDA is $A9. The programmer loads the accumulator with the constant $C8 by entering $A9 $C8.

The program to print "HI" in the upper left-hand corner of the Apple (see Fig. 6.8) consists entirely of load and store instructions. This program can be transformed into assembly language (see Fig. 6.11), to make it easier to understand (for humans).

```
$A 9      $C 8      $8 D      $0 0      $0 4
LDA       "H"       STA       $400

$A 9      $C 9      $8 D      $0 1      $0 4
LDA       "I"       STA       $401
```

Fig. 6.11   Machine language into assembly language.

```
LDA    $C8
STA    $400
LDA    $C9
STA    $401
```

Fig. 6.12   Assembly language program to print "HI" in upper left of Apple screen.

The program in Fig. 6.12 is in assembly language. To actually run this in the machine, the assembler converts it to the machine language hexadecimal code in Fig. 6.8 and stores it in specific locations in memory. In this case we will store the program in locations $300-$309. Fig. 6.13 shows the contents of memory locations $300 through $309 after the program is stored there.

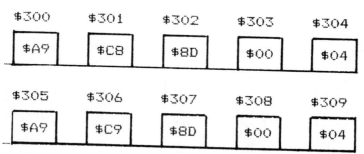

Fig. 6.13   Program to print "HI" in upper left of Apple screen stored in memory locations $300–$309.

To run the "HI" program, three locations will be used: 1) $400 2) $401 and 3) the accumulator. Before the program is run, these locations all have random sequences of 1s and 0s, as in Fig. 6.14. Actually, these may or may not be random, since if the previous program used these addresses, the contents of these addresses reflect whatever happened in the previous program. Always assume that the content of a location is "garbage," and that it is not, for example, equal to 0.

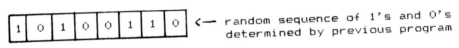

Fig. 6.14   Accumulator before program.

The hexadecimal value of the bytes in the accumulator, locations $400 and $401, and the program counter, before the program is run, are shown in Fig. 6.15.

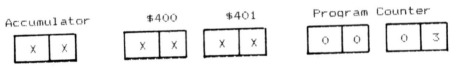

Fig. 6.15   Contents of locations at beginning of program ("X" indicates unknown).

To run this program the programmer must tell the computer the starting address. The program counter is then set to $300 (reading from right to left), and the machine fetches the operation code stored in location $300. The op code tells the computer several important pieces of information. First, it automatically resets the program counter, in effect telling the computer how many bytes long the instruction is, so that the program counter knows where to look for the next instruction. Second, it tells the computer what the instruction is, so the computer knows how to interpret the succeeding bytes. The contents of $300 ($A9) is a two-byte instruction. The first byte has "$A9" in it, and the second byte has the constant value "$C8". The program counter is therefore set to $302 to show where the next instruction can be found. Then the computer carries out the instruction "$A9 $C8", that is, it loads $C8 into the accumulator (see Fig. 6.16).

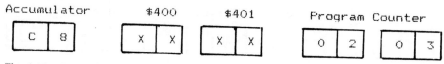

Fig. 6.16　Contents of locations after LDA $C8.

The machine now returns to the program counter to find the address of the next instruction, $302. The instruction beginning at $302 is three bytes long—$8D $00 $04—or, in assembly code, STA $400. The program counter is therefore set to $302 + $3, or $305. STA stores the contents of the accumulator in location $400. The contents of the locations now are shown in Fig. 6.17.

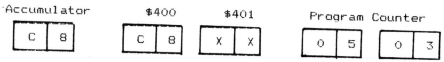

Fig. 6.17　Contents of locations after STA $400.

Storing $C8 in $400 has done something on the screen, as shown in Fig. 6.18.

Fig. 6.18　The Apple screen after executing STA $400.

The machine now returns to the program counter to find the address of the next instruction, $305. The instruction beginning at $305 is two bytes long—$A9 $C9—in assembly code, LDA $C9. The program counter advances to $307. LDA loads $C9 ("I") into the accumulator. The contents of the locations are shown in Fig. 6.19.

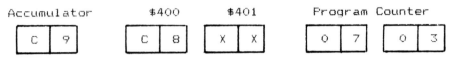

Fig. 6.19   Contents of the locations after LDA $C9.

Returning to the program counter, the computer finds the next instruction is in location $307. The instruction beginning at $307 is three bytes long—$8D $01 $04—or in assembly code STA $401. This loads the contents of the accumulator into location $401, and is the end of the program. The final contents of the locations are shown in Fig. 6.20.

Fig. 6.20   Final contents of the locations after STA $401.

The computer now goes back to the program counter to find the next line of the program (we know the program is over, but the computer does not!). An instruction is needed at the end of the program to stop execution. One way to handle this is to think of the program to print "HI" on the screen as a subroutine—a chunk—and to put an instruction to "RETURN FROM SUBROUTINE" at the end of it. In assembly code this is "RTS", in machine language it is a single byte instruction "$60". Putting a $60 in location $310 makes "Print HI" a subroutine.

The full hexadecimal program (with the final return from subroutine) is shown in Fig. 6.21.

$A9 $C8 $8D $00 $04

$A9 $C9 $8D $01 $04 $60

Fig. 6.21   Final hexadecimal subroutine to print "HI" in upper left of Apple screen.

BASIC NUMBER SYSTEMS

Two questions remain that should have occured to the reader with some programming experience: How do I get the program in there in the first place? and, if this is a subroutine, how do I call it, that is, how does it actually execute? There are several ways to store and run a machine language program depending on how the program is entered on the machine. If the program has been saved onto a disk, then it can be run by using the "BRUN" command. If the program is entered directly into memory, using the monitor, then typing "300G", which stands for $300 GO", will get the program to go. It is also possible to put a machine language program into memory from BASIC—using the POKE instruction. The programmer can then look at it—using the PEEK instruction—and run it as a subroutine—using the CALL instruction.

However, the BASIC language only accepts numbers in decimal. Therefore, the programmer must convert the hexadecimal machine language program into decimal. The programmer can look up the hexadecimal numbers in Table 6.4, and dutifully record all of the corresponding decimal values. In the table, the high-order nibble is on the left side, and the low-order nibble is on the top.

We hope you have not yet looked up the decimal equivalents of this program. Some of you impetuous readers who jumped into the table, and already looked everything up, will be rewarded for your efforts by a deep sense of accomplishment—and a real appreciation of the value of having a computer. Because, it is easy to write a program to do this conversion for you.

HEX	$0	$1	$2	$3	$4	$5	$6	$7	$8	$9	$A	$B	$C	$D	$E	$F
$0	0	1	2	3	4	5	6	7	8	9	10	11	12	13	14	15
$1	16	17	18	19	20	21	22	23	24	25	26	27	28	29	30	31
$2	32	33	34	35	36	37	38	39	40	41	42	43	44	45	46	47
$3	48	49	50	51	52	53	54	55	56	57	58	59	60	61	62	63
$4	64	65	66	67	68	69	70	71	72	73	74	75	76	77	78	79
$5	80	81	82	83	84	85	86	87	88	89	90	91	92	93	94	95
$6	96	97	98	99	100	101	102	103	104	105	106	107	108	109	110	111
$7	112	113	114	115	116	117	118	119	120	121	122	123	124	125	126	126
$8	128	129	130	131	132	133	134	135	136	137	138	139	140	141	142	143
$9	144	145	146	147	148	149	150	151	152	153	154	155	156	157	158	159
$A	160	161	162	163	164	165	166	167	168	169	170	171	172	173	174	175
$B	176	177	178	179	180	181	182	183	184	185	186	187	188	189	190	191
$C	192	193	194	195	196	197	198	199	200	201	202	203	204	205	206	207
$D	208	209	210	211	212	213	214	215	216	217	218	219	220	221	222	223
$E	224	225	226	227	228	229	230	231	232	233	234	235	236	237	238	239
$F	240	241	242	243	244	245	246	247	248	249	250	251	252	253	254	255

Table 6.4   Hexadecimal to decimal conversion table.

The program for converting a two-digit hexadecimal number to a decimal number uses a straightforward algorithm.

1. Look at the left digit.
2. If it is a letter, convert it to its decimal equivalent.
3. Multiply the digit by 16.
4. Look at the right digit.
5. If it is a letter, convert it to its decimal equivalent.
6. Add the number to the earlier result.

The key to doing the conversion easily is to use ASCII codes, since we are converting alphanumeric characters (both letters and numerals) into numbers.

PROBLEM #9

Write a subroutine to convert a hexadecimal digit to its decimal equivalent.

ANSWER

The ASCII codes for the numerals "0" through "9" are 48 through 57, and the ASCII codes for the letters "A" through "F" are 65 through 70. In the conversion in program #1, the routine relies on these codes.

This BASIC subroutine first checks the ASCII value of a hex digit (HEX$). Line 600 says: when the ASCII value is between 47 and 65, it is a numeral, whose value, in decimal, is the ASCII value less 48. Line 610 says: when the ASCII value is between 64 and 71, it is a letter A to F whose value, in decimal, is the ASCII value less 55. And line 620 says: When the ASCII value is anything else, it is not hexadecimal.

```
590 REM
CONVERSION ROUTINE

600 IF ASC (HEX$) > 47 AND ASC (HEX$) < 65 THEN DIGIT = ASC (HEX$) - 48: RETURN : REM  IT IS A NUMERAL
610 IF ASC (HEX$) > 64 AND ASC (HEX$) < 71 THEN DIGIT = ASC (HEX$) - 55: RETURN : REM     IT IS A LETTER FROM A-F
620 PRINT "THIS IS NOT A LEGAL HEX NUMBER": POP : GOTO 500

]
```

Program 1.

This conversion is set up as a subroutine because it is used twice—for both the high and low nibble. We can now think of this routine as a single chunk embedded in a program that converts two-digit hex numbers.

PROBLEM #10

Write a program to convert a two-digit hexadecimal number to its decimal equivalent.

ANSWER

The first version of the program is in program #2.

```
10  HOME
490  VTAB 21: PRINT "TO QUIT ROUTINE TYPE 'Q' FOR HI DIGIT"
499  REM
MAIN LOOP
 FOR HEX-DECIMAL CONVERSION

500  HEX$ = "": VTAB 2: PRINT "ENTER THE HI DIGIT OR ZERO $";: GET HEX$
505  IF  ASC (HEX$) = 81 THEN  END
510  VTAB 6: HTAB 4: PRINT "$"HEX$: GOSUB 600
515  HIGH = DIGIT
520  HEX$ = "": VTAB 2: PRINT "ENTER THE LOW DIGIT $";: GET HEX$
530  VTAB 6: HTAB 6: PRINT HEX$;: GOSUB 600
540  NUMBER = (16 * HI) + DIGIT
550  PRINT " = ";NUMBER
560  GOTO 490
590  REM
CONVERSION ROUTINE

600  IF  ASC (HEX$) > 47 AND  ASC (HEX$) < 65 THEN DIGIT =  ASC (HEX$) - 48: RETURN : REM  IT IS A NUMERAL
610  IF  ASC (HEX$) > 64 AND  ASC (HEX$) < 71 THEN DIGIT =  ASC (HEX$) - 55: RETURN : REM     IT IS A LETTER FROM A-F
620  PRINT "THIS IS NOT A LEGAL HEX NUMBER": POP : GOTO 500

]
```

Program 2.

To understand this program, think of this subroutine as a single operation, a chunk, which does the appropriate conversion. You may want first to look at the subroutine and convince yourself that it succeeds, or you may assume it does and then fill in the steps only after you understand the whole program. Either way, you must see this whole subroutine as a single step.

If you have not already done so, and you have access to an Apple, enter the above program into your machine. There are a couple of problems with this program. Fortunately they all revolve around the same issue. When you run the program, the opening screen looks like Fig. 6.22.

If you now enter a high digit, such as "8", the top line overwrites the previous line without erasing it. In screen two (Fig. 6.23), notice the "R ZERO $" that remains from screen one.

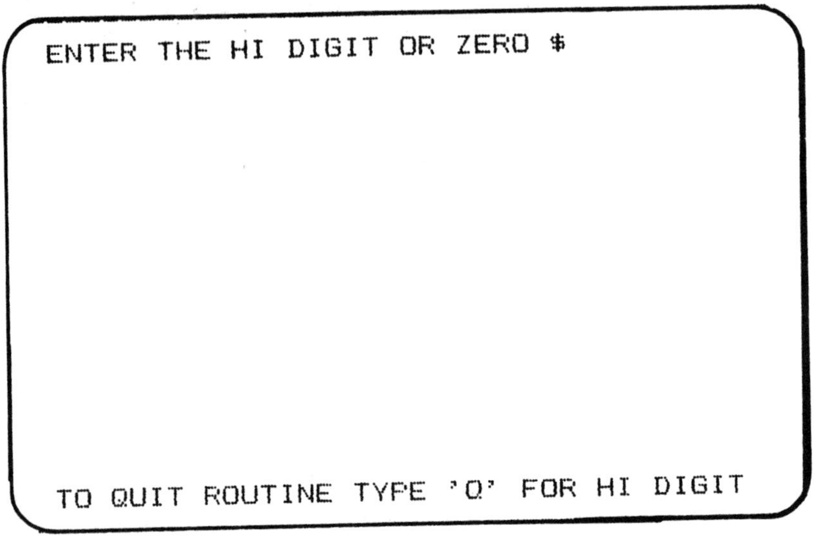

```
ENTER THE HI DIGIT OR ZERO $




       TO QUIT ROUTINE TYPE 'Q' FOR HI DIGIT
```

Fig. 6.22   Screen 1.

This erasing problem comes up in two other places: first, when one answer is a decimal number that is three digits (like 255), and a succeeding answer is only one or two decimal digits (like 1 or 23); and, second, when the program prints the error message: "THIS IS NOT A LEGAL HEX NUMBER", the phrase is left on the screen, and must be erased.

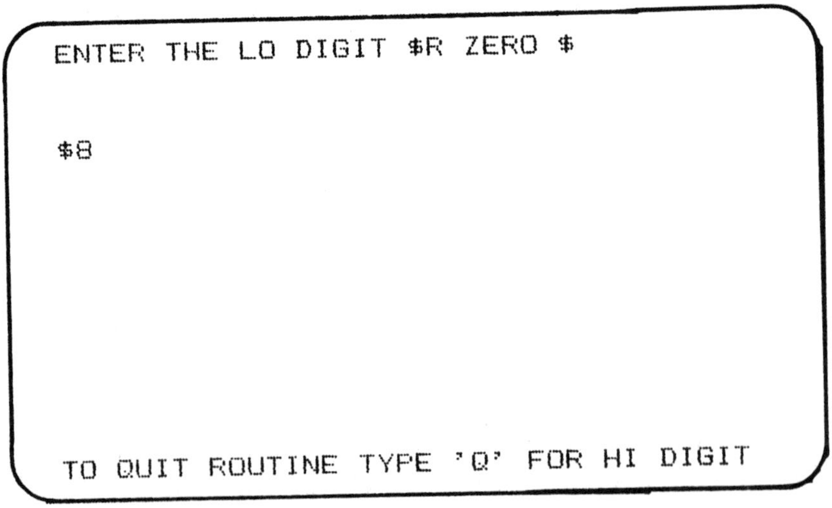

```
ENTER THE LO DIGIT $R ZERO $

$8




       TO QUIT ROUTINE TYPE 'Q' FOR HI DIGIT
```

Fig. 6.23   Screen 2.

PROBLEM #11

Correct the above program.

ANSWER

The Apple has a machine language subroutine that allows you to erase a line from the position of the cursor to the right of the screen. It is located (always) at location 64668 in memory. You can invoke it in a BASIC program by typing "CALL 64668" in a program line. You do not need to know—and in fact you have no idea of—the precise nature of this subroutine. You can simply insert it in a program and it does the appropriate job.

The corrected program below also contains a pause subroutine that is called before we take away the error message. In this case, you can see the content of the subroutine on line 700; again, you can ignore it if you want to. The corrected listing is in program #3.

```
10  HOME
490  VTAB 21: PRINT "TO QUIT ROUTINE TYPE '0' FOR HI DIGIT"
499  REM
MAIN LOOP
 FOR HEX-DECIMAL CONVERSION

500  HEX$ = "": VTAB 2: PRINT "ENTER THE HI DIGIT OR ZERO $";: GET HEX$
505  IF  ASC (HEX$) = 81 THEN  END : REM  '0' ENDS INPUT
510  VTAB 6: HTAB 4: CALL 64668: PRINT "$"HEX$: GOSUB 600
515  HIGH = DIGIT
520  HEX$ = "": VTAB 2: CALL 64668: PRINT "ENTER THE LOW DIGIT $";: GET HEX$
530  VTAB 6: HTAB 6: PRINT HEX$;: GOSUB 600
540  NUMBER = (16 * HI) + DIGIT
550  PRINT " = ";NUMBER
560  GOTO 490
590  REM
CONVERSION ROUTINE

600  IF  ASC (HEX$) > 47 AND  ASC (HEX$) < 65 THEN DIGIT =  ASC (HEX$) - 48: RETURN : REM  IT IS A NUMERAL
610  IF  ASC (HEX$) > 64 AND  ASC (HEX$) < 71 THEN DIGIT =  ASC (HEX$) - 55: RETURN : REM       IT IS A LETTER FROM A-F
620  PRINT : PRINT "THIS IS NOT A LEGAL HEX NUMBER";:PAUSE = 2000: GOSUB 700
630  HTAB 1: CALL 64668
640  POP : GOTO 500
690  REM
PAUSE SUBROUTINE

700  FOR T = 1 TO PAUSE: NEXT T: RETURN

]
```

Program 3.

PEEKS, POKES, AND CALLS

Now that we have a program to convert two-digit hexadecimal numbers to decimal, we can use the PEEK and POKE commands in BASIC. To run the program we need to use the CALL command and again, this uses the decimal equivalent of the address at which the program was stored. Recall that the "HI" program was stored at location $300, so we need to convert three-digit hex numbers to decimal.

PROBLEM #12

Modify the conversion program to accept three-digit hex numbers. Modify it again to accept any hex number.

ANSWER

Do it yourself. We're not telling.

It is, of course, possible to do this the old fashioned way:

$$(0 \times 16^0) + (0 \times 16^1) + (3 \times 16^2) = 768$$

To run the PRINT "HI" program on line 220 of a BASIC program, you need to enter:

220 CALL 768

The BASIC command POKE puts a value in a memory location. The instruction

POKE 768, 169

places the hexadecimal equivalent of 169 ($A9) in the hexadecimal equivalent of 768 ($300). You can now take the BASIC program that converts from hexadecimal to decimal, and consider it as a chunk, as a subroutine, in a program that pokes into memory the machine language program to print HI. The full program takes a hexadecimal number, converts it into decimal (using the old program as a subroutine), and pokes it into a specific address (see program #4).

```
10  HOME
90  REM
MAIN PROGRAM LOOP

100 ADDRESS = 768: REM STARTING ADDRESS OF PROGRAM
110  GOSUB 500
120  IF QUIT = 1 THEN  GOSUB 200: END
130  POKE ADDRESS,NUMBER
140  ADDRESS = ADDRESS + 1: GOTO 110
190  REM
RUN MACHINE LANGUAGE PROGRAM

200  PRINT : PRINT "WHEN YOU ARE READY TO RUN THE PROGRAM": PRINT : PRINT "HIT ANY KEY. ";: GET A$
210  CALL 768: RETURN
490  VTAB 21: PRINT "TO QUIT ROUTINE TYPE 'Q' FOR HI DIGIT"
499  REM
MAIN LOOP
 FOR HEX-DECIMAL CONVERSION

500 HEX$ = "": VTAB 2: PRINT "ENTER THE HI DIGIT OR ZERO $";: GET HEX$
505  IF  ASC (HEX$) = 81 THEN QUIT = 1: PRINT : RETURN : REM      'Q' ENDS INPUT
510  VTAB 6: HTAB 4: CALL 64668: PRINT "$"HEX$: GOSUB 600
515  HIGH = DIGIT
520  HEX$ = "": VTAB 2: CALL 64668: PRINT "ENTER THE LOW DIGIT $";: GET HEX$
530  VTAB 6: HTAB 6: PRINT HEX$;: GOSUB 600
540  NUMBER = (16 * HI) + DIGIT
550  PRINT " = ";NUMBER
560  RETURN
590  REM
CONVERSION ROUTINE

600  IF  ASC (HEX$) > 47 AND  ASC (HEX$) < 65 THEN DIGIT =  ASC (HEX$) - 48: RETURN : REM  IT IS A NUMERAL
610  IF  ASC (HEX$) > 64 AND  ASC (HEX$) < 71 THEN DIGIT =  ASC (HEX$) - 55: RETURN : REM      IT IS A LETTER FROM A-F
620  PRINT : PRINT "THIS IS NOT A LEGAL HEX NUMBER";:PAUSE = 2000: GOSUB 700
630  HTAB 1: CALL 64668
640  POP : GOTO 500
690  REM
PAUSE SUBROUTINE

700  FOR T = 1 TO PAUSE: NEXT T: RETURN

]
```

Program 4.

The major addition to the hexadecimal-decimal conversion program is in the beginning program lines. In lines 100–140 the programmer gets a number, pokes it into an address, increments the address by one, and goes back for a new number. After the programmer enters the program, he or she calls it (lines 200–210). The old conversion program is changed into a subroutine (lines 500–590). In the previous version, line 560 sent the computer back to begin the program circle. The new program changes line 560 to RETURN. The old subroutine ended when the user typed "Q" (line 505). In the revised program typing "Q" sets a Flag (QUIT = 1) that the user is done entering the program, and is ready to CALL it. The old subroutine at 590 is now a subroutine within a subroutine, and the details are forgotten.

MACHINE LANGUAGE SUBROUTINES

Although it is now possible to print "HI" in the top left of the screen, the screen is filled with whatever preceded the running of the program. Like the subroutine that erases a line, a permanent subroutine in the Apple can clear the whole screen (like HOME in BASIC). This subroutine begins in location $FC58. To call it from the machine language program, add the instruction, "JUMP TO SUBROUTINE at $FC58". In assembly language this is JSR $FC58, and in machine code it is $20 $58 $FC. The final machine language subroutine and the addresses in which it resides are shown in Fig. 6.24.

```
$300 $20    $301 $58    $302 $FC    Subroutine to clear screen

$303 $A9    $304 $C8    $305 $8D    $306 $00    $307 $04

$308 $A9    $309 $C9    $310 $8D    $311 $01    $312 $04

$313 $60    Return from subroutine
```

Fig. 6.24   Machine language subroutine to clear screen and print "HI".

To see this program in memory you can make another BASIC program. Just as "POKE Address, Number" places a value into a memory location from a BASIC program, "PEEK Address" shows you what is there. The program we typed in, including the clear screen instruction, was fourteen bytes long. Entering program #5 into an Apple will show you the entire machine language program as it is stored in memory.

```
100 FOR I = 0 TO 13

110 PRINT PEEK 768 +I

120 NEXT
```

Program 5   Basic program to display machine language program.

CONCLUSIONS

The short course is now over. But this was only the beginning. There is so much more to explore—and still, wherever you look, numbers and mathematical concepts are fundamental to the explanation. This course was designed to provide you with a little insight into how the computer really works, and to show you how you might use just such a course with your students. The course can give them the experience of using mathematical concepts and problem-solving skills they have developed to understand something as complex as how a computer works at the machine level.

For a computer scientist, the computer is a hierarchical machine. There are many different ways to think about what is occurring when the machine is operating. Each layer, from bits, nibbles, bytes, and even sandwiches, to machine language, assembly language, and even high-level programming languages, has a unique set of problems associated with it. Each set demands a different level of understanding of logic, mathematics, and formal languages. All involve a constant process of "chunking," or taking small complex pieces and considering them as wholes, as a single primitive element. In each case this is for the benefit of people, not the machine. In all aspects of computing, numbers and number systems continually reappear. What might, at first glance, seem arbitrary—for example, that some machines are limited to 64K of memory—is a direct result of the numerical restrictions imposed by the binary number system. When addresses are two bytes, 64K is all the possible combinations.

There is a wealth of mathematics in the machine. It is, and should be, an enormous source of actual problems for the mathematics teacher. Programming and programming theory is only one aspect of that source.

Programming and Computer Languages

7

To most people, computer literacy means a course in programming. To most students, programming means a course in BASIC for the top group in mathematics. And to most schools, educational computing means computer labs. Programming generally has been taught to ten or fifteen students at a time in computer labs, either at terminals or on microcomputers with limited graphics and no color capability. It has been taught without regard to other subjects, and it is rarely used by students or teachers in their other courses. But just as there is much more to the use of computers than teaching programming, there is much more to programming than traditionally has been offered in schools. Programming should be viewed as involving more than simple language mastery, and it should be taught and learned in new and varied contexts.

THE OLD VIEW— PROGRAMMING AS LANGUAGE TEACHING

As described in Chapter 2, programming has traditionally been viewed and taught as a foreign language. Most students learned only one language, usually BASIC. They learned that language by a combination of copying programs out of books and developing their own simple programs, using each new command as it was parcelled out to them like new vocabulary in a French class. Each new command was taught with the proper syntax.

The programs that were copied or written generally duplicated some kind of mathematical function, like the compound interest formula or the method of finding prime numbers. The emphasis was on mastering the language, not on the nature of programming.

Teaching programming in this way is like teaching foreign languages in traditional ways. Progress is slow and often tedious, and usefulness is limited. Soon after the course is over, most students forget most of what they learned. Often they remember the words, but forget the ways of putting them together. And even students who have mastered this kind of language-based programming course do not carry with them a useful, workable understanding of programming. They do not know how to turn their own ideas into programs.

This traditional view of teaching programming as a foreign language also suggests the narrowest view of programming itself. It fulfills our skewed image of programmers as translators who simply take ideas and translate them into words that computers understand. It leaves out the creativity and the problem solving that are so fundamental to all programming. It centers on general purpose programming languages like BASIC or FORTRAN, and fails to include simple and specialized languages that may be parts of specific programs like *Delta Drawing*. Viewed in this way, the prime question becomes, "What language should students learn?"

Programming courses have also traditionally been taught on a single computer, often a mainframe, and have ignored the differences in language between machines. More importantly, they have ignored the **operating systems** of computers, whose mastery is often the hardest part of learning to program. To do any useful programming, students must master not only the commands and **syntax** of the language but also the **disk operating system,** the screen editing system, the printer operating system, perhaps the monitor of the computer, and often a debugging system, each of which has its own commands and syntax. To make matters even more complicated, each of these systems programs is usually separate in BASIC, while they are collected as a large integrated whole in Pascal, and come in different versions of Forth for the same machine. All of this can seem to the new student of programming a forbidding learning experience, which may be why traditional programming courses generally ignore these matters.

THE NEW VIEW— PROGRAMMING AS CONSTRUCTION

Educators and program designers are beginning to put together a new view of programming: as a construction and problem-solving activity, rather than as a translation into a foreign language. The program itself is seen as a construction like a house, a machine, or a dress. It performs certain functions and reacts to certain commands, be they the push of a button or the turn of a knob. Many of these computer constructions are similar to those we make with tools other than computers, such as: filing cabinets, automatic typewriters, graph paper, pinball games, flight simulators, player pianos, and canvases.

This new view of programming is more than just semantic. It is a fundamental change in emphasis from one that concentrates on learning the components of the language to one that concentrates on the acts of programming. For as every programmer knows, the hard part of programming is not what words to use or what the right syntax is, but rather the design of the ideas and the implementation of that design into a program structure. Like any other kind of construction, from producing an oil painting to manufacturing a new car to writing an essay to building a new house, a good program has to be designed with good ideas and then built soundly and with good form. Without these fundamentals of good construction, any product either will not work well or will break down and need constant repair. A computer program constructed without creative design and good craftsmanship will be difficult to use and to debug. Good creative programming designs and well-formed, well-crafted implementations should be the goals of any course in programming.

As in any construction, there are tools of the trade that make it easier to perform the task. One of the tools required for programming is the language. The more facile a person is with a computer language, the easier it is to design and craft a program. Along with languages, there are simple programming routines that, once understood, provide powerful tools as well. And then there are those dreaded operating systems, each of which is, again, a tool. A programmer who has command of these tools can work more economically than one who does not have that command, although being able to use these tools does not mean that a person will necessarily by a good programmer.

COMPUTER LANGUAGES

Computer languages are amazingly flexible. Any program, from the very simplest to the most complex, can be written, even in the same language, in a surprising number of different ways. Some ways are much better than others. Similarly, the same programs can be written in many different languages, and for a given purpose, some languages are better than others. Each language offers its own benefits and each has its own difficulties. A student who understands programming as a construction and programming languages as construction tools will not have much difficulty learning alternative languages or using different languages for different purposes. A student who has learned programming with this view will be able to program in a specialized language that may be part of another program or in a general purpose language like BASIC.

The various general purpose languages available today can each play a variety of roles in a mathematics classroom for different kinds of problems and different kinds of students. There is little need for most students to master any of these languages. But there is a great need for all students to understand what constitutes a language and how, if they desire, to learn a computer language. But where is there time for such learning in the currently crowded curriculum? Fitting a new topic, much less a new subject, into a curriculum that is all too often forcing out subjects like science and social studies does not make sense. Instead, we should use new ideas to join subjects together, to connect ideas so that our curriculum is more economical and so that our students learn ideas in a connected way. One way to do this is to emphasize the interconnectedness of computer languages and mathematics skills and ideas.

When we think of languages as tools for problem solving and as tools for the construction of ideas, we can then turn to different languages as different ways of looking at the ideas we want to teach. Once a student understands what programming is and how programs are constructed, learning a new language is not difficult. And each new language just adds to one's available tools.

BASIC

BASIC (Beginners All-purpose Symbolic Instruction Code), as its acronym and full name imply, was designed to be a general purpose language. BASIC, while it has grown as a language significantly over the years, remains easy to use and useful for most programming activities. Unfortunately, it is not exceptionally good for any of them. Working in BASIC is like working in a good home workshop: the tools are there to do most jobs, but they make it more difficult and time consuming to do high-quality work than the tools in a professional shop. One reason BASIC is easy to use is that it does not require much in the way of operating systems. It comes with the simplest built-in editor, in the form of line numbers. A programmer can correct line 670 by typing a new line with that number. Of course, this simple procedure can become very tedious in large programs, so programmers generally use sophisticated screen-oriented editing systems that allow them to change lines without rewriting them. Disk operating systems are also usually separate in BASIC and can be learned later.

BASIC works well for doing simple arithmetic or algebra problems because it uses an algebraic format. It is thus an easy and "natural" computer language for the mathematics classroom. Forth, by contrast, uses **Reverse Polish Notation.** One of the first and easiest programs for a student to write in BASIC performs a series of calculations like finding the squares of the numbers from 1 to 100.

```
10 FOR I = 1 TO 100
20 PRINT I, I*I,
30 NEXT I
```

Such programs are easy to write and provide instant gratification when run. Students could also modify this program to print out the square roots of the numbers from 1 to 100. Such a program could be used to begin a discussion of accuracy and rounding off, since the computer has a procedure for rounding off numbers that can sometimes produce very funny results. The next step could be a program that would produce the entire multiplication table. This could be used to discuss arrays and matrices. BASIC is an excellent way of beginning these difficult topics, even though most forms of it make later handling of matrices difficult. But with BASIC, students can get a sense of the process of working with array elements and the labeling of those elements.

The flexibility of BASIC makes it a particularly easy language to show how the same programming idea can be done in a number of different ways. It is important for students to think from the very beginning in terms of program designs that are fundamentally simple, run as fast as they can, and use as little memory as possible. Timing contests can add to the fun of programming while at the same time showing students that there are many different ways of accomplishing the same programming task. Students could compete to write the fastest possible program for a given programming problem. They could race using two similar machines or by timing their programs on the same machine.

A similar contest could be held to find the shortest program that would solve a particular problem. For example, students could be asked to write programs to find the prime numbers from one to a thousand. These programs could be measured to determine their length simply by counting up the number of variables and the number of commands, or by looking up the start and end points in the program as they are stored in the computer.

Again, ideas involved in teaching BASIC also apply to the teaching of mathematics. Just as with programming, there are a number of different ways to write or approach any mathematics problem. A multiplication problem can be done as repeated addition. The Romans performed multiplication and division by a doubling procedure. Similarly, as with programming, the solution to algebraic equations is a process of simplifying equations for solutions, although it often seems to students that algebraic algorithms and procedures they are taught are the right ones. Coupling the teaching of mathematics and computing can show students that the procedures they have been taught are usually the fastest or the shortest, but not the only ones.

As with speed and length, students can learn to control program simplicity by practicing writing programs. Unnecessarily complicated programs are known in the profession as spaghetti code, meaning that the programming ideas would be difficult to follow for anyone having to work on the program. Spaghetti code makes it easy for bugs to creep in and difficult for others to edit the program. Programming is, again, no different from any other construction. Some designs are simple, elegant, and well executed and some are not. We value those beautiful designs. In the same way, we should teach our students to value simple, elegant programs, not only for the aesthetic pleasure they elicit, but for their practical superiority. Perhaps the easiest way to recognize such simplicity is for one student to try to follow another's work. Students should be encouraged to share their programs and to try to understand each other's code.

BASIC comes in many different versions. A version worth considering for use in the mathematics classroom is Integer BASIC. Integer BASIC seems at first glance a poor relation to decimal or, as it is usually called Floating Point BASIC, but it has its very valuable purposes. It is easier for students who have not had decimal experience to use. And it can be used to teach **MOD arithmetic** because it has a MOD function that returns the remainder of a division. MOD arithmetic makes it particularly easy for students to use a computer to find the factors of any number, simply by dividing that number by all possible integers and picking out those that have a MOD of 0. A BASIC program to do this appears in Fig. 7.1.

This program could in turn become a basis for other programs, such as one to find the prime numbers.

```
>LIST
    1 REM   FACTORING PROGRAM
   10 INPUT "NUMBER",NUMBER: REM   CHOOSE A NUMBER
   12 IF NUMBER=0 THEN 10
   15 FACTRCNT=0: REM   CHECK FOR PRIMES
   18 FACTR=0
   20 FACTR=FACTR+1
   30 RMAINDER=NUMBER MOD FACTR: REM   THIS DOES THE WORK
   40 IF RMAINDER<>0 THEN 20: REM   LOOKING FOR MOD 0'S
   50 IF FACTR=NUMBER THEN 100: REM   DON'T INCLUDE NUMBER ITSELF
   60 IF FACTR=1 THEN 20: REM   DON'T INCLUDE 1
   70 FACTRCNT=FACTRCNT+1
   80 PRINT : PRINT FACTR
   90 GOTO 20
  100 IF FACTRCNT<1 THEN PRINT "THIS IS A PRIME NUMBER"
  110 PRINT : PRINT : GOTO 10: REM   START ALL OVER AGAIN

>
```

Fig. 7.1

Logo

One of the motivations behind the development of Logo was to make programming accessible to young children. To accomplish this, the developers set out to create a language with an easy and interactive graphics component. They succeeded. While Logo may be used to work with numbers (and letters) just like BASIC, it is best known for the ease with which students can use graphics to explore numerical and geometric ideas. Students can use Logo to study mathematics, and they can learn mathematics as they program in Logo.

Logo includes its own operating environment and many of its own operating systems whose commands students must master along with the language. At the same time, its simple command structure for graphics makes it easier for children to learn.

At one end of the K–12 curriculum, Logo can help young children learn geometry, especially many significant intuitive geometric ideas, simply by playing with turtle graphics. At the other end of the curriculum, Logo's great power as a language can be used to develop significant ideas in geometry and physics. Because it is a language that uses arithmetic and algebraic notation, Logo is an excellent vehicle for integrating arithmetic and algebra with geometry, and for representing numerical ideas graphically. For example, instead of constructing a table of squares numerically, as we did in BASIC, a student could write a Logo program that constructs the square numbers graphically, as in Fig. 7.2.

The visual impact of the rapid increase in size of the square numbers, especially if this figure were animated, would add much more to most students' intuitive sense of number than any list of square numbers. The

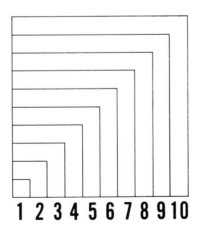

Fig. 7.2

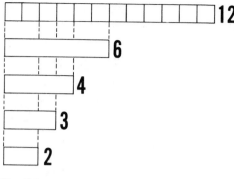

Fig. 7.3

same visual impact makes it easier for many children to understand factors and primes when they are presented graphically, as a series of line or bar segments that can be matched to a given number (see Fig. 7.3).

Assembly Languages

To most people, assembly languages are the province of the real computer experts, far from the ability of ordinary mortals to comprehend. Yet, they are fundamentally no different from other languages, and for many students, programming in assembly language may actually be easier to understand than programming in a high-level language. The construction of programs in assembly language is somewhat different than for high-level languages because the fundamental ideas are simpler. But the act of programming is the same.

Assembly commands are mnemonics, short expressions representing the fundamental machine language commands built into the CPU. An assembler in the computer translates these mnemonics into numeric (machine language) codes to instruct the computer on what to do. Assembly language commands are much closer to the actual functioning of the computer than high-level languages. Different machines have different assemblers, each with its own vocabulary and syntax. But all are conceptually simpler than languages like BASIC or Logo because they do not use the idea of a variable. Students who are not yet at the stage of formal operations (generally reached at 12 to 14 years) cannot fully understand the notion of a variable. To program in assembly language, students need only understand that they are putting numbers into memory locations and taking them out of memory locations. They can only add or subtract these numbers or move them to other locations. They are working entirely with concrete quantities.

Besides being cognitively easier to manipulate, assembly languages can give students a much better sense of what the computer is actually doing. And, because most assembly languages have only the operations of addition and subtraction, any mathematical programming requires the student to develop new mathematical operations as well. For example, to write a program that would generate the square numbers a student would first have to write a program to multiply two numbers together. Once again, there are different ways of doing this, such as a program that uses repeated addition or one that is based on the Roman system of doubling. The development of such programs involves creating "new" operations, and so is a means for students to explore the essence of familiar mathematical operations. One possible assembly language program to multiply two one-digit numbers appears in Fig. 7.4.

Like BASIC and Logo, assembly languages are tools for the construction of programs, but using them is more like building programs from a balsa wood model kit than from a plastic pre-formed model kit like BASIC.

```
 1 ***** PROGRAM TO MULTIPLY ONE DIGIT NUMBERS ******
 2 ***** PUT NUMBERS INTO LOCATIONS $800 AND $801 *****
 3 ***** RUN PROGRAM ($80AG) *****
 4 ***** FIND ANSWER IN $802 *****
 5            ORG    $80A
 6 FACTOR1    EQU    $800
 7 FACTOR2    EQU    $801
 8 PRODUCT    EQU    $802
 9 ********************************
10            LDX    #00        ;START THINGS OFF AT 0
11            LDA    #00
12            STA    PRODUCT
13 START      CPX    FACTOR2    ;CHECK TO SEE IF DONE
14            BEQ    DONE
15            CLC
16            LDA    PRODUCT    ;REPEATED ADDITION
17            ADC    FACTOR1
18            STA    PRODUCT
19            INX
20            JMP    START
21 DONE       RTS
```

Fig. 7.4

The elements are simpler and less determined. There is a real delight which students experience writing assembly language programs, and an ease that is surprising. There are also a number of excellent books on the subject.

Pascal and Forth

There are two newer languages, along with Logo, that are widely available and have recently received a great deal of attention: Pascal and Forth. As programs become longer, they become more difficult to design, follow, keep straight, and understand. To make it easier to work with large and complicated programs, these newer languages have powerful ways of keeping ideas separated and of keeping the programmer oriented. The price for this is that the internal design tools in the language are more complex, and the language itself is tied to its operating system, so that both must be learned simultaneously. Indeed, the newest and most exciting addition to the stable of programming languages, Smalltalk, does not distinguish its language component from its operating system. Pascal and Forth, therefore, require a different level of educational commitment, including a reasonable amount of time to learn and a degree of ongoing use to remember. Thus, they are probably best taught in advanced programming courses in which students will do a fair amount of programming, although there is no reason why teachers familiar with them cannot show examples of programming in Pascal and Forth to their students in any mathematics course.

PROGRAMS WITHIN PROGRAMS

Subroutines

The real power of programming languages, the reason so few commands can produce such complex programs, comes from their capacity to grow. Long programs can be constructed from a series of shorter ones. "New" operations like multiplication can be programmed from existing ones like addition. Complex ideas can be built up out of simpler ones. Programming languages can be used as building blocks to construct new building blocks to construct programs. In traditional languages like FORTRAN and BASIC, these building blocks, called subroutines, are small programs designed to work within larger ones. For example, a program may require the input of a certain set of numbers in several different locations. A subroutine to input these numbers would be written once and called up each time the numbers were needed. In FORTRAN, the first high-level language, libraries of subroutines were created. Some of these subroutines would perform simple operations or would act as functions, like sine or tangent. Others would be more complex, like finding the analysis of variance of a collection of statistics. FORTRAN thus began as a very simple language and grew through its subroutines.

When BASIC was developed, its creators built many of these kinds of subroutines into its command set. But, although BASIC is constructed in many ways like FORTRAN, it does not pass variables between the main program and subroutines in the same way. Each variable used in a BASIC subroutine automatically becomes part of the variable listing of the program, and the program must use the same variable name that the subroutine uses for the same purpose. This is not too difficult if the programmer writes both the main program and the subroutine at the same time. But if they are written at separate times, or if they are written by different people, confusion rapidly sets in. To add to the confusion, the subroutine has to be numbered in a nonconflicting way with the program.

Logo and Forth handle subroutines in a more powerful way by automatically incorporating them into the language as new words or commands. Languages to which new words can be added in this way are called **extensible** because they can be extended by the user. Programs in such languages are made up of a series of words, some of which come from the core or kernel of the language and some of which are added by the programmer. In this way, programmers participate in the construction of the language, fabricating new commands for their own purposes.

In Logo, writing a program or procedure, as it is called in Logo, means adding words to the language. A program to draw a hexagon simply starts with the command TO and then the name of the program.

```
TO HEXAGON
  REPEAT 6 (FD 20 RT 20)
```

HEXAGON is both a program and a new word that can be used in another program just like the kernel words REPEAT, FD, and RT are used. The program BEEHIVE uses the new word, HEXAGON, as well as the kernel words REPEAT, PU (pen up), PD (pen down), and RT.

```
TO BEEHIVE
  REPEAT 6 (PU FD40 PD HEXAGON PU RT 60)
```

Pascal handles subroutines in a different way. The programmer can define variables as local or global. As a result, local variables in a subroutine do not conflict with global variables used in other parts of the program. Also, in Pascal, programs are structured without line numbers so it is possible to insert subroutines without paying attention to possible conflicts in line numbers. Pascal programs are thus much easier to separate into subroutines and to build out of subroutines than are BASIC programs. This simplicity of separation facilitates what is called a structured program, a program whose structure allows it to be easily separated into discrete parts.

Forth treats subroutines much like Logo does, by adding new words to the language. But, it handles the passing of variables between words by putting them on a stack and taking them off a stack. A stack is like an old-fashioned spindle on which notes are placed. Forth does not need to provide a means for the program to tell the subroutine where it keeps variables or what they mean. It simply places the values on a stack and expects the next word in the program to use them in the order in which they come off, which is of course opposite to the order they were put on.

All languages are fundamentally similar. They allow the construction of more complex ideas out of simpler ones. The virtue of new languages like Logo, Forth, and Pascal is that they make this building process an easy one. Logo and Forth build new vocabularies. Pascal builds global procedures out of local procedures. Both kinds of languages allow variables to be easily passed between subroutines and the main programs. It is this process of construction that is the most significant programming idea to teach. Students should understand that programming is a process of building new blocks from simpler old ones. Blocks can be stacked vertically so that one block is used after another, or they can be grouped horizontally so the program can choose one block or another, or they can be nested so the program uses first one block then the block within that block, and so on.

If we look across the spectrum from the machine language to high-level languages to programs, we see a similar process of construction out of building blocks. A program is built of subroutines. Each subroutine is built of commands in a high-level language. Each command in the high-level language is a subroutine, a block of commands, in machine language, and finally each machine language command is a subroutine written into the CPU as a series of electronic signals.

Programmable Programs

An exciting new wrinkle has been added lately to programs, particularly those used in education. It is the programmability of the program itself. *Songwriter* and *Delta Drawing* not only allow the student to use the simple commands built into the program, but they also allow the student to build new commands out of these simple ones. These programs are thus programmable, extensible, and transformable by the student. They provide students with a new and simple language to work with and to program, a language designed for just one purpose, for example to write songs or to draw pictures. Students can then take such a language and program with it in new and exciting ways, in ways the developers may never have thought of.

We are likely to see more and more of this kind of program which itself is programmable. Instead of programs with built-in, inflexible menus and commands, future programs will incorporate flexible mini-languages that can be used to control and build on to the program. These programs will grow with students and become tools for them to use in constructing new ideas and new programs. This is the new direction in educational software. And this is not a futuristic vision: it is happening today.

Educators will, thus, soon have an increasingly broad selection of languages for students to use, everything from the large programming languages like Logo and Pascal to more specialized languages, like a problem-solving language with which students may develop their own problem-solving programs, to more narrowly specialized languages as in *Songwriter* which allow students to create very specific constructions in a narrow area. To take maximum advantage of this range of languages, students will need to have a basic understanding of the nature of programming as a construction process and the nature of languages as tools for such constructions. Although programming in each language is a specialized construction process, it is akin to all other such processes, including many that are purely mathematical. Thus, knowledge of programming may be gained by using large-scale languages like Logo or more limited programmable programs like *Delta Drawing*. The key is the underlying process of construction, not the details of the building blocks.

THE ELEMENTS OF LANGUAGES

All languages are made up of the same kinds of elements. These building blocks can be found in all computer languages and throughout the study of mathematics. Although we do not have the space here to look at the extent of these connections, the discipline of using a computer language can and should carry over to the use of mathematics language. Students should be encouraged to develop good work habits in mathematics just as they do in programming.

Languages are surprisingly similar when their skin is lifted off. Thus, programs in all languages are constructed in similar ways. To start with, all languages have elements that hold information, such as numbers, variables, strings, and matrices. In assembly languages, information is stored as, and is often viewed as, memory addresses. Some languages, like BASIC, handle each kind of information element as a distinctly different item. Thus, integers are followed by % signs and strings by $ signs, while matrices have their indices in parentheses. Each kind of element also often has its own commands. Other languages, like Pascal, are much more flexible, requiring the nature of each variable to be declared at the beginning of the program, but allowing them to be named in any way. Pascal also allows new elements to be constructed.

All languages also have ways of operating on these elements, ways of joining and separating them, comparing them, and shifting (transforming) them. In every language, students will encounter operations and a variety of elements to use them on.

Joining and Separating

The joining and separating commands are most familiar. They can be operators like $+, -, *, /$ for numbers, concatenation for strings, and logical operations for numbers or strings. These operations put two elements together or separate one element into two. Each of these operations has corresponding operations in mathematics that can be taught when teaching the language. For example, most BASIC interpreters include logical operators like NOT, AND, OR and relational operators $=, <, >$, which will return 0 or 1 depending upon the Boolean relationship. These provide a way to study mathematical logic in a way that students can actually apply and see reasons for.

Comparing

The comparing operations, IF...THEN and IF...THEN...ELSE, are common to many languages. To accomplish the same purposes, assembly languages use a combination of "compare" and "branch." Comparing commands change the direction of a program: "If the input is a certain letter, then perform the following"; "If the value of a variable is the same as another, then branch to a new place in the program". To do this, the computer needs to constantly test every outcome. This routine testing and comparing of outcomes is the kind of behavior that we would hope to instill in our mathematics students. We would like them to question the answers to the computations. "Is the answer in the right ballpark?" "Are the dimensions of the answer correct?" "What would I estimate that answer to be?" "What would happen if I did the following?" We would like them to see problem solving as a series of questions whose answers direct their next step. Programming provides students with a model for good mathematical problem-solving behavior.

Shifting

There are also a variety of shifting operations. Some shift the number at one address to another or from one variable to another. Others shift the numbers within a byte or within a string. But the most used form of shifting moves programs around. In BASIC, GOTO and GOSUB shift the program's operation to different locations in memory. In assembly language, JMP and JSR accomplish the same result. In Logo and Forth there is no need to "jump" around the program since the routines are sequenced simply by listing them by name or by procedure. But all languages have the shifting commands that call for a particular set of instructions to be repeated. In BASIC, FOR...NEXT repeats a set of instructions, Logo uses REPEAT, Forth has a DO...LOOP, and Pascal has FOR...DO and WHILE...DO.

Shifting is a very important aspect of mathematics as well as programming, and once again a teacher can join these two subjects together around a common theme. For example, the notion of a repetitive activity links addition to multiplication, subtraction to division, and multiplication to exponents. In mathematics we perform shifting activities all the time. When we regroup we shift, when we change from fractions to decimals we shift, and when we use number lines we shift.

One of the more interesting shifts in assembly language programming rotates the bits of a byte. On the 6502 microprocessor, this shift is called ROL and ROR, rotate left and rotate right. These shifts change the binary place value of the bits. Thus, ROL multiplies a number in a memory location by 2, and ROR divides it by 2. ROL, ROL multiplies by 4 (2 squared). Although these operations are carried out on binary place values, they work exactly the same way as shifts in decimal place values, except that instead of shifting by powers of 10 the computer shifts by powers of 2. Students could write a short assembly language program that stored a number in a memory location, rotated left the bits in that location, and then printed the number out. Such a program would give the powers of two of that number for as many rotations as the program specifies.

Surprising as it may seem, these three types of operations, joining and separating, comparing, and shifting are *all* the fundamental activities computers and their languages perform. There are, of course, additional higher levels of commands, but these are really just built upon these three building blocks. To understand programming languages and the essence of programming is to understand joining and separating, comparing, and shifting, each of which has significance and usefulness in teaching mathematics, and each of which provides ways of constructing cognitive ties between programming and learning mathematics.

THE ELEMENTS OF PROGRAMS— THE SIMPLE ROUTINES

Most of the other commands available in a language produce routines to accomplish special programming tasks. These may include printing on the screen, drawing a picture, saving information on the disk, or running the program. And these tasks are just the beginning. Most novices experience difficulty creating programs because they do not understand these and other constructions that are an integral aspect of programming. They have to think about and construct the entire program from scratch, re-inventing the wheel each time. They have no ready-made parts to bring to their task to make it less formidable.

Teachers can make it much easier for students to construct new programs by providing them with some of these parts, either as short programs or as ideas. Just as in building a house, it is useful to understand how walls are framed and roofs are constructed, so too is it helpful for students to understand how to use commands and simple routines, the building blocks of programs. Though a library of these simple routines are useful, a structure for breaking down programs is much more important. It gives students a sense of where to start and of the kinds of building blocks to construct.

Flowcharts are one way to break down programs into meaningful blocks, but they require the novice programmer not only to understand the building blocks, but also to define the sequence in which they will be used, even before the program is constructed. Like an outline for a story, it is often more useful to flowchart a program after it has been written and before it is rewritten.

Another way for students to break down programs, which may be more useful to them, is into functional sections: an output section, an input section, a filing section, and a calculation or do something section.

CONCLUSIONS

Programming and programming languages can be viewed as constructions based on very simple ideas. At each stage in the process we put together a new building block, fabricated from the smaller, simpler ideas of the previous stage. Thus, we build new languages and new words in these languages all ultimately from the elements the machine uses. We put together subroutines in each of these new languages from the commands in that language. Then, we combine these building blocks to fashion portions of programs. And finally, we join the programs themselves together. This process is not like using a child's set of blocks, for each time we create a new building block, it becomes a new entity with which to work and more importantly with which to think.

This view of programming provides students with a powerful image of how computers function, how their languages work, and how programs are put together. Armed with such an image, students need never master a programming language and teachers need never ask which programming language they should teach. Instead, students will program at whatever level of complexity seems appropriate and teachers will provide whichever programming tools are needed to facilitate this.

The Mathematics Teacher as Computer Sponsor

8

Mathematics teachers in secondary and elementary schools across the country have begun to recognize the vast potential of computers to address a range of teaching and learning needs in the K–12 mathematics curriculum. Not that computers are new to mathematics education, but in recent years educators have had access to a new generation of machines that make extensive computer interaction possible for more mathematics teachers and their students. Spurred on by the low cost and relative ease of use of microcomputers, more and more schools are buying and using computers of all kinds and sizes. This rapid influx of computers into schools creates special pressures on and special opportunities for mathematics teachers.

The pressures arise because computers are regarded by most people as mathematical machines. They expect mathematics teachers to know more about computers, to run school computer programs, to know which computers to buy, to teach programming, and to train their colleagues—in short, to be the school's computer sponsor.

Where some mathematics teachers welcome this role, others resist it. After all, why should any group of teachers be forced to act in a certain role, especially one based on popular misconceptions? In some ways, there is no more reason for mathematics teachers to be school computer sponsors than business teachers, vocational education teachers, social studies teachers with strong social science backgrounds, science teachers, English teachers

217

who have used word processors, administrators, secretarial staff, students with home computers, or parents or local citizens with computer experience. Nevertheless, the expectation is there, and mathematics teachers may wish to view it as an occasion to expand their educational skills and roles.

The opportunities for mathematics teachers arise because computers *are* mathematical machines; they are ideally suited to doing, learning, and teaching mathematics. Computers can provide mathematics teachers with the means to improve their teaching, to expand the scope of mathematics learned in schools, to transform the nature of the school mathematics curriculum, and perhaps ultimately to produce the first mathematically literate generation.

We hope in this book we have built your enthusiasm and started you thinking about your possible role in using computers for these goals. Let us conclude with some practical suggestions and cautions for you as a potential computer sponsor in your school. These suggestions are based on our own experiences and those of others we know about, such as the mathematics teachers who acted as computer sponsors in the following fictionalized case studies.

THREE COMPUTER SPONSORS

In 1964, a private high school in Connecticut became one of the first schools to purchase a computer. Bob Jaworski, a faculty member who had recently come to the school from the National Aeronautics and Space Administration, was convinced of the potential power of computers as pedagogical tools. The school gave him $20,000 to purchase a state-of-the-art minicomputer, two teletype terminals, a paper-tape reader, an assembler, and a FORTRAN compiler.

When the president of the computer company heard about the sale, he was so concerned about possible misuse of the computer he insisted a rider be included in the contract, giving the company the right to visit the school within 90 days of delivery to make sure everything was going well with the installation. If the company did not find things to its liking, it could cancel the sale. Company representatives visited the school within the first two months. After spending less than an hour in the computer room, they commented that, if they closed their eyes, they could imagine they were in their own shop.

The students at this school were initially introduced to computer programming through their introduction to physical science course. More advanced programming was part of the mathematics curriculum. The geometry teacher took time out of his geometry course to teach FORTRAN, adding assembly language for those students ready for an advanced topic. In those days it took four minutes to read the FORTRAN compiler into the computer memory. This process usually had to be repeated two or three times before the compiler was read without error. Doing this in the morning allowed the students to run their programs in the afternoon. Within two years, Bob left the school to join the computer company as an educational consultant, touring the area to show other teachers what they could do with computers.

* * * * *

Another teacher/computer sponsor went on to become the K–9 director of curriculum and technology for his school system. Once again leadership for introducing computers into the school was provided by a mathematics teacher, Sam Marx, who purchased his own personal computer and experimented with it in his junior high school mathematics classes. As Marx learned more about computers through this very practical experiential approach, he began collecting, modifying, and even developing software.

Marx introduced computers to his colleagues on an informal basis in his free time. As the computer bandwagon picked up speed, the school system established a committee to determine school policy. Because he had the most experience with microcomputers, the committee turned to Marx for leadership. They decided that the junior high school was the most appropriate level to introduce computers system-wide; that was where Marx had experience.

Under Marx's leadership, the committee decided to create a curriculum for a three-week junior high school "computer literacy" unit that would introduce BASIC to every seventh-grader in the city as part of the mathematics curriculum, and to establish a six-week, advanced BASIC unit for eighth-graders that would serve as the prerequisite for the high school first-term BASIC course. They also made plans to introduce all junior high school mathematics teachers to teaching these units, and created a new position of computer specialist to implement this program. Naturally, Sam Marx was hired to fill the position.

These plans were approved by all the appropriate persons. The school committee was pleased that one of the lower-priced computers had been chosen, not a great deal of equipment requested, and the plan modest, but that each part of the city—as represented by each junior high school—

would receive an equal share of equipment. The junior high school mathematics coordinator was relieved to have the responsibility taken over by Marx. The senior high school mathematics department which had been using a larger, timesharing computer to teach some students programming felt the junior high school units would make their job easier and require few changes in their curriculum.

All seemed well, but when the plans were circulated, several elementary school teachers asked the committee for guidance and support in introducing computers into their schools. The computer curriculum committee told them to wait: there was only enough money to purchase equipment for the junior high program, which the committee felt was equitable since it would introduce every student in the district to computers in the seventh grade.

This memo did not sit well with some people at the elementary level. Like Marx, elementary teachers who had purchased their own computers had begun experimenting with their students. Parent-Teacher Associations had given schools computers, and parents had volunteered to help with the process. However, the elementary school people had to wait for official sanction and financial support until the committee felt comfortable with the success of the junior high school program. After three years of implementing seventh- and eighth-grade programs, the committee decided to include the elementary schools. Marx became Director of Curriculum and Technology, K–9, officially assuming the leadership position he had taken since the beginning.

$$* \quad * \quad * \quad * \quad *$$

In 1965, Ray Walters, another mathematics teacher, this time from a medium-sized suburban public high school, wrote a grant proposal allowing a consortium of high schools in the school district to buy and timeshare a DEC PDP-8. For the previous few years, he had taught programming to his mathematics classes, bringing his students to local industrial and municipal computer sites to run their programs on donated time. With the jointly owned computer, Walters integrated programming into several high school mathematics courses.

In 1967, the district superintendent of schools realized that the central administration could benefit from computer support. He gave Walters funds to hire a programmer and clerk to carry out administrative tasks on the PDP-8. By 1970, with accountability (and the attendant record-keeping) as the primary educational issue, administrative use of the computer became much greater. In 1975, with Individual Education Plans now required for all special needs students, the district developed a management information system under a state Department of Education grant for its new DEC PDP-11.

By 1978, town parents had become interested in seeing computers integrated into instruction. Elementary school students were bused to the high school to use its computer. All instructional use was in the mathematics resource area. Soon, however, terminals began turning up everywhere, including at the elementary and junior high schools. With the computer power available between the PDP-8 and PDP-11, parents were encouraged to work with the teachers. However, the resulting activities were unstructured and generally unrelated to the curriculum. Further, students were pulled out of their classes to go down the hall to use the computer and parents began to object to the disruption this caused. It became clear that a computer resource person was needed to study, plan, and coordinate activities in the school system. However, Walters was not interested in moving out of the mathematics classroom into this role, and did not apply for the new position.

The town hired a computer resource person in 1979 to organize computer use in the school system. Her task has been primarily to remove the computer curriculum from the mathematics department and set up a new curriculum area called computer literacy, scheduled for full implementation by 1985. This new structure will put librarians in charge of the computer curriculum in the elementary schools, using Logo as the computer language taught. At the junior high school level, BASIC will gradually be replaced by Pascal as the language taught. A full computer science department, including courses in machine level language, software systems, and computer electronics is planned for the high school. Parallel to these plans is the integration of computers into all aspects of the curriculum K–12 with the computer resource person being responsible for supervising and training all faculty in educational computing.

These case histories show three different ways in which mathematics teachers have become computer sponsors. The first computer sponsor left education and went to work for industry, a scenario repeated all too often. The second mathematics teacher assumed a leadership position in his school system, moving up to director of curriculum and technology. The third computer sponsor chose to continue his career as a secondary mathematics teacher, allowing the leadership role to be assumed by someone else.

BACKGROUND AND TRAINING
OF A COMPUTER SPONSOR

Your first responsibility as a potential computer sponsor is your own education. Often taking a leadership role is not a conscious decision, but a gradual move made by a person who has slowly built up a level of confidence and expertise with computers. As the second case history illustrates, such persons have more and more opportunities to move into leadership positions because of their knowledge and experience. As a potential leader of educational computing in your school, you should be prepared to spend a good bit of time—perhaps as many as one thousand hours—studying (the equivalent of a graduate degree program). However, people with strong mathematics or science backgrounds can prepare themselves for leadership with fewer courses and/or by working closely with a computer professional. About half of this time might be in formal classes and workshops, and half might be spent working independently.

Degree programs designed for using computers in education are beginning to appear with almost daily frequency (see the Resource Section of the *Practical Guide to Computers in Education*). Alternatively, people with mathematics or science undergraduate degrees probably could qualify for a computer science graduate program. Although, unfortunately, often people who complete such degrees are lured away from teaching by the financial rewards of working for industry.

After completing some variation of an advanced program of study in educational computing, a person assuming a leadership position should:

- Be familiar with three or four computer languages and feel comfortable programming in at least one.
- Be able to act as a consultant to administrators and teachers on administrative applications of computers.
- Be familiar with instructional applications of computers in all discipline areas.
- Understand computer hardware so as to interpret manuals for others and act as a consultant for decisions about such activities as networking and peripheral interfacing.
- Be familiar with the state-of-the-art technology as well as computer-related social issues such as employment patterns and ethical behavior.

- Be prepared to take an active role with others in planning the integration of computers into the curriculum, K–12.
- Contribute significantly to the education of the rest of the school staff.

STAFF DEVELOPMENT

Creating an Interest

To create an interest in educational computing, you, the computer sponsor, might begin by offering colleagues workshops of various kinds. You might decide, for example, that the best introduction to computers is to teach some simple programming. Teachers could then use the machine as a true tool, making it do what they want it to do. The highly accessible graphics capability of Logo makes it an excellent language for first-time computer users. People begin programming in the first few minutes and can explore Logo with the support of a resource person for some time before encountering any conceptually difficult material. If Logo is not available for your machine, a version of BASIC or PILOT with graphics capabilities is a reasonable substitute.

A second approach to introducing computers, if you decide programming is an inappropriate activity for your teaching staff, could be to show the computer's power as a general purpose machine. You might run a series of sessions demonstrating the computer's capabilities for word processing, record keeping, report generating, data entry and retrieval, and laboratory data gathering. (See the Resources Section of this book for software suggestions.)

Finally, a very low-key non-threatening approach to interest other teachers is simply showing them how computers can make their teaching jobs easier. You can focus either on the teachers' specific disciplines or on their students' age level. Introduce them to the best available commercial software, software they could use in their classes the next day. These could include drill and practice routines, tutorials, games, and simulations. Focus discussions on evaluating the software to insure that your colleagues become critical consumers.

When starting such staff development, you need to remember that some staff members are likely to express their lack of interest in quantitative activities. Some may even demonstrate a fear of math or a distrust of machines. Don't give up on these people. Everyone can learn meaningful and exciting ways to use computers. Start slowly and give them a great deal of support. Perhaps you can have a student demonstration to show them how easy the computer is to use. Or you might have teachers and students learn together.

Reading lists can also provide background and can help teachers consider important issues such as:

- Equity of access to technology in schools and society: poor versus rich, male versus female, science versus humanities.
- Societal concerns about computers and technology, such as privacy and the restructuring of traditional lifestyles, including the relationship of school and home.
- Educational issues: the potential danger of students believing computers do not make mistakes; implications for restructuring classroom management; the difficulties in introducing students to vocational possibilities when the job market sixteen, ten, or four years hence will be so different; defining and implementing computer literacy.

Educating Your Colleagues

Once you have created an interest among your colleagues, you should provide them opportunities to increase their expertise. Not everyone will want or need to acquire as much expertise about computers as you have, in your role as computer leader. You and your colleagues could establish a reasonable minimum as an appropriate overall goal. Branching off from this minimum, people can pursue a variety of directions, applications, and areas of expertise. As the resources become available to your school, reasonable goals for educators K–12 might be:

- An ability to use word processing.
- An ability to query a data base, especially one that contains information about your school system and community. (For example, when a teacher needs junior high school science books that discuss earthquakes, and the school system has created a data base containing this information, the teacher should be able to query it and find, in seconds, the whereabouts of these books.)

- A familiarity with the software available for a given discipline or student age group. This implies that every member of the teaching staff should be involved in evaluating software for purchase by reading software reviews, directory descriptions, and promotional copy and, whenever possible, by testing out actual software sent on approval.
- An ability to use a computer to keep class records, if that is a goal of the teacher and school.
- An ability to help students use computers.

At this time, few schools have the computer resources necessary to allow all staff members to pursue on site the goals listed above. However, many schools are making rapid strides toward having an environment in which teachers are developing such a level of computer literacy.

As computer sponsor, you can help build such an environment by skimming as much of the relevant literature on educational computing as possible and dispensing it to others as appropriate. Suggest books, journals, and software that faculty might wish to look at more closely. (See Resources Section of this book.) Insure that general interest journals are available in common meeting areas, such as the teachers' room. Circulate articles of special interest. Tell people about new hardware and software, and arrange demonstrations. In addition, you might prepare and distribute a monthly one- or two-page newsletter on computers-in-education related developments.

Finally, there are numerous opportunities for teachers to learn about computing in more formal settings.

- In-service courses sponsored by the school system.
- Adult education, available in the community.
- College courses, for credit offered at local universities.

CREATING AND MAINTAINING A COMPUTER RESOURCE CENTER

One of the most important roles of the computer sponsor is to assist in the development and maintenance of a computer resource center. Each school needs one location for its software collection, computer-related books and magazines, and computer supplies such as disks and paper for the printers. This room might, in addition, house all or most of the computer hardware, in which case there must be some supervision, whether by adults or peers. To provide the greatest amount of access to the most members of the school community, the hours the computer resource center is open should be similar to those of the library, and it should be located in the general stream of school traffic. (See *Practical Guide to Computers in Education*, Chapter 7.)

Purchasing Hardware

As a minimum, you will need one computer system which would be composed of:

- A central processing unit (CPU) and the **logic** and **memory units**.
- A device for storing information, such as a **disk drive**.
- **Input and output (I/O) devices** for sending information into the computer and/or receiving information. Such devices include **keyboards**, **printers**, and **monitors**.

In addition to this minimum hardware, you can use many other **peripheral devices** to expand the computer's educational applications. These include **voice** and **music synthesizers**, robots such as a mechanical turtle, **light pens**, and **graphics tablets**. (See *Practical Guide to Computers in Education*, Chapter 3.)

To determine what you should purchase, ask yourself and your colleagues what you want to do with the computer immediately and in the next few years. Ask yourselves who will use the hardware and for what:

- The resource room teacher with special needs students?
- Mathematics teachers for mathematics applications?
- A computer teacher to teach programming?
- The English Department for word processing?
- The Social Studies Department for simulations?

If you have no computer experience, start small to keep your mistakes small. After you gain experience and have time to learn more, you can make longer-range, more ambitious plans.

Besides taking into account hardware requirements for the school system in general (as discussed in the *Practical Guide*, Chapter 4), consider the graphics capability of the machine, the relative speed of computation, and the number and ease of attaching peripherals capable of a variety of data gathering tasks. For example, you can construct light- and heat-sensing devices and attach them to a computer chip which can then be plugged into a game paddle—an inexpensive project. With these devices and a few lines of BASIC programming, students can observe data from a variety of experiments relating to light and heat and can analyze them effortlessly. This type of activity can be as simple or sophisticated as is appropriate for the students.

Other hardware concerns involve the quality of the output on the monitor and the printer. Is color output crucial for your uses? What quality **hard copy** will you need? Do you need to generate hard copies of graphics such as those discussed in Chapter 4? This is often both a hardware and a software question.

Purchasing Software

As you determine what you want to do with the computer, you will find that software is as important, if not more, than hardware. Software can be grouped into three general types:

1. **Applications software:** programs that allow the computer to do a particular task, such as word processing or drill and practice.
2. **Systems software:** programs necessary to use the computer at all. Most important is the operating system which, among other tasks, allows the user to move data between disk and memory.
3. Computer languages: the means by which the user communicates with computers. As discussed in Chapter 7, lower level languages are closer to the signals that the machine understands while high-level languages are closer to what people understand. High-level languages, of which there are hundreds, have different purposes. APL (A Programming Language) is better for solving mathematics problems than DYNAMO (DYNAmic MOdels), which is better for developing simulation models. FORTRAN (FORmula TRANslator) is better for solving science problems. BASIC (Beginners All-purpose Symbolic Instruction Code) is a general purpose language.

Sometimes the line between applications software and a computer language is not obvious. For example, *VisiCalc*, a business applications program, is successful because it has the characteristics of a computer language. On the other hand, DYNAMO, a simulation "language," is actually a program written in another language. For the Apple II, DYNAMO is written in Pascal, while for other machines it may be written in FORTRAN or ALGOL.

Budget as much for your software purchases as for your hardware. Shop for both together—they are not independent purchases. The *Practical Guide to Computers in Education* provides a planning sheet for these purchases in its Appendix.

Evaluate all software before purchasing it. Try it and make sure it does the task you expect it to do in an appropriate way. Read through the manuals that accompany the software. Are they understandable? Do they appear to be thorough? You will not be able to answer these questions completely until you have used the software for some time, but you should begin the evaluation process before purchasing anything.

Special mathematics software concerns center first around language requirements. The version of BASIC on the machine you are considering should be mathematics-oriented. It should have available floating point computation and mathematical functions such as logs, sines, and shape tables. Next you should consider mathematics-oriented languages and software that run on the machine you are considering: *TK!Solver*, DYNAMO, FORTRAN, or Logo, for example. One of the languages should have high resolution graphics capabilities if you are going to need them, and software tools that make manipulating graphics easier. (See the Resources Section of this book.)

Maintenance

When dealing with a number of machines, you must assume that they will need regular maintenance. So that this task does not become a burden, you can follow guidelines such as those in Chapter 7 of the *Practical Guide to Computers in Education*. Here are the key points:

- Identify a close, reliable repair shop.
- Consider the benefits of negotiating, in advance, a yearly maintenance contract for your machines, figuring 10 to 12 percent of the cost of your hardware, including the replacement of parts.
- If you cannot get 24-hour service, buy at least one extra of everything so you can replace the part that needs repair.

- Provide the best possible physical environment for the machines: a dust-free (including chalk dust) and well-ventilated room with a minimum of static electricity (no carpets or plastic chairs).
- Learn to do some maintenance, such as disk drive cleaning, peripheral connection cleaning, changing broken switches, and pushing down chips.
- Make sure users know how to use the machines and handle disks. Insist on proper storage and order of materials in the computer room.
- Back up all software, if possible. Rotate your backup copies so that you know you always have a working piece of software. Throw out bad disks: don't try to stretch the life of your disks.

Security issues go hand-in-hand with maintenance. In a national survey done for the *Computers in Education Series*, inner-city schools and new computer users voiced the most concern about security. If this issue is important to your school, you can easily lock computer cases, bolt them to tables, and lock them in the computer room when supervision is not available. However, as personal computers are becoming more common, many schools are allowing staff and students to take computers home overnight and over weekends and vacations.

CURRICULUM PLANNING AND DEVELOPMENT

At some point soon, your school system will need to do some K–12 planning for computer infusion into the curriculum. Some administrators may insist that this be done before any computers are purchased or used with students. However, the chances are that for most school systems K–12 planning will follow a period of less systematic infusion carried out by innovative individuals in a few schools. In either case you, as computer sponsor, will need to be centrally involved.

Integration of Computers into the Curriculum

Every curriculum area will be impacted by computers. Some, like mathematics, will change more quickly than others. As you gain experience integrating computers into your teaching, you will be in a strong position to help your colleagues do the same. Remember, no one likes to be told what to do. The more your peers feel ownership of curriculum revision ideas, the more they will accept and implement changes.

One school system established a procedure for encouraging teachers to share their curriculum development efforts and experience. Teachers with reasonable proposals for integrating computers into their curriculum were the first to be given computer equipment to use with their classes, with the provision that they would:

1. Allow their project to be evaluated by another person;
2. Agree to revise their project should the evaluation suggest change is needed; and
3. Teach another teacher how they used computers, should their project be a success.

Either prior to or after the computer integration process has been underway for awhile, your school system will need to do some systematic long-term planning. The distribution of currently limited resources and the direction of future purchases both require decisions to be made about how computers will be used throughout the school system. One planning approach is to devise a gradual implementation plan such as the following:

WESTON (MA) TWO YEAR PLAN

By September 15, 1981	Summer workshop members meet with their respective cabinets to discuss workshop report and seek endorsement of computer education goals.
By October 1, 1981	Report presented and discussed at faculty meetings.
By October 15, 1981	Curriculum Council discusses report and endorses computer education goals.
By November 1, 1981	Report presented to School Committee along with Superintendent's recommendations for its implementation.
By November 15, 1981	Standing Committee on Computers formed. (We recommend composition of one high school student, one middle school student, one teacher from each building, one elementary principal, the Computer Coordinator and the Assistant Superintendent for Curriculum.)
October, 1981	Invite consultant to demonstrate the use of computers in the classroom.

December, 1981	Begin pilot programs using existing resources (co-ordinated by Standing Committee on Computers).
Spring, 1982	Offer computer literacy course for teachers and administrators.
March, 1982	Devote 50 percent of Workshop Day to integration of computers into the curriculum.
April, 1982	Conduct "swapshop" for sharing results of pilot programs.
Summer, 1982	Evaluate results of computer integration efforts during 1981–82.
Summer, 1982	Offer workshop on curriculum development in a specific discipline(s) with a view toward computer applications.
September, 1982	Introduction of ten-week computer module in high school mathematics department (requires expansion of computer facilities).
September, 1982	Devote 50 percent of Workshop Day to presentation of first year's results and development of strategies for the future.
September, 1982	Expansion of Computer Coordinator's role to permit K–12 support to teachers and students.
September, 1982	Begin new pilot programs (assumes expanded computer capability).
Fall, 1982	Offer computer literacy course for teachers.
Summer, 1983	Evaluate results of 1982–83 computer integration efforts to establish (a) where we are and (b) where we go.

A K–12 Computer Curriculum

One of the tenets of our democracy is the right of all citizens to an education that will enable them to support themselves as adults. In this day and age, such an education must include exposure to, knowledge of, and skills with computers. Your school system will need to consider the competencies you intend students to have before they graduate. These might include the following:

• A useable level of skills in one programming language.

- The ability to use a variety of computer tools such as word processing, financial packages, data entry and retrieval software, music synthesizers, and graphics packages.
- A basic knowledge of how a computer works, including computer mathematics, logic, and electronics.
- The ability to engage in problem-solving activities, drawing on the computer as an aid, when appropriate.
- Experience with using at least two kinds of computers.
- Feeling comfortable in a high technology environment and understanding the potential of technology for raising the quality of life.
- Being aware of and concerned about the social and moral issues relating to science and society.

Students headed for careers in computer science, engineering, mathematics, or other sciences might need to attain additional competencies at the pre-college level besides these minimums.

In order for students to attain competencies such as these, you and your colleagues will need to provide them with a wide range of appropriate experiences with computers. This means deciding when, where, and how computers will be used in the curriculum. As computer sponsor, you should play a major role in making these decisions, along with appropriate administrators, faculty, and local citizens. Other resources you might be wise to consult are the computer science and education departments of local universities and local computer industry representatives.

Fig. 8.1 shows one way to conceptualize and present a K–12 computer curriculum. It lists the ways computers might be used (programming, tools, and CAI) and topics to be discussed (computer science and other), indicating a range of grade levels over which this might be most appropriate.

MAKING AND BREAKING IMAGES

Ultimately, your most important role as computer sponsor may be making and breaking images. Image-breaking was one of the reasons the school system in the third case history at the beginning of this chapter hired as the computer resource person a woman whose educational experience was teaching high school English. The computer as a mathematics machine

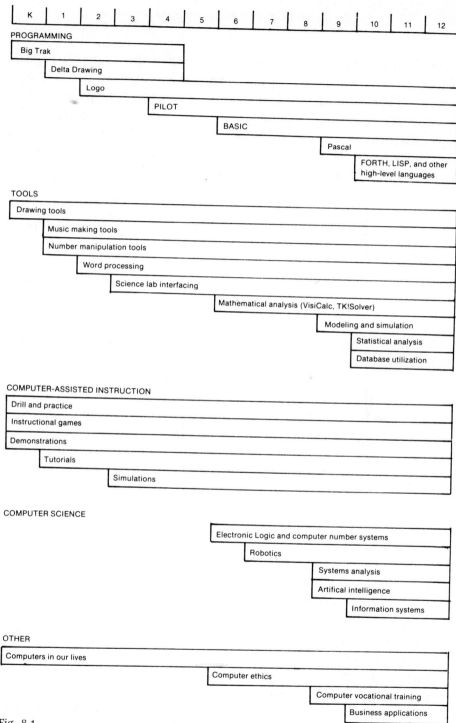

Fig. 8.1

233

dominated by male computer enthusiasts is a common stereotype. The advent of personal computers is changing this, but there is still a long way to go before computers lose their male mystique. The educator with a leadership role in computing should work to change such restrictive and even negative images. Here are some suggested image-making and breaking dos and don'ts, gathered over the past few years from teachers who have taken leadership roles in their schools.

DO	*DON'T*
• Introduce programming as a general-purpose tool (e.g., write a program that generates musical tunes).	• Give programming assignments that presuppose an understanding of or fascination with mathematics (e.g., write a program to generate the fibonacci number series).
• Place the machines in shared areas of the school such as the library.	• Place the computer in the mathematics lab or basement of the school.
• Provide enough variety in the software so that everyone can find a useful program.	• Limit the software to programs for the gifted or for remediation of basic skills.
• Encourage everyone to use the computers (teachers, students, staff, administrators).	• Require students to take a programming course before they may have unlimited access to the computers.
• Have adult supervision for reasonable amounts of time each day to insure equity of access.	• Let boys exclude girls or computer experts exclude beginners.
• Set up firm rules as to handling of equipment, order of room, sharing of software.	• Allow illegal copying of software and misuse of hardware.
• Encourage teamwork on student program development.	• Exaggerate privacy issues, such as privacy of files.
• Start an introductory programming course with no prerequisite.	• Require one year of algebra or the equivalent as a prerequisite for an introductory programming course.

- Include all staff in supervising the computer facility and ordering hardware, software, and related literature.

- Designate the computer facility as the responsibility of the mathematics or science department.

POST SCRIPT

In Chapter 1 we presented a futuristic vignette to illustrate the challenging possibilities computers offer for teaching and learning mathematics. We end the book with a more modest vignette, based on actual cases of what is being done today with limited resources by novice computer sponsors.

Gloria Finn, an eighth-grade mathematics teacher at Elm Street Middle-High School, was just completing the first year of her masters program in computer education at the nearby state college. She had twelve credits under her belt: introduction to computers in education, BASIC programming, computers in the elementary mathematics curriculum, and Pascal for educators. Gloria certainly didn't think of herself as a computer expert, particularly not after the Pascal course, which she found quite difficult. So it was with apprehension that she accepted her principal's request that she be the computer coordinator for the middle school's fledgling computer program. At the same time, the prospect of doing so excited her tremendously. Gloria had definite ideas about what computers should be used for in education and what they shouldn't be used for. This would give her the opportunity to put her ideas into practice.

Gloria's first task was to purchase equipment and supplies, using the $7,000 grant the school had received through state funding for the handicapped. She had virtually free reign in deciding what to buy. No one else in the middle school knew a thing about computers, and few of them seemed to care. After consulting with the high school computer coordinator and her faculty advisor, Gloria decided to purchase machines capable of using Logo, the "child-appropriate" programming language that had so impressed her in her course in computers in the elementary mathematics curriculum. For software, having decided to limit activities in this first year to programming, she ordered only Logo in addition to the BASIC that came with the machines.

Gloria knew parents and some teachers would pressure her to order drill and practice programs to reinforce basic skills, but she was determined to resist these pressures. With her limited budget, she had to make choices that reflected the priorities she and the principal had agreed upon: handicapped students first, since the grant was intended to help them; gifted and talented students next, as a political maneuver to assuage parents who had been clamoring for a gifted and talented program in the school; and finally, students experiencing motivational or learning problems because Gloria wanted to demonstrate to her colleagues and to parents that Logo and other "open" computer activities were more appropriate uses of the computer and more effective than drill and practice. After two months, however, Gloria partially relented and bought a few mathematics learning games like *Darts*, *Buggy*, and *Lemonade*, which she felt helped teach skills in a more effective way than drill and practice programs.

That first year was an exciting one, with plenty of ups and downs. Once, two of the three computers were down—inoperative—for three weeks. But when the computers were up and running—which was most of the time—the spirits and accomplishments of the children who used them were up as well. Three stories from that first year exemplify how each of the school's priorities was served.

Mathophobic

Howie hated school. He much preferred watching TV, or even reading a book at home in his room, to sitting in class studying, especially mathematics. Unfortunately this attitude was getting him into big trouble. His grades were poor, his teachers frustrated, his parents angry, and he was bored out of his mind. Lucky for Howie, his eighth-grade mathematics teacher, Laura Jones, recognized mathophobia when she saw it—she'd been mathophobic herself in elementary school. Also, luckily, Laura had an idea, and the school had the resources to help Howie overcome his fear and loathing of mathematics.

One day, she suggested to Howie that, rather than sit in class doodling and squirming, he go to the computer lab and play the mathematics fractions game, *Darts*, which he could get from Mrs. Finn. Howie was only too glad to get out of class, but his real excitement came when he played the game. He got very good at it, which meant, as he realized, that he did know how to do fractions. The period was over before he knew it. The next day he asked Ms. Jones if he could play *Darts* again. She said, "Yes, but first let's work out a deal. I'll let you work on the computer two days a week—Tuesday and Friday—provided you complete your regular mathematics work for the previous week by Monday." Howie was dubious about this condition, but said he'd give it a try.

After a month, the deal was a solid success. With the computer, Howie soon moved far beyond playing *Darts*. First he tried other educational games—no arcade games were allowed in Mrs. Finn's computer lab. He found most of the mathematics games captivating and educational. He realized he was learning mathematics and was actually proud of it! Soon he became interested in how these games worked. He wanted to modify some of them and even create his own. So, with the help of one of the high school students who helped Mrs. Finn run the middle school computer program, he learned a variety of BASIC computer commands and was soon creating his own simple games.

The more Howie worked on the computer, the more mathematics he realized he needed to know. This recognition provided him with an even stronger motive for learning mathematics than the deal he and Ms. Jones had made. Howie's performance in mathematics class began to improve dramatically. There were even days when he skipped working on the computer because he didn't want to miss an important discussion in class. When Ms. Jones teased him about this, Howie explained simply, "I can always work by myself on the computer after school, but class discussion helps me understand how me and the other kids think about math problems. I can't do that by myself." Howie and Ms. Jones grinned at each other, two former mathophobes, exploring mathematics through the computer.

Gifted and Talented

Karen loved mathematics. She enjoyed working problems, and more importantly, she had a drive to understand mathematical concepts. She saw mathematics as beautiful in a concrete, visual sense and in its most abstract forms. Karen was also very good at mathematics. Her ability to perceive and appreciate its rhythms allowed her to attain a very high level of competence in a short period of time. Topics that her classmates labored over for frustrating weeks were often grasped by Karen in a few minutes. This sometimes caused friction between her and her friends. Being a girl made it worse, a lot of the sophomore guys viewed her as a "brain," not a prospective date.

Karen's algebra II teacher, Bill Finch, recognized Karen's gift for mathematics and worried that she might become bored with the pace at which he taught even his advanced course. He suggested to Karen that she stop coming to class and instead work at her own rapid pace through some more challenging materials. In addition, Mr. Finch proposed that Karen learn how to program on one of the middle school microcomputers and then on the high school's minicomputer. Karen liked both of these ideas and began at once.

Within a very short period of time, Karen had mastered BASIC on the micros and had gone on to learn Pascal on the high school system. Karen was soon writing programs that allowed her and other students to explore a variety of mathematical concepts, and she taught a number of her appreciative classmates how to use the computer to assist them with their schoolwork. In the computer, Karen had found an almost limitless mathematical world to explore and a way of converting her mathematical aptitude from a social liability to a social advantage.

Handicapped

Willy and Jake had both been diagnosed as being hearing-impaired at an early age. Since entering school six years before, they had taken all of their academic subjects in special classes. Frank Renaldi, the special education consultant, felt that Willy might eventually be able to be fully mainstreamed—his hearing wasn't totally gone and he seemed to be quite bright. But Jake was another story. He was totally deaf and tested out as borderline mentally retarded. He learned sign language slowly and seemed incapable of reading lips. Dr. Renaldi felt that Jake was unlikely to learn much in school or lead a functional life.

In October of their sixth-grade year, Willy and Jake began to spend third period in Gloria Finn's "computer lab," a small conference room adjoining and visible from her classroom. Third period was one of five periods in which Gloria did not have a class; she taught only three classes to allow her to spend time with students on the computers. Gloria had read Frank Renaldi's reports on Willy and Jake, but, with no special education training, she didn't know where to start with them. Her college program advisor suggested that she just show them the few basic Logo turtle graphics commands and let them play.

The first time Willy and Jake entered the little computer lab Gloria's heart sank. She started to speak to them, but the sound of her voice struck her as terribly loud next to the silence of these two shy boys. Unused to working with handicapped children, Gloria forced back her tears, beckoned to the boys to approach one of the computers, and began showing them how to turn it on, how to load the Logo disk, and how to type in several simple commands which caused the turtle to move on the screen. When she was done, she turned the machine off and indicated to Willy that he should do what she had done. To Gloria's surprise, when Willy hesitated Jake sat down in front of the computer, regarded it sternly, and quickly replicated Gloria's actions. Then, almost before Gloria knew what was happening, Jake began typing in a series of commands to the Logo turtle on the screen. He was making it dance! Willy looked on in fascination, while Gloria watched in utter surprise. At the end of twenty minutes Jake looked up from the screen, a broad smile on his face. Gloria had tears in her eyes for a second time.

As the weeks went on, Jake continued to explore the world of Logo, mastering more commands and creating a whole catalogue of his own programs. Willy was pretty good with Logo, as well, but not as good as Jake. Dr. Renaldi came in to observe the boys at work on the computers. He was astounded, and he had to admit that his diagnosis and prognosis for Jake had been totally wrong. Far from being retarded, Jake was obviously a very bright youngster. Logo had provided him with a means for using his keen mind and curiosity. Previously his parents and school people had focused exclusively on teaching him to communicate in terms of basic needs: eating, sleeping, going to the bathroom, responding to requests or orders. They hadn't realized that to Jake such matters were of little importance compared with his urge to problem solve. Unfortunately, their well-meaning efforts had caused Jake to turn inward where his mind could roam freely, giving them the impression that he was retarded. For Jake, Logo became a bridge to the outside world, one over which his mind travelled swiftly and with great power.

Glossary

Accumulator or "A" register A temporary memory location used for all arithmetic and logical functions.

Address or memory address The location of a computer word in the computer's memory, or the location of a record on a disk storage medium.

Alphanumeric characters All the different symbols the computer can represent: letters, numerals, and punctuation marks.

Applications software See Software.

ASCII characters The American Standard Code for Information Interchange, an acronym pronounced "as-key," a binary code using 8 bits to represent 128 text and control characters.

Assembler A primitive language translator that facilitates instructions to the central processing unit.

Assembly language See Assembler. A language made up of three-letter mnemonics rather than numbers.

Bit Acronym for *binary digit*. The smallest unit of digital information.

Bug An error in a computer program. The process of eliminating such program errors is known as *debugging*.

Byte The number of *bits* required to store one character of text. A byte is most commonly, but not always, made up of 8 bits in various combinations of 0s and 1s that represent text and control characters in computer code. The smallest addressable unit of a computer.

Central processing unit (CPU) The "brains" of a computer. The CPU controls what the computer does. It contains the circuits that interpret and execute instructions.

Computer assisted instruction (CAI) Sometimes called computer aided instruction. Originally applied only to computerized tutorials, now also refers to any instructional application of computers. Used here to mean computer applications applied to traditional teaching methods such as drill, tutorial, demonstration, simulation, and instructional games.

Computer managed instruction (CMI) Primarily classroom management systems that use computers to help teachers organize and manage teaching and record-keeping for classes.

Courseware Educational *software*, usually accompanied by a range of ancillary materials.

Digital computer A computer that works with numbers, usually expressed in binary form. Operations are carried out in discrete steps, in contrast with a continuous solution as performed by an analog computer.

Disk drive or **magnetic disk drives** See Hard disk drive and Floppy disk drive.

Disk operating system (DOS) An operating system for a disk drive. See operating system.

Extensible Computer languages which can be extended by the use by adding new words or commands.

Flip-flop A computer circuit that can be in one of two states. The mechanism that allows a computer to "remember." The circuit remains in one state until a new signal is passed through it.

Floppy disk drive A peripheral device for storing programs or other information on disks made of a thin flexible plastic with a magnetic recording surface (called a floppy disk or diskette). Floppies are more reliable than simple audio tape, but hold less information and operate more slowly than hard disks.

Graphics tablet A computer peripheral that allows the user to input data, generally pictures, directly on a writing surface.

Hard copy A copy of computer printout printed on paper; e.g., a listing of a program or printout of text.

Hard disk drive A peripheral device for storing programs or other information on disks made of rigid aluminum, coated with a magnetic recording surface (called hard disks). The most common form of storage on large computer systems due to the large amount of information hard disks can hold, the speeds at which the disk drives operate, the ease at which information can be accessed, and their reliability.

Hexadecimal A number system with a base 16.

High bit See Most significant digit.

High-level languages Languages such as FORTRAN, BASIC, COBOL, Logo, APL, and others that use English-like commands instead of commands in machine code to communicate with the central processing unit. Typically, one high-level language statement is equal to several machine-level instructions.

High order byte The byte that is most significant in determining the size of the number.

Indexing A programmer's word meaning keeping count. A procedure that enables the computer to add or subtract a constant amount over and over again.

Input device   A peripheral device allowing the user to enter information into the computer (e.g., a keyboard).

Input/output (I/O) device   Peripheral devices that have both input and output components (e.g., video terminal).

Iteration   Repetition of one set of instructions, often with changed variable values in each iteration.

Keyboard   A set of keys, similar to typewriter keys, used to input information to a computer.

Least significant bit (LSB)   The bit that is least important in determining the size of a binary number.

Light pen   A computer peripheral that allows the user to input information by positioning a wand on the computer screen.

Loading   Entering information into memory locations or registers of the computer. The assembly language word "load" means specifically to put some information into a register.

Logic unit   One of the parts of the central processing unit.

Low bit   See Least significant bit.

Low order byte   The byte that is least significant in determining the size of a binary number.

Machine language   The lowest level language of the computer. The "native" language of the central processing unit, coded in hexadecimal or octal number systems, depending on the CPU.

Mainframe   A category of computer, determined to some extent by size, usually occupying a significant part of a room. Mainframes generally have more capabilities than micros of minicomputers, such as greater speed and a larger memory.

Memory   (Also called main memory, core memory, or main storage.) The integrated circuits of a computer in which information is stored that is directly accessible to the CPU, as opposed to peripheral storage, which is accessible only via interfaces. See Random access memory (RAM) and Read only memory (ROM).

Memory addresses   See Addresses.

Memory locations   A piece of memory that holds one word of information.

Memory unit   That portion of the computer consisting of a collection of randomly addressable memory locations.

MOD arithmetic   Modular arithmetic. An arithmetic number system that focuses on the remainder in a number problem.

Monitor   Otherwise known as a cathode ray tube (CRT) or video display unit, a monitor is an output device that is essentially a TV screen, although it generally has much finer resolution than an ordinary television.

Most significant bit (MSB)   The bit that is most important in determining the size of a binary number.

Music synthesizer   A machine, when under computer control, which produces computer-generated music. Some synthesizers are not operated by computers.

Nibble   Four bits considered together as one unit.

Octal   A number system with a base of 8.

Operating system   Systems software that manages the computer and its peripheral devices, allowing the user to run programs and to control the movement of data to and from the computer memory and peripheral devices. See Software.

Operation code (op code)   The binary or hexadecimal numbers representing the different sets of directions a particular computer can carry out.

Operations   The specific set of directions a particular computer can perform. The operations of a computer are determined by its central processing unit (CPU).

Output device   A peripheral device allowing the user to receive information from the computer (e.g., printer).

Peripheral devices   Devices for communicating with the central processing unit or storing data in CPU accessible form (e.g., keyboard, printer, disk drive).

Printer   An output device that allows the computer user to obtain a paper copy of work.

Program counter   The means by which the computer keeps track of where it is in the execution of a program.

Random access memory (RAM)   The computer's general purpose memory, sometimes called read/write memory. RAM may be written to or read from by the central processing unit. Information on RAM is usually volatile: it disappears when power to the computer is turned off.

Read only memory (ROM)   Integrated circuits on which are programmed special system programs that will be used often or will provide a set of simple commands enabling more powerful programs to be loaded. ROM has the following features: data may be read from ROM to the central processing unit but may not be read back to ROM; data in ROM is fixed, not volatile.

Registers   Locations inside the central processing unit that store temporary results or intermediate calculations and are used repeatedly by the CPU.

Reverse Polish Notation   A logical system that groups all the operations together at the end of a statement.

Software   The list of instructions that tell a computer to perform a given task or tasks. There are two basic types of software. Systems software enables the computer to carry out its basic operations. Examples include operating systems, language interpreters, and utility programs. Applications software consists of programs that instruct the computer to perform various real-world tasks such as writing checks, playing chess, and testing students.

Source code   For assembly language, the annotated code that the programmer writes. It is transformed into object code to run.

Store   An assembly language command that takes the information from one of the registers and moves it into a particular memory location.

Subroutine   A piece of programming that is considered a unit when accessed by another part of the program. After the subroutine is executed, the program returns to the step following the subroutine call. Useful for pieces of code that are used repeatedly.

Syntax   The grammatical structure of a language.

Systems software   See Software.

Timesharing   The concurrent use of one computer by several users. Generally, timesharing is the connection of several users at different terminals to a shared computer. The connections are either through direct wires or through modems and telephone wires.

Turtle graphics   A way of producing graphics on the screen that includes relative polar commands such as "move forward a distance" and "turn by so many degrees."

Voice synthesizer   A machine that, under computer control, produces computer-generated speech.

Resources

INTRODUCTION

The information provided in the final portion of this book represents a sampling of resources available to inspire and support the use of computers by mathematics teachers and computer sponsors. Periodicals, Reviews, Directories, and Associations provide avenues for staying current in the field. Books, Projects, Resource Centers, and Software can aid in establishing or expanding the computer applications in a school, since they offer information about others' successful experiences.

For those who want a broader range of resources than is offered here, two sources are recommended. Both the *Classroom Computer News Directory of Educational Computing Resources* and the resource section in the *Practical Guide to Computers in Education* provide comprehensive listings of educational resources, including the types of sources offered in this book, along with sections that include sources of funding, databases, user groups, continuing education, and more. The *CCN Directory* is available from Classroom Computer News, 341 Mt. Auburn Street, Watertown, MA 02172, (617) 923-8595, and the *Practical Guide to Computers in Education*, the first in this *Computers in Education* series, is available from Addison-Wesley, Reading, MA 01867, (617) 944-3700.

The resources used in Addison-Wesley's series on *Computers in Education* are drawn from an extensive database of educational computing resources, maintained at Intentional Educations by Carol Nuccio who also has responsibility for organizing and updating resources for each book just prior to publication. Special thanks to Nancy Via for her research of the Books section.

RESOURCES CONTENTS

ASSOCIATIONS AND ORGANIZATIONS
  Mathematics
  Educational Computing

RESOURCE CENTERS

PROJECTS AND PRACTICES

PUBLICATIONS
  Journals
  Periodicals
  Books
    Educational Computing
    Mathematics Applications
    Computer Literacy: Programming

SOFTWARE SOURCES
  Reviews
  Directories

RECOMMENDED SOFTWARE
  Mathematics Applications
    Primary Level
    Middle School Level
    High School Level
  Instructional Tools

ASSOCIATIONS AND ORGANIZATIONS

Membership in a professional association or organization can provide you with a wealth of resources and knowledge via its publications and regional and national conferences. Listed below are two categories of associations, Mathematics and Educational Computing. Both provide mathematics teachers with the opportunity to expand their professional capabilities. The mathematics associations regularly address computer applications in their publications and their conferences provide extensive coverage including hands-on workshops and seminars. Educational computing associations frequently address issues in the mathematics curriculum, and many of the general resources they provide can be applied to mathematics.

Mathematics

Association for Computers in Mathematics and Science Teaching (ACMST)
P.O. Box 4455
Austin, TX 78765
(512) 258-9738

The goal of ACMST is to provide a forum for exchange of ideas and experiences about new computer materials, methods, and issues that are of interest to mathematics and science instructors at all levels through college. Members are encouraged to submit articles for their quarterly publication, *The Journal of Computers in Mathematics and Science Teaching*. Discounts on books about computing are also available through ACMST.

National Council of Teachers of Mathematics (NCTM)
1906 Association Drive
Reston, VA 22091
(703) 620-9840

This is a nationwide organization for K–12 teachers with smaller affiliate groups in each state. Besides a national convention each year, NCTM sponsors several regional meetings, all of which have major commitments to presenting current information about computer use to support mathematics instruction. Two of its journals, the *Mathematics Teacher* and the *Arithmetic Teacher*, now contain software and book reviews, as well as many articles of interest to computer users. The Nov. 81 *Mathematics Teacher* and the Feb. 83 *Arithmetic Teacher* are special issues devoted to computers. The NCTM Technology Advisory Committee has produced a *Guide to Resources in Instructional Computing* which contains current information about applications of computing in the mathematics curriculum. Another endeavor of the organization includes a publication, *Guidelines for Evaluating Instructional*

Materials. They also offer a series of computer seminars throughout the year which are held at various locations across the country.

School Science and Mathematics Association (SSMA)
126 Life Sciences Building
Bowling Green State University
Bowling Green, OH 43403
(419) 372-0151

This group publishes a journal, *School Science and Mathematics,* primarily for secondary school interest, although some articles include elementary and college applications. Some issues have computer information; those in the future will certainly include such information. They have recently published a book, *Microcomputers for Teachers,* which addresses integration of computing in instruction of science and mathematics.

Educational Computing

Association for Educational Communications and Technology (AECT)
1126 Sixteenth Street, NW
Washington, DC 20036
(202) 833-4180

AECT promotes the effective use of media and technology in education. It supports a special task force on microcomputers and is currently working on Project BEST which includes a microcomputer program database and computer networking. AECT's purpose is to increase understanding and information sharing of educational computing and its use in basic skills education. Its publications include *Educational Communication and Technology Journal, Journal of Instructional Development,* and *Instructional Innovator.*

Association for the Development of Computer-Based Instructional Systems (ADCIS)
ADCIS Headquarters
Computer Center
Western Washington University
Bellingham, WA 98225
(206) 676-2860

ADCIS membership includes elementary and secondary school systems, colleges, universities, businesses, and government agencies. The Association's purpose is to advance the use of computer-based instruction and/or management by facilitating communication between product developers and users. It seeks to reduce redundant activities among developers of CAI materials. Publications are *The Journal of Computer-Based Instruction* and *ADCIS Newsletter.* This organization also has a special interest group, SIG/Math, which publishes a bimonthly newsletter for mathematical science educators. The October 1982 issue has a particularly useful section on Computers in Math Courses, including calculus, algebra, and trigonometry, and a bibliography of related articles. Call Dr. Ronald Winger at (302) 738-2140 for information about this subgroup specifically.

Computer-Using Educators (CUE)

Box 18547

San Jose, CA 95138

The goal of this organization is to assist the promotion and development of instructional uses of computers in all disciplines and at all educational levels from preschool through college. CUE's primary contribution is facilitating communication among its members by publishing the bimonthly *CUE Newsletter* and sponsoring timely meetings and conferences. The *Newsletter* includes articles covering new product announcements, software and hardware evaluations, essays by CUE members, digests of articles from computing journals, notifications of meetings and conferences, and new ideas for classroom computer applications.

CUE cosponsors SOFTSWAP (see page 283) and the Microcomputer Center (see page 254) with the San Mateo County Office of Education. Educators can visit the Center on any weekday and use any of several brands of microcomputer systems. SOFTSWAP has gathered a collection of donated software available for copying at the Center or through mail order for a small fee. In addition, a previewing library of commercially available software is open to visitors of the Center.

Council for Instructional Computing in Iowa (CI)

AEA 1 Instructional Computing Network

Luther College

Decorah, IA 52101

(319) 387-1178

This group is working to promote a coordinated state response to the challenges of instructional computing including a clearinghouse for educational software and documentation. Representatives from fifteen state area education agencies, teachers, and professionals are all involved in supporting these collaborative endeavors.

Educational Computer Consortium of Ohio (ECCO)

Teacher Center 271

4777 Farnhurst Road

Cleveland, OH 44124

(216) 291-5225

Sharing educational software, books, journals, and computer-related audiovisual materials is a service provided by this group. ECCO also prints a newsletter, sponsors workshops, and holds an Annual Educational Computer Fair.

International Council for Computers in Education (ICCE)
135 Education
University of Oregon
Eugene, OR 97403
(503) 686-4408

ICCE has both individuals and organizations as members, and aids in the formation of other groups working to facilitate instructional uses of computers. Individual members receive the publication, *The Computing Teacher*, which is published nine times annually. Organizational memberships include announcements to meetings and activities, discounts on books, and opportunities to participate in the direction of ICCE.

Michigan Association for Computer Users in Learning (MACUL)
Wayne County ISD
P.O. Box 807
Wayne, MI 48184

MACUL publishes a bimonthly newsletter and holds several conferences each year. The goal of the group is to coordinate statewide instructional computing activities.

National Association for Educational Computing (NAEC)
33 Knutsen Street
Tappan, NY 10983

This is a nonprofit organization dedicated to the use of computers in education. Its members are educators, students, parents, or school board members. NAEC considers itself to be a national forum for discussing important issues in educational computing. It offers a curriculum service and a regular report of organizational news, which appears as a column in *Educational Computer* magazine.

Texas Computer Education Association (TCEA)
P.O. Box 42808, Dept. B
Houston, TX 77242
(713) 462-7708

TCEA encourages interest in K–12 computer education, provides information on current trends, promotes professional cooperation and communication, serves as a liaison for other computer organizations, and works to improve teacher training. It also supports a software exchange, conferences, and a quarterly newsletter.

Young People's Logo Association (YPLA)
1208 Hillsdale Drive
Richardson, TX 75081
(214) 783-7548

YPLA is a nonprofit association which publishes *Turtle News* and the *Logo Newsletter*. It offers a software exchange library of public domain programs. YPLA recently published

The Turtle's Sourcebook, a guide to learning and teaching Logo in the classroom. Currently under development are two projects—a series of books for children about Logo, PILOT and BASIC and a series of educational games to enhance the use of Logo and PILOT. All YPLA products incorporate activities to be done both on and off the computer. Turtle Learning Centers are the local chapters of the YPLA where members can meet informally. TLC members receive a bimonthly newsletter, *TLComputing*.

RESOURCE CENTERS

At both the local and national level, resource centers provide a variety of services. Many review, develop, or disseminate software, offer workshops and seminars, or compile resource information. The centers listed below are a sampling of what is available throughout the United States. For additional listings, check the *Classroom Computer News Directory of Educational Computing Resources*, (see page 247).

Board of Cooperative Educational Services (BOCES)
Statewide Instructional Computing Network
Oswego County BOCES
Mexico, NY 13114
(315) 963-7251

Boards are set up in various regions throughout the state to provide support to the school systems in each region. They are now helping teachers with computer-related projects and needs. Coordination of educational computing applications is provided by the Oswego County BOCES.

California Teacher Education and Computers (TEC) Centers

The TEC Center program divides California into fifteen regions, each with a TEC Center responsible for providing teachers in-service training in science, mathematics, computer literacy, and other subject areas. The Microcomputer Center (see page 254) in the SMERC Library of the San Mateo County Office of Education has been designated the statewide Software Library and Clearinghouse to provide support services to the TEC Centers. Information requests from teachers should be forwarded to your regional TEC Center. For the location of your local TEC Center, contact the Microcomputer Center (see page 254).

Consortium for Mathematics and Its Applications (COMAP, Inc.)
271 Lincoln St.
Suite #4
Lexington, MA 02173
(617) 863-1930

This organization provides a variety of excellent mathematics materials which apply to pre-calculus, calculus and other university level subjects. Many of the modules they have developed directly lend themselves to computer use. They publish a journal, titled the *UMAP Journal* (Undergraduate Mathematics Applications Program), and they also have a catalog of their materials available upon request.

Educational Resources Information Center (ERIC)

National Institute of Education
1200 19th St., NW
Washington, DC 20208
(202) 254-5500

ERIC provides access to educational research findings through a nationwide network of clearinghouses that abstract, index, store, and disseminate information. A list of the topics covered may be obtained from ERIC at the above address. The clearinghouses listed below are directly involved with information on classroom computer use.

ERIC Clearinghouse on Information Resources
Syracuse University
School of Education
130 Huntington Hall
Syracuse, NY 13210
(315) 423-3640

ERIC Clearinghouse on Elementary and Early Childhood Education
University of Illinois
College of Education
Urbana, IL 61801
(217) 333-1386

Microcomputer Center

SMERC Library
San Mateo County Office of Education
333 Main Street
Redwood City, CA 94063
(415) 363-5472

The Microcomputer Center is a joint project of Computer-Using Educators (CUE) and the San Mateo County Office of Education. Besides maintaining SOFTSWAP, 400 public domain programs available for exchange, the Center has a variety of computers for educators to examine and a collection of commercial educational software for evaluation. The Center has published *Courseware Reviews 1982*, which is a compilation of reviews of fifty software packages (see page 280). Also, the Microcomputer Center has been designated as the statewide software library and clearinghouse to provide support services to The Teacher Education and Computers (TEC) Centers throughout California (see page 253).

Microcomputer Education Applications Network (MEAN)

256 N. Washington Street
Falls Church, VA 22046
(703) 536-2310

MEAN aims to help educators develop and sell software and provide information on microcomputer applications in education. MEAN encourages software development in areas delineated by their members. Programs are available to school officials and other interested individuals for purchase. MEAN publishes a quarterly newsletter, *MEAN Brief*, which provides information on other software sources and industry news and contains a subscriber exchange of particular microcomputer applications and requests. MEAN also helps local districts and state agencies develop specific educational computing programs.

Microcomputer Evaluation and Resource Centers

State Department of Public Instruction
Room 229 State House
Indianapolis, IN 46204
(317) 927-0296

This Center, sponsored by the State Department of Public Instruction, offers in-service programs as well as the opportunity for teachers to preview software and hardware. Microcomputer technology is also used here to link nine state regional centers through online databases, such as BRS.

Microcomputer Resource Center

Library of Michigan
P.O. Box 30007
Lansing, MI 48909
(517) 373-7538

The Microcomputer Resource Center maintains a library of administrative and instructional software for schools and libraries, in all subjects, and for all grade levels. A computerized database has been developed to disseminate information about the holdings of the Center, free to all school systems within the state. The Center also contains resources for computer literacy and facilitates training of teachers and librarians.

Minnesota Educational Computing Consortium (MECC)

2520 Broadway Drive
St. Paul, MN 55113
(612) 376-1101

MECC, supporting the nation's only statewide instructional computing effort, is organized to coordinate and provide computer services for the students, teachers, and administrators in Minnesota public schools and colleges. MECC provides in-service training and curriculum guides, and develops and distributes educational software. They are an excellent source of software and written materials for use with Apple II and Atari microcomputers, although other hardware is under consideration for conversion. Both *Users*, a bimonthly instructional newsletter listing available materials, and their organizational newsletter, *Dataline*, are free upon request. Non-Minnesota customers to MECC pay extra for MECC products. Individual programs designed by MECC are also available through many commercial software distribution houses.

Pennsylvania Service Centers

Allegheny Intermediate Unit
200 Commerce Court Building
Pittsburgh, PA 15219
(412) 394-5760

Thirteen Intermediate Units throughout Pennsylvania provide consulting, in-service, repair, and centralized bidding procedures for the use of computers in schools. Many review and disseminate software as well.

Technical Education Resource Center (TERC)

Computer Resource Center (CRC)
8 Eliot Street
Cambridge, MA 02138
(617) 547-3890

The Computer Resource Center (CRC) of TERC houses information on microcomputer hardware and software and a library of technical and educational publications. It also maintains various microcomputers and educational software for inspection and sample use. CRC conducts workshops nationwide on classroom computer use which include: Logo use, Pascal programming, BASIC programming, the use of computers in educational administration, and computer use in mathematics and science instruction. CRC membership is open to educators and other interested people for a nominal fee and allows use of the CRC facilities. CRC also holds an open house once a week during which nonmembers may use the Center. TERC has recently developed a report on mathematics and science software opportunities and needs for the U.S. Department of Education.

Texas Education Agency

Sandy Pratscher
201 E. 11th
Austin, TX 78701
(512) 475-2479

The twenty regional Education Service Centers of Texas provide technical assistance and teacher training for the public school districts of the state, including training in educational computing. For two projects directly related to mathematics, see pages 260 and 261.

Wisconsin Instructional Computer Consortium (WICC)
725 W. Park Avenue
Chippewa Falls, WI 54729
(715) 723-0341

WICC is an institutional member of MECC and consists of nine educational institutions which provide instructional computing services to Wisconsin schools. Services include planning, trouble-shooting, software review, and a software library.

PROJECTS AND PRACTICES

This section provides a selection of the exciting practices and projects going on across the country in which computers are being used for mathematics teaching and learning. Many are funded at the local level, as well as through federal and state agencies. Detailed information about these projects may be helpful to educators wishing to learn from others' experiences.

Supplementing the ones noted here is an excellent source of additional projects, the *Microcomputer Directory: Applications in Educational Settings*, available from the Gutman Library, Graduate School of Education, Harvard University, Cambridge, MA 02139. Over 900 entries are organized by state and indexed by subject area. Also, *Mathematics Teacher* and *Arithmetic Teacher*, journals of NCTM (see Associations section), list projects of interest to mathematics educators and computer specialists.

Brookline Schools
Brookline Schools
333 Washington Street
Brookline, MA 02146
Hardware: Apple II
Grade Range: 4–8

Grade 4 and 5 students have year-long programs learning about programming, geometry, design, problem solving, and computer literacy through the use of Logo graphics. This school system has had the opportunity of early linking with MIT in their initial Logo explorations. Grade 8 students begin BASIC programming especially with hi/lo resolution graphics. Computers are generally located in the school libraries providing a computer lab setting.

CAI for Basic Algebra
Department of Mathematics
University of Wisconsin—Oshkosh
Oshkosh, WI 54901
(414) 424-1059
Hardware: TRS-80 III
Grade Range: 9–college

This project promotes teaching of concepts in an introductory algebra course. The software provides both short sections of instructions and drill-type exercises.

CAI for Secondary Mathematics
Asbury Park Board of Education
1506 Park Avenue
Asbury Park, NJ 07712
(201) 774-0888
Hardware: Apple II; TRS-80 I, II
Grade Range: 9–12

Federal funding enabled this community to develop software for seven topics in each of their high school mathematics courses: algebra I and II, geometry, trigonometry, and calculus. A combination of microcomputers and terminals is available so students are actually able to have daily access when needed.

Inter-disciplinary Triad
Okaloosa Learning Center
130 Lowery Place
Fort Walton Beach, FL 32548
(904) 243-4934
Hardware: PET
Grade Range: 4–6

The project goal is to improve teaching and learning mathematics through the use of new technology in the classroom. Several teachers use the same lesson plans, and REGENT, a computer network, allows individual confidential programming. There is also an independent study program with gifted students in grades 4–6.

MNCP-Math Network Curriculum Project
San Francisco State University
1600 Holloway Avenue
San Francisco, CA 94132
(415) 469-1104
Hardware: PET
Grade Range: 5–8

This group, under NIE and NSF funding, has developed seven two-week units that guide students in using the computer as a tool to learning. They include input-output, strategies, business, sampling, data analysis, turtle geometry, and turtle symmetry topics. Besides teacher's guides for each topic, they have also developed a *Guide for Master Teachers* to use in planning and conducting in-service workshops for teachers in using the curriculum.

Mathematical Modeling Through Simulating

Academic Support Center
St. Olaf College
Northfield, MN 55057
(507) 663-3114
Hardware: Heath/Zen H89
Grade Range: 10–12

NSF and NIE have funded this project for developing innovative software for use in school mathematics instruction. The three prototype units involve simulating some physical or theoretical situation to aid in introducing, reinforcing, or extending curriculum topics at the high school level.

Mathematical "Story Problems"

Dept. of Mathematical Sciences
Northern Illinois University
DeKalb, IL 60015
(815) 753-0566
Hardware: Apple II
Grade Range: 4–7

Teachers of mathematics are provided assistance in utilizing micros for instruction. The project is also researching format effects, such as graphics and animation, with story problems in grades 4–7.

Microcomputer Curriculum Project

Price Laboratory School
University of Northern Iowa
Cedar Falls, IA 50613
(319) 273-2548
Hardware: Apple II Plus
Grade Range: 5–12

MCP is a nonprofit "of the teacher, by the teacher, and for the teacher" project dedicated to providing curriculum integrated mathematics software at all levels. Seventy-one programs are currently available to schools throughout Iowa through area education agencies, and to schools out of state by contacting MCP.

Microcomputer Programs in Algebra Instruction
Education Service Center, Region XIII
7703 N. Lamar Boulevard
Austin, TX 78752
(512) 458-9131
Hardware: Apple II
Grade Range: 9–12

Title IVC funds were used to develop a series of algebra programs. These programs address concept development as well as the more traditional aspects of tutorial guidance and practice.

Microcomputers for Math Instruction in the Primary Grades
Department of Education
Wittenberg University
Springfield, OH 45501
(513) 327-7101
Hardware: Atari
Grade Range: K–3

This project has mathematics games available to purchase for students in the primary grades. The mathematics content of the games ranges across the ten basic skill areas identified in the National Council of Supervisors of Mathematics position statement on basic skills in mathematics.

Motivation Lab
Oakley Middle School
6031 N. Montana Avenue
Portland, OR 97217
(503) 285-3601
Hardware: PET
Grade Range: 6–9

Although this school is currently using computers only for diagnosis and prescription in reading and mathematics, future directions should be very interesting. They hope to explore the use of cable TV with micros. Artificial intelligence and robotics uses are also being considered.

The Phoenix School
300 Putnam Avenue
Cambridge, MA 02139
(617) 492-3817
Hardware: Apple II; Atari
Grade Range: K–6

The Phoenix School is a private school which stresses the use of computers as a learning tool. Students can explore programming and word processing in a Logo environment as well as in their regular subjects.

TABS—MATH

Ohio State University
College of Education
1945 N. High Street
Columbus, OH 43210
(614) 422-3449
Hardware: Apple II Plus; IIe
Grade Range: 4–8

Federal funding is providing this group the opportunity to develop innovative computer based materials to help elementary school children in areas of mathematics other than arithmetic. These include such areas as intuitive geometry, probability, statistics, estimation and use of the computer in concept learning as well as problem solving. Curricular materials and related in-service materials are also provided.

TABS-Related Courseware for Microcomputers Project

Education Service Center, Region IV
P.O. Box 863
Houston, TX 77001
(713) 462-7708
Grade Range: K–12

The TABS-Related Courseware for Microcomputers Project has designed a database (available in hard copy and disk form) of microcomputer courseware evaluations which meet the Texas Assessment of Basic Skills (TABS) objectives for mathematics and reading in grades 3, 5, and 9. The second phase of the project involves expanding the evaluations into different subject areas and the K–12 levels of instruction. Texas teachers have access to this information through the twenty Education Centers in Texas. Funding is provided by the Texas Education Computer Cooperative.

Teams-Tables for Math Skills

Richfield Elementary School
Box E
Richfield, IN 83349
(208) 487-2790
Hardware: TRS-80
Grade Range: 3–6

A computer plus mathematics games and manipulatives are contained on a portable lab table shared by two grade levels—one in the morning and one in the afternoon. Children are assigned materials from the lab table to work on specific skills as identified on a list that is organized for the teacher. Several schools in Lincoln County use this approach.

Transformational Geometry on Microcomputer Geoboard
Southern Oregon State College
1250 Kiskiyou Boulevard
Ashland, OH 97520
Hardware: Apple II
Grade Range: 5–9

An Apple Foundation grant has provided funding for the development of microcomputer software to teach transformational geometry skills and concepts by using computer graphics. The software teaches students in grades 5–9 the concepts of slides, flips, and turns on a 25-pin geoboard. Input by the students is through the Apple Graphics Tablet. Field testing of the software was completed in spring, 1982.

Word Problem Solving Using Micros
Florida A&M University
Laboratory School
P.O. Box A-19
Tallahassee, FL 32307
(904) 599-3151
Hardware: Apple II Plus
Grade Range: 9–12

Apple computers are used with students in grades 9–12 for practice in problem solving. Such skills as analyzing, abstracting elements, and identifying relationships are reinforced during this program.

PUBLICATIONS

The following are sources of reading materials helpful in keeping you up-to-date in the field of educational computing with a focus on mathematics applications. The Journals are publications of some of the associations mentioned above. Most of the Periodicals listed focus on educational computing and are the most popular and innovative in the industry. If you are interested in subscribing to any of these magazines, you should request a sample copy for review. Also, there are two publications, *Micro ... Publications in Review*, Vogeler Publishing, P.O. Box 489, Arlington Heights, Il 60006, and *COMPendium*, Epicurious, P.O. Box 129, Lincolndale, NY 10540, which are indexes of computer magazines.

Books are listed in three areas: Computer Literacy, Mathematics Applications, and Programming. Although this is only a partial listing of what is available, these books cover a range of areas of computing and mathematics. Some of the books were mentioned earlier in this book, so reference is made to the page on which they appeared. Many new books are published each year, so you may wish to consult the *Annual Bibliography of Computer-Oriented Books*, Box 7345, Colorado Springs, CO 80933.

Journals

Arithmetic Teacher
National Council of Teachers of Mathematics
1906 Association Drive
Reston, VA 22091

The *Arithmetic Teacher* is published by NCTM nine times a year to address concerns of those involved in mathematics instruction in K–8. The February 1983 issue is focused on computer uses to aid instruction. Members of the National Council of Teachers of Mathematics receive this publication as part of their membership fee. For an additional $10, a subscription to the *Mathematics Teacher* is included.

Computers in Mathematics Sciences Education Newsletter (CIMSE Newsletter)
National Consortium on Uses of Computers in Mathematical Sciences Education
014 Memorial Hall
University of Delaware
Newark, DE 19711
(302) 738-2140

The purpose of the CIMSE Newsletter is to promote the exchange of information about curriculum, sources of expertise, projects, materials, courseware and equipment; and to encourage, monitor and share research concerning the use of information sciences technology in the teaching and learning of the mathematical sciences. Those interested in receiving the consortium's newsletter should send the request to the address above. CIMSE also plans sessions at most national conferences of mathematics educators, and is affiliated with the Association for the Development of Computer-Based Instructional Systems.

Journal of Computers in Mathematics and Science Teaching
Association for Computers in Mathematics and Science Teaching
P.O. Box 4455
Austin, TX 78765

This journal was developed to provide a forum for the exchange of information among the members of ACMST about teaching mathematics and science with computers. Articles are of interest to secondary and college teachers. Bibliographies and other listings, as well as book and software reviews, are useful to most educators. Ideas about using simulations or graphics to teach mathematics are typical of the journal entries. The annual association membership fee of $15 includes this journal.

Mathematics Teacher

National Council of Teachers of Mathematics
1906 Association Drive
Reston, VA 22091

The *Mathematics Teacher* is published for members of NCTM, especially teachers of grades 7–12, to present ideas and materials to support mathematics instruction. Recently many articles in this journal address computer issues such as software evaluation and classroom uses of the computer. The *Mathematics Teacher* is always useful for those involved in mathematics instruction and will probably continue to offer its membership more information about computer education. The nine-issue subscription to the journal is included in the NCTM membership fee of $30 or $40. The latter fee entitles members to the *Arithmetic Teacher*, the journal for teachers of grades K–8.

The Computing Teacher

135 Education
University of Oregon
Eugene, OR 97403
(503) 686-4429

This journal of the International Council for Computers in Education (ICCE) is a valuable resource for those interested in the instructional use of computers. Articles are solicited from members and other practitioners so they often highlight actual classroom computer usage or other very practical concerns. Films, books, and software are also reviewed each issue. A one-year subscription costs $16.50 for nine issues and automatic membership in ICCE.

Periodicals

Classroom Computer News

Intentional Educations, Inc.
341 Mt. Auburn Street
Watertown, MA 02172
(617) 923-8595

CCN is a magazine that presents many ideas which aid the educator in considering and resolving issues that evolve as computer use continues to expand. Regular features include teacher-developed classroom applications, interviews with renowned computer educators, program listings, software and book reviews, administrative and library uses, new products, and worksheets for classroom use. CCN also publishes the annual *Directory of Educational*

Computing Resources (see Introduction to the Resources section, p. 247). A year's subscription is $19.95 for seven regular issues and the Directory.

Creative Computing
Creative Computing
P.O. Box 789-M
Morristown, NJ 07960
(800) 631-8112

Creative Computing was one of the earliest and currently is one of the most widely read magazines dealing with applications for the microcomputer. Though it is written for a diverse readership, part of each issue is devoted to educational uses of computers, and special issues have focused on educational applications, resources, and software. Articles range from general to technical and include topics such as programming techniques, comparison of high-level languages, the latest in games, and the impact of computers on society. Subscriptions are $24 a year.

Educational Computer Magazine
Edcomp Inc.
P.O. Box 535
Cupertino, CA 95014
(408) 252-3224

This is a general purpose bimonthly magazine for educators who use computers. It serves several audiences, including the teacher, librarian, administrator, and special education staff. Articles address a myriad of topics and are especially suitable for those just beginning to investigate or expand computer applications. Courseware and book reviews as well as conference information help the educator to stay current. A year's subscription is $15.00.

Electronic Learning
Scholastic Inc.
902 Sylvan Avenue
Box 2001
Englewood Cliffs, NJ 07632
(201) 567-7900

Although primarily aimed at school administrators, this magazine has many interesting regular features that may be of interest to the classroom teacher, including: national news of significance, spotlights on people, technology in the classroom, the computing student, and reviews of new products and software. The eight issues each year provide K–12 teachers with nontechnical introductions to varied educational uses of electronic technology. The subscription rate is $19.00 per year.

InfoWorld
375 Cochituate Road
Box 880
Framingham, MA 01704
(800) 343-6474

For the latest in hardware, operating systems, software, and peripherals, *InfoWorld* is a good choice, since it is a weekly. Though articles are not aimed at educators specifically, there is much in this publication that will be of interest to the computer specialist or others who are trying to be well informed about changes in the computer industry. Regular features focus on computer literacy, hardware/software news, and reviews, as well as a large classified ad section. The cost is $25 per year.

Teaching and Computers
Scholastic Inc.
730 Broadway
New York, NY 10003
(212) 505-3000

This is a magazine for elementary school teachers which is devoted to helping teachers learn and teach about how to use computers effectively. Each issue features non-technical information about how computers work, examples of how other teachers are using computers, and teacher-developed lesson ideas for using the computer as a teaching tool. Plus, there are reproducible student activity pages. The subscription price is $15.95 and includes eight issues during the school year.

T.H.E. Journal
Information Synergy Inc.
P.O. Box 992
Acton, MA 01720

The *Technological Horizons in Education Journal* features theoretical perspectives and reports on applications of educational technology, as well as a plethora of new product information. Educators interested in state-of-the-art developments or international happenings should consider this publication. *T.H.E. Journal* is published eight times a year and is free to those who qualify.

Window
Window, Inc.
469 Pleasant Street
Watertown, MA 02172
(617) 923-9147

Window is an educational magazine on a 5 1/4 in. floppy disk for Apple II computers, although plans are in the works to make it available for other machines. This format allows for interactive reviews of new software and program development. Each issue has a Feature Program which is an actual piece of software that can be used by the educator. A subscription includes five issues and costs $95.00.

Books

Educational Computing

Bits 'n Bytes About Computing: A Computer Literacy Primer
Rachelle Heller and C. Dianne Martin
Computer Science Press, Inc., 1982
11 Taft Court
Rockville, MD 20850
(301) 251-9050
Price: $17.95

For teachers in grades 4–6, this book outlines activities for students covering history of computers, how they run, social aspects, applications, and careers.

Computer Literacy: An Introduction
Center for Learning Technologies,
State Education Department, Albany, NY
Northeast Regional Exchange, 1982
101 Mill Road
Chelmsford, MA 01824
(617) 256-3987
Price: $6.00

This is a collection of articles, program proposals, and curriculum guides on computer literacy. Published as an aid for educators trying to define computer literacy programs.

Introduction to Computers in Education for Middle School and Elementary Teachers
David Moursund
ICCE (International Council for Computers in Education)
135 Education
University of Oregon
Eugene, OR 97403
(503) 686-4408
Price: $7.00

A self-instruction or in-service course for teachers which includes over seventy-five activities for teaching about and using computers in the classroom.

Microcomputer Use and Software Design
Frank DiGiammarino, Donald Johnson, and Beth Lowd
Milton Bradley Co., 1982
Education Division
Springfield, MA 01101
(413) 525-6411
Price: $5.00

This guide for teachers introducing microcomputers in the classroom gives practical advice on location of the computer, suggestions for lessons and activities, and discussions of the problems that may arise in the classroom. Teachers will find this helpful when designing their own educational software for the classroom.

Microcomputers in Education: An Introduction
Adeline Naiman
Northeast Regional Exchange, 1982
101 Mill Road
Chelmsford, MA 01824
(617) 256-3987
Price: $5.00

This is a useful resource book or in-service text to help educators plan ways to use computers as instructional aids. It includes planning, uses in education, hardware, software, teacher education, assessment, and resources.

Mindstorms
Seymour Papert
Basic Books, Inc., 1980
10 East 53rd St.
New York, NY 10022
(212) 593-7078
Price: $14.50

This important book is devoted to new ways of thinking about computers, children, and learning. Rather than using computers to program children, Papert and his colleagues in the LOGO group at MIT created learning environments that enabled children to program and communicate with computers in a natural and easy way. Papert's eloquent vision of future education is "must" reading for anyone with an interest in these issues.

The Practical Guide to Computers in Education
Peter Coburn, Peter Kelman, Nancy Roberts, Thomas F. F. Snyder, Daniel H. Watt, Cheryl Weiner
Addison-Wesley, 1982
One Jacob Way
Reading, MA 01867
(617) 944-3700
Price: $9.95

This is the first book in the Computers in Education series. It is designed to assist educators in exploring the potential of computers in education—a basic primer. Through vignettes and pragmatic suggestion, the authors relate nontechnical information about such issues as introducing the computer to the school, limits and potentials of microcomputers, using the computer creatively, and finding effective resources.

RUN: Computer Education
Dennis O. Harper and James H. Stewart
Brooks/Cole Publishing Co., 1983
Div. of Wadsworth, Inc.
555 Abrego
Monterey, CA 93940
(408) 373-0728
Price: $15.95

This is a text or reference book for colleges or school districts offering computer literacy to preservice or inservice teachers. It includes a collection of articles on instructional computing with opinion questions and exercises following each chapter. There is a glossary of terms at the end.

What Makes Things Fun to Learn?: A Study of Intrinsically Motivating Computer Games
Thomas W. Malone
Xerox
Palo Alto Research Center
Cognitive and Instructional Sciences Group
3333 Coyote Hill Road
Palo Alto, CA 94304

This monograph has become a classic in the field since its publication in 1980. Malone reports on the results of his research on why computer games are captivating and how those features can be used to make learning with computers more interesting (see page 55).

Mathematics Applications

Computer Applications for Calculus
Gary Bitter
Prindle, Weber & Schmidt, 1982
20 Providence Street
Boston, MA 02116
(617) 482-2344
Price: $13.50

This book can be used with a calculus text since it isolates topics where microcomputers can be used to illuminate the ideas of calculus. Sample programs are provided in BASIC, FORTRAN, and Pascal for the Apple and TRS-80.

Computer Resource Book—Algebra
Thomas A. Dwyer and Margot Critchfield
Houghton Mifflin, 1975
One Beacon Street
Boston, MA 02108
(617) 725-5802
Price: $6.25

This book is meant to be used as a supplement to a regular algebra textbook. Many of the BASIC programming skills needed in using the book are taught in a 25-page prologue and the rest are interspersed throughout the algebra topics. Altogether there are 125 computer programs covering ten topics in algebra: the language of algebra, operations with real numbers, linear equations in one variable, inequalities, open sentences in two variables, systems of linear equations, quadratic equations and functions, rational expressions and polynomial equations, polynomial functions and complex numbers, and computer-generated simulation.

Computers and Mathematics
James Poirot
Sterling Swift, 1979
7901 South IH-35
Austin, TX 78744
(512) 282-6840
Price: $16.95

This book provides experiences that integrate computers and mathematics through problem-solving. Students will need at least an Algebra I background to work with the challenges provided in the topics about Boolean Algebra, Error Analysis, Logic, and Computer Arithmetic. A student workbook is available for $7.95.

Computers in Mathematics: A Sourcebook of Ideas
David Ahl
Creative Computing, 1979
39 E. Hanover Avenue
Morris Plains, NJ 07950
(800) 631-8112
Price: $15.95

This large-format book contains sections on computer literacy, problem-solving techniques, art and graphing, simulations, computer-assisted instruction, probability, functions, magic squares, and programming styles. The book ranges from a basic introduction to binary numbers to advanced techniques like multiple regression analysis and differential equations.

Every item discussed has a complete explanation, including flowcharts, programs, and sample runs.

The Entelek Computer-Based Math Lab
Entelek
Ward-Whidden House
P.O. Box 1303
Portsmouth, NH 03801
(603) 436-0439
Price: $29.95

This book contains thirty-five computer-assisted instruction programs for use in your high school mathematics course. Once copied into the computer, the programs, written in BASIC, can be used by individual students to deepen their understanding of selected mathematical concepts, or to sharpen their mathematical skills. The programs are keyed to leading textbooks in secondary school math. The programs are of four kinds: tutorial, simulation, data reduction, and classroom demonstration. A diskette of these programs is also available for $150.00.

Geometry: A Transformation Approach
Arthur Coxford and Zalman Usiskin
Laidlaw Brothers, 1975
Thatcher and Madison
River Forest, IL 60305
(312) 366-5320

This is a high school geometry textbook that uses the transformation approach to Euclidian geometry (see page 161). Due to the copyright date and limited supply, this textbook is available only in the following states—Georgia, Kentucky, Mississippi, Oregon, and Texas.

Introduction to Computer Simulation: The System Dynamics Approach
Nancy Roberts, David F. Andersen, Ralph M. Deal, Michael S. Garet, William A. Shaffer
Addison-Wesley, 1983
One Jacob Way
Reading, MA 01867
(617) 944-3700
Price: $19.95

Introduction to Computer Simulation teaches real-world problem solving using the system dynamics methodology. It enables the user to synthesize all important problem-related information into a meaningful whole. In addition, model building and computer simulation allow users to bring to bear on their problems information and knowledge from all areas— and to test their decisions with the aid of a computer model. This text is used as a supplement to the MicroDYNAMO language, also available from Addison-Wesley (see page 302).

Mathematical Problem-Solving with the Computer
Stephen L. Snover, Mark A. Spikell
Prentice-Hall, 1983
Dept. K-80
Englewood Cliffs, NJ 07632
(201) 592-2510
Price: $8.95

This book approaches programming (in BASIC) as a problem-solving activity. It provides the beginning programmer with twenty programming problems, each of which should be solvable in a half hour or less. The problems are designed for use on virtually any microcomputer with at least 1K of memory. The authors provide a brief discussion with some suggestions for each problem, extensions to the original problem, and answers (in the back of the book). The book can be used by individuals or a class with a simple working knowledge of beginning BASIC and the mathematical knowledge usually gained in first-year algebra.

Problems for Computer Solution
Stephen Rogowski
Creative Computing, 1980
39 E. Hanover Avenue
Morris Plains, NJ 07950
(800) 631-8112
Price: $4.95

This book offers ninety problems which are thoroughly discussed and referenced. Computer programs are provided in the following areas: algebra, geometry, trigonometry, number theory, probability, statistics, calculus, and science. The 182-page teacher's edition contains solutions to the problems, with listings in BASIC, sample runs, and in-depth analyses explaining the algorithms and theory involved. The cost of the teacher's edition is $9.95.

Problem Solving and Computer Programming
Peter Grogono and Sharon H. Nelson
Addison-Wesley, 1982
One Jacob Way
Reading, MA 01867
(617) 944-3700
Price: $14.95

The first half of this book (see page 153) develops a systematic methodology for problem solving. In the second half the authors show how this methodology can be applied to programming. The major theme is the integration of problem solving and programming methodologies. The approach is informal. The emphasis is on practical results rather than esoteric theory.

Problem-Solving with the Computer
Edwin Sage
Entelek
Ward-Whidden House
P.O. Box 1303
Portsmouth, NH 03801
(603) 436-0439
Price: $10.95

This text is designed to be used in a one-semester course in computer programming. It teaches BASIC in the context of the traditional high school mathematics curriculum. There are forty carefully graded problems dealing with many of the more familiar topics of algebra and geometry. Programs will run on TRS-80, Apple, PET, and other micros.

Using Computers in Mathematics
Gerald H. Elgarten, Alfred S. Posamentier, Stephen E. Moresh
Addison-Wesley, 1983
Innovative Division
2727 Sand Hill Road
Menlo Park, CA 94025
Price: $16.08

This book is designed to be used as a text for an introductory computer course with a strong emphasis on mathematical applications or as a supplement for high school mathematics courses. It is a particularly good resource for teachers who are looking for ways to use the computer to enrich their programs, since it is segmented by traditional topics such as elementary algebra, geometry, intermediate algebra and trigonometry, number theory, and calculus. The instructional technique emphasizes using flowcharts and determining output requirements before actual programming.

Computer Literacy: Programming

Basic Computer Programming for Kids
Pat Cassidy and Jim Close
Spectrum Books
A Division of Prentice-Hall, Inc.
Englewood Cliffs, NJ 07632
(201) 592-2000
Price: $11.95

This book includes the history of computers and computing, the future of computers, applications, and introduction to programming for elementary students.

BASICcally Speaking: A Young Person's Guide to Computing

Frances L. Cohen
Reston Publishing Co., Inc.
11480 Sunset Hills Road
Reston, VA 22090
(703) 437-8900
Price: $9.95 paperback; $12.95 hardback

This book covers BASIC programming for elementary-aged children, stressing logical problem solving and good program design. Computer history and parts of the computer are also covered.

The BASIC Handbook

David Lien
Compusoft Publishing, 1981
1050-E Pioneer Way
El Cajon, CA 92020
(714) 588-0996
Price: $19.95

This is an indispensable reference for anyone interested in exchanging programs with others. In an encyclopedic statement by statement format, it reveals the similarities and differences between the various versions of BASIC, gives sample programs, and tells what you can do if your BASIC lacks a particular feature. If you will be using more than one microcomputer or trying to convert programs, this will be an important reference to have on hand.

Computer Literacy: A Hands-On Approach

Arthur Luehrmann and Herbert Peckman
Webster/McGraw-Hill, 1983
1221 Avenue of the Americas
New York, NY 10020
(800) 223-4180; (212) 997-2646 in New York
Price: $17.97

Stresses problem-solving through programming. Includes student text, workbook, teacher's resource manual, and copyable diskette for TRS-80 III or Apple II. This book is designed for junior or senior high school students.

Computer Programming for Kids and Other Beginners

Royal Van Horn
Sterling Swift, 1982
7901 South IH-35
Austin, TX 78744
(512) 282-6840
Price: $9.95

An introduction to programming for TRS-80 and Apple II with simple examples and sample programs. The book introduces graphics early in the book for motivation. Terms, parts of the computer, operating instructions, and glossary are also included. Geared for third and fourth graders.

Computer Programming in the BASIC Language
Zeney P. Jacobs, Francis G. French, William J. Moulds, Jacob G. Schuchman
Allyn and Bacon, Inc., 1983
7 Wells Ave.
Newton, MA 02159
(617) 964-5530
Price: $10.02

Includes introductory activities, exercises, summary and activities, and problem sets for each lesson in BASIC programming. Minitopics are included throughout the book and provide basic information on the history and development of computers, careers, capacities, and modern uses. A teacher can learn simultaneously with students; previous experience not necessary. This is a secondary level text, and a teacher's guide is available.

Discovering Apple LOGO: An Invitation to Computer Art and Programming
David D. Thornburg
Addison-Wesley, 1983
One Jacob Way
Reading, MA 01867
(617) 944-3700
Price: $14.95

The author introduces Logo's unique graphics features, and demonstrates how to teach children the rudiments of programming. Mathematics and geometry skills, plus programming skills are reviewed.

Elementary BASIC
Elementary Pascal
Henry Ledgard and Andrew Singer
Vintage Books, 1982
201 E. 50th Street
New York, NY 10022
(212) 572-2188
Price: $12.95 paperback; $20.00 hardback

Each of these books teaches BASIC or Pascal using Sherlock Holmes cases as a teaching tool. Computer programs in the book sift through clues to illuminate principles of programming. This is a step-by-step primer for fundamental ideas of programming in a motivating format.

Every Kid's First Book of Robots and Computers
David D. Thornburg
COMPUTE! Books, 1982
625 Fulton Street
Greensboro, NC 27403
(919) 275-9809
Price: $4.95

This book helps children develop skills in computer programming through the use of the Big Trax vehicle by Milton Bradley. It relates Logo commands and procedures to Big Trax programming. "Turtle Tiles" can be detached from the back of the book and used to mark pathways if a child doesn't have a Big Trax to program. Those who read can easily follow instructions in the book, or instructions could be read aloud for younger non-readers. For grade levels 1–6.

The Genie in the Computer: Easy BASIC Through Graphics
Rachel Kohl, Laura Karp, and Ethan Singer
John Wiley & Sons, Inc., 1982
One Wiley Drive
Somerset, NJ 08873
(201) 469-4400
Price: $12.95

Includes programming concepts taught with a motivating genie. Workbook includes simple programs, exercises, projects, and quizzes. TRS-80 edition.

Introducing LOGO for the Apple and Texas Instruments 99/4A
Peter Ross
Addison-Wesley, 1983
One Jacob Way
Reading, MA 01867
(617) 944-3700
Price: $12.95

This book introduces Logo as a language and shows the wide range of its capabilities. The author offers valuable programming techniques and suggests several open-ended projects that demonstrate the potential of this language.

An Introduction to Programming and Problem Solving with Pascal
G. Michael Schneider, Steven W. Weingart, and David N. Perlman
John Wiley & Sons, Inc., 1982
One Wiley Drive
Somerset, NJ 08873
(201) 469-4400
Price: $23.50

This is an introductory programming course covering all aspects of programming process, good programming style, and syntax of Pascal. Exercises and answers are included.

Kids and the Apple
(also available for Atari, VIC, or TI)
Edward Carlson
Datamost, Inc.
8943 Fullbright Ave.
Chatsworth, CA 91311
(213) 709-1202
Price: $19.95

A machine specific book to help children learn about the computer.

Learning TRS-80 BASIC
David Lien
CompuSoft Publishing
1050-E Pioneer Way
El Cajon, CA 92020
(714) 588-0996
Price: $19.95

David Lien has developed several good books that allow the reader interactive learning about and on the microcomputer. This book is a compilation of Lien's original *TRS-80 User's Manual* and *Learning Level II*, plus extensive new material including the Model 16. It provides step-by-step instruction including sample programs, and teaches you to write custom software. A question and answer section at the end of each chapter tests your knowledge of new material.

Learning With Logo
Dan Watt
McGraw-Hill Book Company, 1982
Princeton Road
Hightstown, NJ 08520
(609) 426-5254
Price: $14.95

This book is an introduction to Logo for children and adults. There are special sections throughout the book to highlight activities suggested in the book. It also features detailed instruction for creating a Logo Procedures Disk which contains sample programs and a number of "tool procedures" needed to carry out the projects included in the book. The later chapters in the book offer mathematical explorations in turtle geometry.

Logo: An Introduction
J. Dale Burnett
Creative Computing Press, 1983
39 East Hanover Avenue
Morris Plains, NJ 07950
(201) 540-0445
Price: $7.95

This book is designed to aid any Logo beginner (child or adult) to introduce the philosophy and purpose of the Logo language. It is open-ended and exploratory, providing a minimum of expository detail, but acting as a catalyst for further individual activity.

Logo for the Apple II
Harold Abelson
McGraw-Hill Book Company, 1982
Princeton Rd.
Hightstown, NJ 08520
(609) 426-5254
Price: $14.95

The author introduces programming through turtle geometry—a series of exercises involving both Logo programming and geometric concepts. Later chapters illustrate more advanced projects, such as the Instant program that enables parents and teachers to create a programming environment for preschool children. Also included is a reference material of enduring value to the sophisticated user.

One, Two, Three, My Computer and Me: A Logo Funbook for Kids
Donna Beardon
Reston Publishing Company, 1983
11480 Sunset Hills Drive
Reston, VA 22090
(703) 437-8900
Price: $10.95

Contains Logo activities for the Apple and Texas Instruments versions of Logo. These activities can be completed on and off the computer. The book is easy to use, and has appealing graphics.

Pascal
Paul M. Chirlian
Matrix Publishers, Inc., 1980
11000 SW 11th Street
Suite E
Beaverton, OR 97005
(503) 646-2713
(800) 547-1842
Price: $12.95

An introduction to Pascal for students with little or no programming experience. Program listings are used to explain proper usage of language features.

Picture This! (Atari version)
Picture This Too! (Apple version)
David D. Thornburg
Addison-Wesley, 1982
One Jacob Way
Reading, MA 01867
(617) 944-3700
Price: $14.95

Each of these books explores possibilities of teaching children how to use the computer using PILOT and turtle geometry to solve problems, invent games, and create pictures. There are step-by-step approaches with projects throughout the books.

Simple PASCAL
James J. McGregor and Alan H. Watt
Computer Science Press, Inc., 1981
11 Taft Court
Rockville, MD 20850
(301) 251-9050
Price: $12.95

This is an introductory text for high school beginners. The book concentrates on central parts of Pascal that are adequate for writing a wide range of useful programs. Examples introduce general ideas with simple programs.

Spotlight on Computer Literacy
Ellen Richman
Random House, 1982
201 East 50th Street
New York, NY 10022
(800) 241-6402
Price: $6.95

All the parts of this book are well organized, succinct and engaging for students in middle school beginning the study of computers. The first two parts present "How Computers Work" and "Computers in Our Lives." Neither requires access to computers, but both help students to understand the parts of the machine and the role it plays in many aspects of society. The third part is an introduction to BASIC programming that includes simple activities with INPUT, Looping, Strings, IF. . .THEN, and Graphics. Students are expected to explore concepts first at their desk, then at the keyboard. Appropriate modifications for Atari, Apple, TRS-80, and PET are explained.

SOFTWARE SOURCES

In order to make your job of finding quality educational software easier, listed below are sources of software: Reviews and Directories. Reviews of software are invaluable, given the number of programs available and the difficulties in gaining access to review copies of software. Most sources of reviews listed here are provided by educational organizations and represent teachers' perspectives. Good sources of reviews are periodicals, since most of them include three or four reviews in each issue. Also, the book *Courseware in the Classroom: Selecting, Organizing and Using Educational Software* (Ann Lathrop and Bobby Goodson), includes criteria for evaluating courseware, how to organize and maintain a courseware library, plus a resource section with recommended courseware, sources of reviews, and publishers. The book is available for $10.00 from Addison-Wesley Publishing Co., Innovative Division, 2727 Sand Hill Road, Menlo Park, CA 94025.

The directories included in this section cover a range of grade levels, subject areas, and computer hardware. Again, be sure to check your periodicals for new product announcements to keep you abreast of all the new pieces of software on the market.

Reviews

Courseware Report Card
Educational Insights
150 W. Carob Street
Compton, CA 90220
(213) 737-2131
Price: $49.95 per edition; $95.00 both editions

Reviews are published in two editions, elementary and secondary, five times during the school year. Each issue contains 20–25 reviews. Descriptions and evaluations of each program are detailed and comprehensive. Performance, ease of use, error handling, appropriateness, documentation, and educational value are graded A–F as well as in narrative form. Teachers should find the rating system and information very helpful.

Courseware Reviews 1982
SMERC Library Microcomputer Center
San Mateo County Office of Education
333 Main Street
Redwood City, CA 94063
(415) 363-5472
Price: $10.00

There are fifty programs evaluated in this publication in all areas of curriculum. These reviews have been compiled by educators all over California. Besides describing each program, the reviews include noted strengths, weaknesses, and student responses, plus a checklist of evaluation criteria. Wherever applicable, they also list publications which have published critical reviews of the programs.

The Digest of Software Reviews: Education

1341 Bulldog Lane
Suite C9
Fresno, CA 93710
(209) 227-4341
Price: $33.95

This is a new quarterly publication which includes in each issue, abstracts of the published reviews of fifty educational software packages and a guest editorial from a noted computer educator. It is edited by Ann Lathrop, Library Coordinator, San Mateo County Office of Education (see pp. 254 and 283).

Journal of Courseware Review

The Apple Foundation
20525 Mariani Avenue
Cupertino, CA 95014
(408) 996-1010
Price: $5.95

This publication is available from Apple dealers. It reviews commercially available software, gives sources of information, and shows screen displays for each program. Check your yellow pages for your nearest Apple dealer.

Microgram

EPIE Institute
P.O. Box 620
Stony Brook, NY 11790
(516) 246-8664
Price: $48.00 per year

The Educational Products Information Exchange (EPIE) Institute is a huge educational advocacy group that provides detailed analyses of curriculum materials used in elementary and high schools. Along with the Microcomputer Resource Center (MRC) at Teachers College, Columbia University, EPIE has instituted a Microcomputer Software File, which reviews commercially available software programs. The EPIE Software File now has available reviews of six of the larger computer-based instructional programs as well as a number of microcomputer games. A new joint venture between EPIE and Consumers Union, under the title "Consortium for Quality in Educational Computing Products," publishes EPIEgram, an educational consumers' newsletter devoted to consumer issues and product evaluations.

MicroSIFT
500 Lindsay Building
300 S.W. Sixth Avenue
Portland, OR 97204
(503) 248-6800
Price: free

MicroSIFT is a clearinghouse for K–12 software information. It has established procedures for the collection and evaluation of microcomputer instructional materials and information. Reviews available from *MicroSIFT* are each done by several educators at evaluation network sites who review programs for content, instructional quality, and technical quality. Modeled after Conduit, *MicroSIFT* distributes information about software availability and program evaluations. This information is available on RICE—Resources in Computer Education, a data base accessible on BRS Inc.'s computer system. The information is also disseminated in print form through state, regional and local education agencies.

Peelings II
P.O. Box 188
Las Cruces, NM 88004
(505) 526-8364
Price: $21.00

Peelings II is a magazine of Apple software and hardware evaluations published nine times a year. Commercially available programs are described in detail, including the systems setup, instructions, and documentation provided. Errors are noted, and a final evaluation of each program summarizes recommendations and criticisms. Occasional issues of *Peelings II* feature an education section.

Purser's Magazine
P.O. Box 466
El Dorado, CA 95623
(916) 622-5288
Price: $12.00

Purser's began as one of the most complete listings of available software. Currently, *Purser's* reviews programs and publishes separate issues for TRS-80, Apple, and Atari systems. Recent issues have published the results of readers' questionnaires on microcomputer software and a guide to buying specific hardware systems. A brief Atari Software Directory is available from *Purser's* in exchange for a self-addressed, stamped envelope.

School MicroWare Reviews
Dresden Associates
P.O. Box 246
Dresden, ME 04342
(207) 737-4466
Price: $45.00 per year

Produced by the publishers of the *School MicroWare Directory*, this periodical contains in-depth user evaluations of software programs for Apple, Atari, PET, and TRS-80 microcomputer systems. *School MicroWare Reviews* encourages teachers to submit courseware evaluations, and it contains useful critiques written by educators from around the country. A particularly helpful feature of this publication is the inclusion of an index to reviews of educational software in other publications. The reviews are also sorted by subject area which makes looking for mathematics software much easier. It is published three times a year.

SOFTSWAP

San Mateo County Office of Education
333 Main Street
Redwood City, CA 94063
(415) 363-5472

SOFTSWAP is a joint project of the Microcomputer Center (see page 254) of the San Mateo County Office of Education and Computer-Using Educators (CUE) (see page 251). SOFTSWAP receives donations of educational software, evaluates and refines the programs, and makes the programs available free of charge to educators who copy the programs at the Center. Further, SOFTSWAP operates as a software exchange. Any educator who contributes an original program on a disk may request any one SOFTSWAP disk in exchange. SOFTSWAP also sells disks (five to thirty programs per disk) for a nominal fee. Over 400 public domain programs are available on some sixty-four disks, including software for Apple, Atari, Compucolor, IBM, PET, and TRS-80 microcomputers. A complete catalogue and ordering information may be obtained by sending one dollar to SOFTSWAP.

Directories

The Addison-Wesley Book of Apple Computer Software, 1982

Addison-Wesley
One Jacob Way
Reading, MA 01867
(617) 944-3700
Price: $19.95

This directory describes and rates a large section of Apple-compatible software, including educational packages. The descriptions include a summary and numerical ratings of various characteristics of the software. The format is clear and shows occasional representative screen displays for different programs.

The Apple Software Directory, Vol. 3
WIDL Video
5245 W. Diversey Avenue
Chicago, IL 60639
(312) 622-9606
Price: $5.95

This directory lists educational software from over 400 vendors. The programs are briefly described and are cross-referenced by subject matter. WIDL Video also publishes a directory of games software for the Apple; an Apple resource directory listing hardware, boards, and accessories; and *The Apple II Blue Book*, which includes all of this information in one volume.

Commodore Resource Encyclopedia
Commodore Computer
487 Devon Park Drive
Wayne, PA 19087
(215) 687-9750
Price: $9.95

This directory is available from Commodore and lists software for seven different application areas, including education.

Educational Software Directory: A Subject Guide to Microcomputer Software
Libraries Unlimited
P.O. Box 263
Littleton, CO 80160-0263
(303) 770-1220
Price: $22.50

This directory provides subject access to educational microcomputer software (grades K–12). It contains information on programs for many different microcomputer systems. Each entry includes the name of the software package, publisher, grade level, format, language, price, and a lengthy annotation. There is also a publisher and distributor index.

The Index to Computer Based Learning, 1981 Edition
Instructional Media Laboratory
University of Wisconsin
P.O. Box 413
Milwaukee, WI 53201

The *Index*, available either as four paperbound volumes or on microfiche, lists over 4800 computer-based learning programs. Each is cross-indexed by source, programming language, central processor type, and programming category. Programs for primary and secondary school and universities are abstracted according to fourteen characteristics.

Instructor's Annual Computer Directory for Schools
Instructor
P.O. Box 6177
Duluth, MN 55806
(212) 888-3344
Price: $19.95

Software listings in this annual publication are organized by content area, machine, and alphabetically by company. Information about selecting computers, peripherals, books, and other resources are also provided.

Radio Shack TRS-80 Educational Software Sourcebook
Radio Shack Educational Division
1400 One Tandy Center
Fort Worth, TX 76102
Price: $4.95

Software is described and grouped by instructional techniques, user level, and subject categories in this book. Listings of schools that were used as test sites are provided by some software publishers. The 1983 edition will be available in July 1983.

School MicroWare Directory
Dresden Associates
P.O. Box 246
Dresden, ME 04342
(207) 737-4466
Price: $25.00 per year

This semi-annual directory includes software for Grades K–12 in most subject areas and for administration. Programs for TRS-80, Atari, and Apple II are listed and briefly described. Over 250 software suppliers are listed, and programs are indexed alphabetically and by grade level within subject/department. Separate listings for individual computer systems are also included.

Swift's 1983–84 Directory of Educational Software, Apple II Edition
Sterling Swift
7901 South IH-35
Austin, TX 78744
(512) 282-6840
Price: $16.95

This directory contains a listing of most of the educational programs for the Apple microcomputer. The contents are divided into commercial and noncommercial publishers of educational software, and software is further classified by grade level. The directory is available from Sterling Swift and from most computer stores.

RECOMMENDED SOFTWARE

The following software was selected to provide the reader with a variety of materials currently available in the marketplace. Each has educational merit as well as some limitations. Any products previously mentioned in this book are listed with reference to the page(s) on which they appear. The software is divided into grade levels: Primary, Middle, and High School; and Instructional Tools. Those programs that span more than one level are listed in the lowest of the appropriate levels. Each listing specifies hardware requirements and price when information was available. For detailed information, contact the publisher or your local vendor. Before purchase, potential users should submit the software to their own evaluation procedures if possible. A sample of guidelines may be obtained from the National Council of Teachers of Mathematics in their publication, *Guidelines for Evaluating Instructional Materials.*

You should never buy software unless the distributor permits thirty-day approval purchasing. This allows you to evaluate the software and return it if you are not satisfied for any reason. Most distributors now honor such arrangements. All should. You, as consumers, can insist upon this as a condition of purchase. For your part, you should see to it that no one in your school makes illegal copies of software.

Mathematics Applications

Primary Level

Arithmagic
Quality Educational Designs (QED)
P.O. Box 12486
Portland, OR 97212
(503) 287-8131
Hardware: Apple II Plus
Grade Range: 3–8
Price: $35.00

This disk contains three arithmetic games that encourage logical thinking while reinforcing computational skills. *Diffy* (see pages 55–57) encourages youngsters to find four special numbers whose repeated differences continue to produce more than zero. This game helps students to develop skills employed in thinking many moves ahead or backwards, depending upon the method of thinking chosen. *Tri Puz* is a very simple game that reinforces finding addends, sums, or factors, given products. The triangular arrangement of the given answers, however, requires the user to focus on the outcomes of not one but three related operations.

Magic Squares leads students individually, in pairs, or as teams step by step in discovering the mysteries behind what makes a magic square work.

Building Estimation Skills
Cuisenaire Co. of America, Inc.
12 Church Street, Box D
New Rochelle, NY 10805
(914) 235-0900
Hardware: Apple II Plus
Grade Range: 4–8
Price: $65.00

The two disks included in this package provide practice with rounding whole numbers, as well as estimating sums, differences, products, quotients, and percents. A piece of a picture is disclosed on the screen when the student makes the correct response. Choice of topics and levels of difficulty are left to the user. On-disk documentation is good and tutorials are also available on the screen for students who exhibit difficulty. Worksheets and a Teacher Information Sheet are provided with the package and are very usable. Though the activities are basically drill and practice, they do provide the teacher with a range of problems that are often tedious to develop. The design and range of the program is good. Since students often need encouragement to use estimating rather than finding the exact answer, this software should be very useful in the mathematics classroom.

Bumble Games
The Learning Company
4370 Alpine Road
Portola Valley, CA 94025
(415) 851-3160
Hardware: Apple II Plus
Grade Range: K–5
Price: $60.00

This disk contains six colorful number plotting games. Bumble, the featured creature, gives clues as students guess secret numbers on a number line, or locations on maps. In the game Tic Tac Toc, two players choose points on a grid, until someone gets four in a row and sees a surprise. In the game Bumble Dot, players make dot-to-dot pictures using Bumble's designs or make their own computer graphics for themselves or a friend.

Bumble Plot
The Learning Company
4370 Alpine Road
Portola Valley, CA 94025
(415) 851-3160
Hardware: Apple II Plus
Grade Range: 3–8
Price: $60.00

This disk includes five games that build on skills learned in Bumble Games (see previous description). Players, using negative numbers as well as positive numbers, become fluent number pair plotters as they set up roadblocks to trap a robber, read a sonar map to find treasure with Bumble, and draw Bumble and other computer graphics on a grid.

Change/Elem—Vol I Math

MECC Distribution Center
2520 Broadway Drive
St. Paul, MN 55113
(612) 638-0611
Hardware: Apple II; Atari
Grade Range: 3–6
Price: $24.95

Change is a simple single-purpose program that tests students' ability to make change with amounts up to $20.00. They must use a "counting back" technique, as is done in the store. There is an opportunity to change a response and to exit the program after each turn.

Clock

Hartley Courseware, Inc.
P.O. Box 431
Dimondale, MI 48821
(616) 942-8987
Hardware: Apple II Plus
Grade Range: K–3
Price: $39.95

This is a simple program that allows students to set clock hands or indicate time in digital format. A tutorial mode is also available which could be used for demonstration of the movement of the clock hands and the related time in digital format. Documentation in the program could be better, but with some preteaching children can practice their skills at the level of their choice: hour, half hour, quarter hour, five minutes, or one minute. The teacher may select to run the lessons, review the students' progress—using the management system, select a design option or check the catalog.

Darts

Control Data Publishing Company
P.O. Box 261127
San Diego, CA 92126
(800) 233-3784
(800) 233-3785 in CA
Hardware: Apple II Plus; Atari 800
Grade Range: K–6

This game is designed to teach fractions. Balloons appear on a number line and students guess where the balloons are by typing in mixed numbers. Each time they guess an arrow shoots to the specified position. The arrow pops the balloon when the guess is correct (see pages 58 and 236).

Elementary Mathematics Classroom Learning System
Whole Numbers and Fractions/Decimals
Sterling Swift
7901 South IH-35
Austin, TX 78744
(512) 282-6840
Hardware: Apple II Plus
Grade Range: 5–8
Price: $495.00 per package; $49.95 per disk

This system offers two complete CAI/CMI packages, *Whole Numbers* and *Fractions/Decimals.* Each package contains six diskettes, including one for the management system and one for games. The teacher is able to maintain records for 200 students in a maximum of five groups. As a student uses each disk s(he) must sign on and is then directed to take a diagnostic test or is given the lesson that was indicated as appropriate the last time s(he) used the package. Tutorials are provided when necessary and usually include some graphic representation or expanded notation. Students who have completed the tutorials can choose to do another drill or try a mastery check. This is a well-organized easy-to-use system and should provide the teacher with a helpful tool for reinforcement of skills. However, the need for initial instruction and concept development by the teacher is still required. (Note: Individual disks for each skill without the management package can be purchased from the publisher as part of the *Arithmetic Classroom.*)

Explorer Metros
Sunburst Communications, Inc.
Room M5
39 Washington Avenue
Pleasantville, NY 10570
(800) 431-1934
Hardware: Apple II Plus
Grade Range: 5–8
Price: $90.00

Explorer Metros: A Metric Adventure is a simulation designed to give students experience in using estimation and the knowledge of different units of metric measurement. The program varies the elements of the simulation each time it is run so that individuals or small groups will enjoy playing the game several times. Students explore a space colony and encounter situations requiring them to choose one of three alternatives based on a given metric length, mass capacity, or temperature. Students must complete the journey within a time limit but they may call up a metric table or solicit assistance from a computer companion—Dugan the robot. One particularly useful feature of this program is the modification option which allows the teacher or students the opportunity to redesign the encounters and the material covered. Use of graphics and on-screen documentation are also a plus.

Factoring Whole Numbers

Quality Educational Designs (QED)
P.O. Box 12486
Portland, OR 97212
(503) 287-8131
Hardware: Apple II; TRS-80 I; PET
Grade Range: 5–8
Price: $90.00

Factoring Whole Numbers is a 3-disk series that takes the student through factoring, beginning at an experimental level with manipulative materials, and moving step by step toward abstraction. Documentation is excellent throughout and provides bypass options. Each topic has a second level choice requiring application of the skill learned at a problem-solving level in a game format.

Junior high school students with good ability should be able to use these programs as tutorials and/or practice for number theory concepts such as: factor pairs, prime numbers, exponents, square roots, least common multiple and greatest common factor.

Green Globs

Conduit
P.O. Box 388
Iowa City, IA 52244
(319) 353-5789
Hardware: Apple II
Grade Range: K–6
Price: $55.00

In this game the player is given coordinate axes on which thirteen green globs are scattered randomly (see page 58). Students type in equations, which are graphed by the computer. Every time a graph hits one of the globs, the glob explodes. The object of the game is to destroy all thirteen globs. The scoring algorithm is carefully structured to encourage students to hit as many globs as possible with each shot. Green globs is part of the disk, *Graphing Equations*, which also includes *Linear and Quadratic Equations*, and *Space Tracker*.

Lemonade

MECC—Volume 4 Diskette
2520 Broadway Drive
St. Paul, MN 55113
(612) 376-1118
Hardware: Apple II
Grade Range: 3–6
Price: $30.00 (disk only)

The Sell series, *Sell Apples*, *Sell Plants*, *Sell Lemonade*, and *Sell Bicycles*, can be used to teach elementary economics to students through simulating a business environment (see pages 49–53). A support booklet may be purchased at an additional $10.50.

Math Ideas with Base Ten Blocks

Cuisenaire Co. of America, Inc.
12 Church Street, Box D
New Rochelle, NY 10805
(914) 235-0900
Hardware: Apple II
Grade Range: 1–7
Price: $49.95

The programs on this disk (see page 48) can be used for demonstration, tutorials, and drill. They are particularly helpful for a child who requires models at the initial learning stages. Students can select the number of problems, level of difficulty up to 1000, and the concept: counting, comparing, adding, subtracting, multiplying, or dividing. The latter two operations are often the most difficult to teach with models because of the amount of materials needed and the organizational skills required of the learner. Since both are provided on the screen the teacher will find students able to progress quickly, often discovering the rules for performing the operations themselves. These programs are an excellent example of how the computer can be used as an instructional tool to aid the learner and to free the teacher to work with others in the classroom.

Minus Mission

Arcademic Skill Builders Series
Developmental Learning Materials Inc. (DLM)
One DLM Park
Allen, TX 75002
(800) 527-4747
Hardware: Apple II Plus; TI 99/4A
Grade Range: K+
Price: Apple version—$39.00 (disk); $220.00 (set)
TI version—$44.00 (disk); $245.00 (set)

This is one program included in a six-program series (see pages 54–55). *Minus Mission* is a drill and practice program in an arcade format. The teacher can adjust the speed so the game can be used by students of varying abilities. The computer provides feedback to "answers" immediately through vivid graphics and sound. Rapid, accurate responses are awarded, and slower and incorrect ones are penalized. The games in the series challenge students to improve their mastery of basic skills by increasing the difficulty of the problems, as the students' proficiency increases.

PLATO
Control Data Publishing Company
P.O. Box 261127
San Diego, CA 92126
(800) 233-3784
(800) 233-3785 in CA
Hardware: Apple II Plus; Atari 800; TI 99/4A
Grade Range: K–12
Price: $45.00/lesson

PLATO computer-based education (see pages 44 and 47) is a highly interactive system of self-paced, one-on-one instruction. Although there are lessons available in all curricular areas, mathematics lessons are available in both basic skills and high school academic skills. The titles of the mathematics lessons are *Basic Number Facts, Whole Numbers, Decimals,* and *Fractions.*

Geometry and Measurement
Cuisenaire Co. of America, Inc.
12 Church Street, Box D
New Rochelle, NY 10805
(914) 235-0900
Hardware: Apple II Plus
Grade Range: 4–8
Price: $49.95

There are six major programs on this disk: reading customary or metric rulers; estimating and measuring the length of segments shown on a geoboard in units, millimeters or centimeters; constructing segments of a given length on a geoboard; naming segments that are parallel or perpendicular to a given segment on the geoboard; finding the perimeter of various polygons on a geoboard; and finding the area of various polygons. Each of these major programs can be accessed through a main menu and each allows for some choice of content within each topic. *Geometry and Measurement* is easily used by people with no programming experience, since the teacher documentation is well developed. The activities provide simple reinforcement for a previously learned skill or an opportunity for students to learn through trial and error.

Gertrude's Puzzles
The Learning Company
4370 Alpine Road
Portola Valley, CA 94025
(415) 851-3160
Hardware: Apple II; Apple II Plus
Grade Range: pre-K–6
Price: $75.00

In this program, Gertrude the goose flies across the screen bringing colored shapes to attribute puzzle rooms. Children pick up, move, and position the shapes on the screen to solve puzzles. They can play with different sets of shapes, or can create their own sets, using a magic shape editor. Solving Gertrude's puzzles involves early logic skills such as same/different relationships, and higher level skills such as deductive reasoning and problem solving.

Moptown

Apple Delivery Software
Apple Computer, Inc.
20525 Mariani Avenue
Cupertino, CA 95014
(408) 973-2222
Hardware: Apple
Grade Range: K–8
Price: $50.00

The disk and courseware with *Moptown* provide the user with eleven attribute games, some of them reminiscent of the Attribute Blocks and other logic models used in many elementary classrooms. The major skills developed with these materials are: pattern or similarity recognition and use, strategy development, hypothesis testing, and analogy logic. Students must discern attributes of height, color, girth, and name while responding to tasks in each game that are increasingly more difficult. The well-executed graphics and animation are very motivating. However, the clutter of the on-screen text might prove difficult reading for some students. Besides good instructions in the teacher's manual, there are also ideas for using the games with different types of groups, including a one-computer classroom. These materials will be particularly valuable to the teacher who sees merit in developing logical skills and in having access to a progression of activities that should be challenging to many students.

Numberforms

(Still under development)
Learningways Inc.
98 Raymond Street
Cambridge, MA 02140
(617) 864-2214
Hardware: Apple II; Apple II Plus
Grade Range: K–12
Price: $50.00

Numberforms is a computer manipulative tool for exploring and learning mathematics (see page 8). Students can move a numberline on the screen and pull off from that numberline a series of blocks, "numberforms," which display the number. They can then add, subtract, multiply, and divide numbers as the blocks visually perform the same operations. *Numberforms* thus provides the bridge between concrete manipulatives and abstract symbols. It provides a visual, pictorial, animated tool for students to understand and explore whole numbers and their operations.

Patternmaker

(Still under development)
Learningways Inc.
98 Raymond Street
Cambridge, MA 02140
(617) 864-2214
Hardware: Apple II; Apple II Plus
Grade Range: K–12
Price: $50.00

Patternmaker approaches art from a symmetry, tiling pattern perspective (see page 23). A person can create a simple design on an 8 × 8 pattern of squares and then put that design into a larger pattern. Each of these simple grids can be manipulated using all of the symmetry operations to produce artistic patterns, which can be colored and animated. *Patternmaker* is so easy to use that even very young children can enjoy it, and so sophisticated that artists, mathematicians, and designers will find it interesting.

Rocky's Boots

The Learning Company
4370 Alpine Road
Portola Valley, CA 94025
(415) 851-3160
Hardware: Apple II Plus
Grade Range: 2–up
Price: $75.00

In this game, players build logic machines to score points in an arcade game setting, using conventional logic symbols for "and," "or," "not," and "flip-flop." These logic machines are animated in a simulation where electrical current flows and operates a kicking boot. Players score or lose points for "booting" particular characters. The object of the game is to build the machine that will win the most points.

Songwriter

Scarborough Systems Inc.
25 N. Broadway
Tarrytown, NY 10591
(914) 332-4545
Hardware: Apple II; Apple II Plus
Grade Range: K–12

Songwriter is a program that helps students to learn and understand music by composing and editing musical scores (see page 23). The program plays music in tune through the Apple or external speaker as the screen scrolls the notes like a player piano. Students are able to adjust the musical notes by adding, subtracting, multiplying, and dividing, therefore learning a great deal about fractions by whole number operations. The program has been carefully designed to be very easy to use and to be fun to play with. It presents a new and interesting perspective on music and mathematics education.

Middle School Level

Buggy
(still in development)
Ginn and Company
191 Spring Street
Lexington, MA 02173
(617) 861-1670
(800) 848-9500

Buggy (see page 57) is an arithmetic skills game in which the player(s) must detect "bugs" in a series of equations.

Fast Freight
(still in development)
Intentional Educations, Inc.
341 Mt. Auburn Street
Watertown, MA 02172
(617) 923-7707

This is one in a series of four simulations called *Big Business* (see page 20). *Fast Freight* simulates a trucking business designed to teach students how to set up and run a business. It involves considerable mathematical application.

Magic Grid
Ideal School Supply Co.
1100 S. Lavergne Avenue
Oak Lawn, IL 60453
(312) 425-0800
Hardware: Apple II Plus; TRS-80 I
Grade Level: 7–10
Price: $24.95

Magic Grid provides students with an opportunity to practice equation solving skills using the addition principle and/or substitution. Students must solve nine different equations selected from a tic-tac-toe-like grid. Each equation requires information from a previously solved equation. Help is given in a friendly manner each time an incorrect response is returned. The answer is supplied after two wrong choices. When the *Magic Grid* is completed a summary of the equations solved, with and without help, is provided, as well as the opportunity to do another *Magic Grid* or to play one of two other games. This program is limited in scope, providing only practice in simple equation solving, but it may be appropriate for some grade 7–10 students.

Multiplying Fractions
Microcomputer Workshops
225 Westchester Ave.
Port Chester, NY 10573
(914) 937-5440
Hardware: Apple II; Atari; PET; TRS-80
Grade Range: 5–8
Price: $24.95 (disk); $20.00 (cassette)

This program's merits are in the sequencing of presentations for cancellation prior to multiplication with fractions, a skill students often have great difficulty acquiring. The student is given a problem, work options, and work space on the screen. Diagonal and vertical reduction is required and often changing the answer to a mixed number. An error summary is provided at the end so students will know whether errors occur because of the reduction process or multiplication. This same author has prepared a program for addition of fractions with similar features, also available from Microcomputer Workshops.

Pollute: The Impact of Pollutants on Bodies of Water
Diversified Educational Enterprises, Inc.
725 Main Street
Lafayette, IN 47901
(317) 742-2690
Hardware: TRS-80
Grade Range: 7–12
Price: $59.95

Pollute (see pages 143–148) is a program which analyzes the oxygen content and waste content of a body of water according to the variables—type of body of water, water temperature, type of waste, rate of dumping waste, type of treatment of waste.

Search Series
McGraw-Hill
Webster Division
1221 Avenue of the Americas
New York, NY 10020
(800) 223-4180
Hardware: Apple II; TRS-80
Grade Range: 5–9
Price: $180.00 (set)

There are five sets of programs available in this series (see pages 75–84). Each set includes software, student workbooks, and a teacher's manual. The individual sets are listed below.
• *Geology Search* simulates an oil exploration. As the computer "performs" geological tests and keeps track of the budget, students learn about rocks, fossils, and underground structures in order to make decisions about where to drill.

- *Geography Search* simulates ships searching for the New World. Students navigate using the sun, stars, ocean depth, climate, and winds.
- *Community Search* simulates an ancient society where students must face choices about migration, occupations, trades, aggression, and building a palace.
- *Archeology Search* simulates an excavation of an historical site. Students collect data and formulate theories about the origins of the people who once lived there.
- *Energy Search* simulates the role of a manager of an energy factory. Students make interdependent decisions as they recreate the steps necessary in the search for new energy sources.

Survival Math

Sunburst Communications, Inc.
Room M5
39 Washington Avenue
Pleasantville, NY 10570
(914) 769-5030
Hardware: Apple II Plus; TRS-80 I, III; Atari 400, 800
Grade Range: 7–12
Price: $50.00

Survival Math is a set of four simulations that provide students with the opportunity of applying and integrating arithmetic skills in realistic situations. All of these simulations are practical, well designed, and challenging. The activities are an excellent way to measure students' abilities to use their arithmetic skills and to work on tasks as a group. Because of the on-screen documentation and the worksheets provided, the first two simulations can be attempted by capable students without much assistance. The latter two, however, will require teacher organization and coaching. Parameters are changed each time the programs are run so that they can be used several times.

Three Mile Island

MUSE
347 N. Charles Street
Baltimore, MD 21201
(301) 659-7212
Hardware: Apple II; Apple II Plus
Grade Range: 5 +
Price: $39.95

This program is a simulation of a nuclear reactor (see page 49). The student controls the reactor, which involves management skills. Their goal is to make a profit, but also to avoid a meltdown.

High School Level

Equations

Microcomputer Workshops
225 Westchester Ave.
Port Chester, NY 10573
(914) 937-5440
Hardware: Apple; PET; TRS-80
Grade Range: 8–12
Price: $24.95 (disk); $20.00 (cassette)

When *Equations* is run, a student is presented with a linear equation in the form $AX + B = C$ and is asked to solve individual steps to simplify for X. The student solves the equation step by step on the screen. After each step, the equation is updated. All errors, including incorrect use of algebraic axioms, are immediately flagged and explained with messages explaining the student's error. Common errors such as dividing by the variable are specifically flagged. Adding a negative number and subtracting, or dividing and multiplying by a reciprocal are interchangeable. The student continues to solve the equation until reaching the correct solution. At the end of the problem, the number of procedural and computational errors are given.

Solving Quadratic Equations (by Factoring)

Microcomputer Workshops
225 Westchester Ave.
Port Chester, NY 10573
(914) 937-5440
Hardware: Apple II; PET; TRS-80
Grade Range: 9–12
Price: $24.95 (disk); $20.00 (cassette)

This program is a well developed CAI package with automatic tutorial help after the second incorrect attempt. The instructional objective is to give students practice in solving quadratic equations of the form $AX^2 + BX + C = 0$ by factoring. A particularly nice feature is the division of the screen into three parts: one to show the equation, another to show the work selected, and the third gives a menu of options to be used in solving the equation. An additional feature is the error summary at the end of each problem, pinpointing whether mistakes are procedural or computational. Many teachers will welcome this aid in helping students to develop the step-by-step process required in solving quadratic equations.

Instructional Tools

Delta Drawing
Spinnaker Software
215 First Street
Cambridge, MA 02142
(617) 868-4700
Hardware: Apple II Plus; IBM; Atari; Commodore 64
Grade Range: K–12
Price: $59.95

This is a good beginning program to aid children in learning about the concept of step-by-step programming as well as in exploring geometric concepts that relate to drawing figures (see pages 96–107). Commands are of eight types usually requiring only one or two keystrokes; for example, D draws a line a fixed length and R turns the cursor 30 degrees. Commands are automatically stored in a program labeled with one of the digits 1–9. These programs can be recalled and reused throughout one session, singly or in nested form, to create elaborate designs. A child need know only a few commands to explore many concepts in plane geometry and graphing. This makes *Delta Drawing* a wonderful tool for demonstration and problem solving. Note: Documentation is outside program.

Function Plotter
Math Software
233 Blackthorn Place
Deerfield, IL 60015
Hardware: Apple II Plus
Grade Range: 9–12
Price: $29.95

Function Plotter is a software tool for the graphic exploration and/or demonstration of most mathematical functions. The opening menu offers students the choice of trigonometry, absolute value, greatest integer, polynomial, and student supplied functions. The user can also define the range and domain. A significant feature for demonstration is its capability for alternating color overlay of graphs. Students or teachers can find help on the screen and in a 30-page manual. This program has rather obvious significance to an Algebra I or II teacher and should save hours of preparation time, while allowing the student to discover intrinsic relationships between functions. It is certainly worth its expense in graph paper and transparencies.

Logo

Two companies, Krell Software Corp. and Terrapin, Inc., have obtained licenses to market the MIT version of Logo. Logo Computer Systems, Inc. (LCSI) and Texas Instruments have produced their own Logo versions although they are based on the original developed at MIT (see pages 107–119).

Krell Software Corp.
1320 Stony Brook Road
Stony Brook, NY 11790
(516) 751-5139
Hardware: Apple II w/64K; Apple II Plus w/64K
Price: $89.95

Terrapin, Inc.
380 Green Street
Cambridge, MA 02139
(617) 492-8816
Hardware: Apple II w/64K; Apple II Plus w/64K
Price: $149.95

LCSI's Apple Logo
Apple Computer Inc.
Cupertino, CA 95014
(800) 538-9696
(800) 662-9238 in CA
Hardware: Apple II w/64K; Apple II Plus w/64K
Price: $175.00

TI Logo II
Texas Instruments
P.O. Box 53
Lubbock, TX 79408
Hardware: TI 99/4A w/memory expansion unit
Price: $129.95

Atari, Inc.
1265 Borregas Avenue
Sunnyvale, CA 94086
(800) 538-8543
(800) 672-1404 in CA
Hardware: Atari 400 w/16K; Atari 800 w/16K; Atari 1200 w/16K
Price: under $100

Digital Equipment Corp.
Maynard, MA 01754
Hardware: DEC Professional Series 300 Personal Computers
Price: not available at press time

Commodore Computer
487 Devon Park Drive
Wayne, PA 19087
(215) 687-9750
Hardware: Commodore 64
Price: $100

Turtle Graphics Packages

Atari Pilot Student Pak
Atari, Inc.
1265 Borregas Avenue
Sunnyvale, CA 94086
(800) 538-8543
(800) 672-1404 in CA
Hardware: Atari 400; Atari 800
Price: $78.95

Atari Pilot Educator Pak
(address above)
Hardware: Atari 400; Atari 800
Price: $128.95

TRS-80 Disk Color LOGO
Radio Shack
Education Division
1400 One Tandy Center
Fort Worth, TX 76102
(800) 433-5682
(800) 772-8538
Hardware: TRS-80 Color Computer w/16K
Price: $49.95

Delta Drawing
(see page 96).

Kidstuff
Thomas R. Smith
P.O. Box 345
Dedham, MA 02026
(617) 326-0917
Hardware: Commodore PET CBM
Price: $59.95

Cyber LOGO Turtle: A First Step in Computer Literacy
Reston Publishing Company
11480 Sunset Hills Road
Reston, VA 22090
(800) 336-0338
(703) 437-8354 in VA
Hardware: Apple II w/48K; Apple II Plus w/48K
Price: $79.95

CyberLOGO

Cybertronics
One Lincoln Plaza
New York, NY 10023
(212) 772-9565
1410 Shrader Street
San Francisco, CA 94117
(415) 566-4556
Hardware: Apple II w/48K; Apple II Plus w/48K
Price: $99.95

MicroDYNAMO

Addison-Wesley
One Jacob Way
Reading, MA 01867
(617) 944-3700
Hardware: Apple II
Grade Range: 9–12; college
Price: $245.00

MicroDYNAMO is a simulation language developed for solving real world, complex interdependent problems. (see pages 84–93) It allows the user to simulate the problems over time, asking a variety of "what if" questions. MicroDYNAMO is a tool that allows individuals, groups, or whole classes to apply mathematical and other concepts in a simulated environment. Note: Requires two disk drives. A supplemental text, *Introduction to Computer Simulation: The System Dynamics Approach*, is also available from the publisher (see page 271).

MuMath

Microsoft Consumer Products
10700 Northrup Way
Bellevue, WA 98004
(206) 828-8080
Hardware: Apple II; TRS-80
Grade Range: 11–12
Price: $250.00

The *MuMath* package is similar to LISP and can be used to do calculus, matrix algebra and some trigonometry. There are lesson files with exercises that help the user learn to use the system. Programming in muSimp requires building complex structures from simple ones and then analyzing and operating on those structures.

PILOT

(PILOT is available for most brands of microcomputers. Check with your local distributor or sales representative for ordering information.) PILOT was the first author language available for microcomputers (see page 48), and it continues to be actively used. A true programming language that is more suited to producing dialogues than to number crunching, PILOT does not offer the structured formats of other author languages such as *Genis* I, *Blocks* or *Shell Games*, and is therefore more flexible but less easy to use. Versions of PILOT exist for all the popular microcomputers, including $100 machines. Some schools have used PILOT as a first programming language because it is easier to learn than BASIC and because students can quickly produce interesting programs.

SemCalc

Sunburst Communications, Inc.
Room M5
39 Washington Avenue
Pleasantville, NY 10570
(800) 431-1934
Hardware: Apple II Plus; TRS-80 III
Grade Range: 6–12
Price: $95.00

The *Semantic Calculator (SemCalc)* (see pages 5–6) is an innovative tool that helps students explore and solve word problems. It has two teaching objectives: to help students focus on correct unit names to avoid inappropriate computations (adding apples and oranges), and to help students focus on units rather than numbers, which enables them to choose the appropriate mathematics operation in a word problem.

TK! Solver

Software Arts
27 Mica Lane
Wellesley, MA 02181
(617) 237-4000
Hardware: Apple; IBM Personal
Grade Range: 9–12
Price: $299.00

TK! Solver is an automatic problem solver (see pages 71–75). Students enter relevant equations, dimensional relationships, and numbers for the given variable. Then they choose the unknown variable, and the program solves for it by picking out the appropriate formulas, converting dimensions as required, and placing the numbers in the proper place.

VisiCalc

VisiCorp
2895 Zanker Road
San Jose, CA 95134
(408) 946-9000
Hardware: Apple II, III; Atari 800; IBM PC; Commodore
Grade Range: 9–12
Price: $250.00

VisiCalc (see pages 61–67) is an electronic spreadsheet, a matrix 260 rows by 75 columns. The computer is like a window through which the user can view any part of the sheet. The cursor indicates the user's position in the matrix. Each row and column name can contain a label, value or formula. As these variables are defined, *VisiCalc* automatically computes numerical values as needed by the user.

VisiPlot

Visicorp
2895 Zanker Road
San Jose, CA 95134
(408) 946-9000
Hardware: Apple II
Grade Range: 9–12
Price: $200.00

Excellent business graphing program especially for time-dependent plots (see page 7). It is a very powerful and easy to use program. It would be useful for both mathematics and business classes. Used along with *VisiTrend*, it has statistical applications.

Index

788020